P9-BHS-003

GUIDE TO ANCIENT NATIVE AMERICAN SITES

by
Michael S. Durham

A Voyager Book

The Globe Pequot Press

Old Saybrook, Connecticut

About the Author

Michael S. Durham was the editor of *Americana* magazine for thirteen years. Since 1986 he has been a freelance writer and editor. His articles have appeared in *Smithsonian, Audubon, American Heritage,* and a number of other magazines. He is the author of several books, including two volumes in the twelve-volume series *The Smithsonian Guide to Historic America.*

Copyright © 1994 by Michael Durham

All rights reserved. No part of this book may be reproduced or transmitted in any form by any means, electronic or mechanical, including photocopying and recording, or by any information storage and retrieval system, except as may be expressly permitted by the 1976 Copyright Act or by the publisher. Requests for permission should be made in writing to The Globe Pequot Press, P.O. Box 833, Old Saybrook, Connecticut 06475.

Library of Congress Cataloging-in-Publication Data
Durham, Michael S. (Michael Schelling), 1935-
    Guide to ancient Native American sites/by Michael S. Durham.—
1st. ed.
        p.   cm.
    "A voyager book."
    Includes index.
    ISBN 1-56440-492-7
    1. Indians of North America—Antiquities—Guidebooks.   2. United
States—Antiquities—Guidebooks.   I. Title.
E77.9.D87   1994
917.304'929—dc20   94-34361
                                                        CIP

Manufactured in the United States of America
First Edition/First Printing

CONTENTS

Introduction vii

The East 1

Alabama 3

Arkansas 11

Florida 17

Georgia 23

Illinois 33

Indiana 41

Iowa 43

Kentucky 47

Louisiana 51

Minnesota 57

Mississippi 61

Missouri 71

North Carolina 79

Ohio 83

Tennessee 103

West Virginia 111

Wisconsin 117

The West 121

Alaska 123

Arizona 127

California 155

Colorado......................................163

Montana..179

Nevada 187

New Mexico.................................191

Oklahoma....................................219

South Dakota...............................223

Texas..225

Utah...233

Wyoming.....................................245

Glossary of Terms....................248
Glossary of Cultures.................250
Index 252

INTRODUCTION

When I look back on all the prehistoric sites visited in preparation for this book, my thoughts often go to Poverty Point, the oddly named complex of prehistoric ridges and mounds on a Louisiana bayou that flows (if that is the right word for this sluggish body of water) into the Mississippi River. I was there on a quiet weekday morning in May, the only visitor except for a Cajun couple from southern Louisiana, who had seen the Poverty Point sign on the interstate and had made the detour on a whim. The sign had given them no indication of what to expect—certainly the name, Poverty Point, although intriguing, is misleading—and their surprise and delight in the discovery made my visit all the more memorable.

With site manager Dennis LaBatt at the wheel, we rode a tram around the site, stopping here and there as he pointed out key features and explained how this ridge or that mound fit into the overall complex, which covers 400 acres and was constructed some four centuries before the birth of Christ. At Bird Mound, an effigy mound so huge that its birdlike shape can only be seen from the air, LaBatt led us up a path until we stood on the bird's head, 72 feet in the air. As we paused for breath, the couple expressed what I had felt many times before: amazement that a prehistoric people could have achieved all this almost twenty centuries before the first Europeans set foot on this continent.

My own fascination with the mystery of prehistoric America came upon me just as unexpectedly, in a quiet canyon in Arizona, where the Sinagua Indians had built cliff dwellings about A.D. 1150. There I began to understand how little I knew about this continent's long past; American history, to me, had always been confined to that relatively short period since Europeans had come to this land. I realized that prehistory is not, as I had always assumed, the exclusive domain of the professional archaeologist and that this country is dotted with sites the public can visit—places that I, like the Cajun couple, had always passed by.

Many books have been written about prehistoric America, but for me reading was simply not enough. The story didn't come alive until I was able to go and see for myself: to climb the mounds, hike through canyons to cliff dwellings, and stand on ledges gazing at images chipped into the rock face by prehistoric artists. For me these sites speak volumes, and this book is the result of my desire and resolve to visit as many of them as I could.

The couple at Poverty Point also posed a question that I had asked myself: What is prehistory? As the dictionary puts it, prehistory is the span of time before man began recording his story. Before the white man arrived in America, the Indians had no written language; therefore, prehistory ended when the Europeans arrived and began writing down what happened. It is a convenient division, this line that divides the past into two periods, prehistoric and historic, but one that creates the false and misleading impression that our past really began "at the time of European contact," to use a phrase that archaeologists favor. At least, that is the impression I took away from my teachers and textbooks when I was a student.

Who were the prehistoric Americans and what happened to them? Certain native peoples had the misfortune to live on the cusp between historic and prehistoric times and be in the way when Europeans laid claim to this continent. These are the Indians that the sixteenth-century explorers Coronado and de Soto encountered and casually slaughtered as they rampaged through the Southwest and Southeast in a fruitless search for riches. We can trace these victims to Indian tribes of modern times; other cultures, like the Anasazi, had disappeared by the time the white man arrived. In the territory that is now southern Ohio, once home to the complex Adena and Hopewell cultures, the native Indian population had completely disappeared by the time white settlers arrived.

Although we are uncertain about their fate, archaeology and related sciences have taught us much about prehistoric people. To a lesser or greater extent, we know how they lived and how they died and were buried, what they looked like, what they wore, and even what they ate. We know about their art and craft, their trade, their architecture, and their skills, and we can make educated guesses about their religion and social organization. We know enough about them to be able to appreciate their diversity and their achievements. We do not know their leaders or their artists as individuals; we do not know events in their histories, such as battles or droughts or famines; and we do not know what they called themselves.

Anasazi, the cliff dwellers of the Southwest, means "ancient ones" in the Navajo tongue; the name Sinagua is from the Spanish "without water," a tribute to this culture's ability to survive in the arid desert; and in Ohio, the Hopewell people were named for the owner of an estate on which an important mound was excavated.

All interpretations of the past are subject to change, but our views of the prehistoric past, where archaeologists have to base their theories on what they find buried in the ground, are in constant flux. In present-day New Mexico, around the Anasazi center known as Chaco Canyon, archaeologists have discovered nearly 1,000 miles of prehistoric roadways spread over some 60,000 square miles. Until fairly recently, these engineering marvels were thought to be thoroughfares linking Chaco and its outlying communities. New evidence provided by aerial photography and remote sensing has caused scholars to change their thinking. Many now believe that this intricate highway system led from Chaco to sacred sites in the surrounding territory—not to other settlements—and must have been used mostly for ceremonial purposes. As one archaeologist pointed out, the roads are too wide, too grand, and too little used simply to move people and goods around.

Similarly, scientists once automatically assumed that the great prehistoric mounds in the eastern half of the country were the work of a large labor force dominated by an all-powerful chief. Today some scientists are speculating that some of the mounds at least were built in stages, by a smaller group of individuals working voluntarily together.

The early European arrivals to this country were intrigued and puzzled by the mounds and other earthworks they found marking the landscape. Most Europeans could not bring themselves to believe that these ancient monuments were built by Indians, whom they considered too uncivilized and backward for such impressive accomplishments. Therefore, they reasoned, the mounds had to be built by someone else, and so arose the belief in an ancient race of superior beings called the Mound Builders, a people presumably more like the settlers in skin color, culture, and maybe even heritage. Some believed that the Mound Builders orignally came from Europe or were descended from the Lost Tribes of Israel.

And what happened to the Mound Builders? No mystery there, at least for believers in this theory. They were wiped out or driven away by invading savages, the ancestors of the Indians that the white settlers found inhabiting this continent. In 1832, in a poem entitled "The Prairies," the New England poet William Cullen Bryant lamented the demise of the Mound Builders, a "disciplined and populous" people who thrived until

> The red man came—
> The roaming hunter tribes, warlike and fierce,
> And the mound-builders vanished from the earth
> The solitude of centuries untold
> Has settled where they dwelt.

As far-fetched as this theory sounds today, it held on until late in the nineteenth century when archaeologist Cyrus Thomas, in an extensive study of mounds and other prehistoric earthworks undertaken for the Smithsonian Institution, concluded that the Mound Builders had never existed and that the mounds were indeed built by ancestors of present-day Indians.

Thomas settled the issue as far as science was concerned, but the thought of a prehistoric race of non-Indians intrigues some Americans to this day. Especially mysterious are the examples of prehistoric "writing" that turned up on tablets at such places as Grave Creek Mound in West Virginia and the Newark Earthworks in Ohio in the early nineteenth century. Since native Indians had no written language, it was assumed that the tablets were the work of a more advanced culture. Scientists have long since dismissed these writings as hoaxes, but attempts to translate them go on. In 1986 an "expert" cryptographer determined that a runestone—

now preserved in a state park in Heavener, Oklahoma—was inscribed by Vikings about A.D. 600 in Futhark, an ancient Germanic language.

Archaeologists and anthropologists like Cyrus Thomas play an important role in the story this guidebook tells. These are the men who excavated, mapped, explored, and helped preserve this country's prehistoric legacy. They include Richard Wetherill, a cowboy turned amateur archaeologist, who discovered an extensive cliff dwelling at Mesa Verde, Colorado, by climbing down a Douglas spruce that grew up a cliff from a ledge; C. B. Moore, a wealthy Philadelphian who explored the backwaters of the Mississippi and other rivers on his own paddle wheeler; and Frederick Ward Putnam of Harvard, who personally raised money to purchase the Serpent Mound in Ohio for the Peabody Museum in order to save it from destruction by agriculture.

A number of the sites date to mankind's earliest days on this continent. Russell Cave in Alabama shows evidence of being first occupied at least 8,000 years ago. Mastodon State Park in Missouri, where a spear point that could be 14,000 years old was found amid mastodon bones, offers early proof of what was not considered possible before: that humans were here at the same time as the mastodon and even hunted the beast for food.

Estimates of how long people have been on this continent are continually being revised backwards. Before the 1930s we still thought of humans as a fairly recent arrival—no more than 4,000 years ago. Then the discovery of ancient projectile points at Clovis, New Mexico, added another 7,000 or 8,000 years to the duration of human presence, and the development of new techniques such as radiocarbon dating helped to provide a clearer picture of how ancient people crossed the land bridge in the Bering Sea from Asia to present-day Alaska and spread down through the continent.

More recently, discoveries in South America and places like the Meadowcroft Rock Shelter in western Pennsylvania have produced artifacts that could be 16,500 years old or even older. In early 1994 a group of geneticists published a study of linguistically related Indians in Central America that estimated, based on a rate of genetic mutation, that the ancestors of these Indians came to the New World from Asia some time between 22,000 and 29,000 years ago.

There are 144 individual sites from twenty-nine states profiled in this book. For convenience, the book is divided into two sections. The East covers the territory known as the Eastern Woodlands, home to the mound-building cultures, and the West, an equally vast area, includes three separate geographic entities: the Desert West (a region of cliff dwellings and pueblos), the Great Plains, and the Far West.

Why some regions have more sites than others is due to a variety of complex causes, among them climate, development, population density, and general attitudes toward preservation and the prehistoric past. In my research I constantly came across cases of our prehistoric heritage being lost to looting, vandalism, development, and neglect. At Death Valley a National Park Service ranger asked me not to pinpoint the location of rock art sites because vandals had already caused so much damage. In Ohio I watched the busy operation of a gravel pit that was eating its way through an archaeologically important Hopewell Indian site.

Increasing public interest in American prehistory is the only sure way of stopping such destruction, but this loss should not diminish our appreciation of the prehistoric heritage that is left. Surely no similar collection of sites in a specialized guidebook could offer such variety. Among the sites are cities hung on cliffs and earthen mounds that rival, in size, the pyramids of Egypt. There are forts, earthworks shaped like animals, and dank and cheerless caves that hunting parties of the ancient Paleo and Archaic Indians used for shelter. There are roads and graded esplanades, undecipherable patterns carved into and painted on rock, astronomical observatories made from wooden posts or arrangements of stone, and sites, called pishkuns, where hunters drove buffalo to their death over cliffs. Many of the sites are spectacular in their size and setting and scope, but not every one. At a few sites all that is left of a mound or settlement are slight undulations in the earth that only an archaeologist or prehistory buff could get excited about.

Some of the sites, like Mesa Verde in Colorado, are national parks with guided tours, well-maintained paths, informed rangers, and informative museums and visitor centers. These are places no traveler should miss. But for me the appeal of prehistoric America is stronger at some of the smaller, less well known places, such as a mound in a small historic cemetery in Tiltonsville, Ohio, an outcropping of petroglyphs in a New Mexican desert, or an Anasazi pueblo ruin at the end of a dirt road near Pleasant Point, Colorado. Here, undistracted by other visitors, you can conjure up a prehistoric scene in your mind, contemplate the vastness of prehistoric time, or simply enjoy the view, for prehistoric Americans had an unusual ability to pick the best vistas for their homes. Perhaps this was for defense, so that enemies could be seen at a distance; but it is also possible that the Anasazi Indians and others appreciated a good view as much as we do.

Doug Jones, director of Moundville Archaeological Park in Alabama, recommends early morning or late afternoon as the best times to appreciate "the pristine mystery" of a prehistoric site. It is then, he has written, that "I can close my eyes and imagine the scene: the people stirring as the village awakens, the women tending the cooking fires, the men repairing their stone tools, the children and old people starting on their daily chores. It's like hearing voices in the wind."

Voices in the wind. I have heard them; the couple from Louisiana heard them. May you, the users of this book, hear them too.

Information regarding hours, fees, phone numbers, and all other information subject to change was believed to be accurate at press time. Neither the author nor the publisher, however, can be held responsible for revisions to this information that occur subsequent to the publication of this guide.

THE EAST

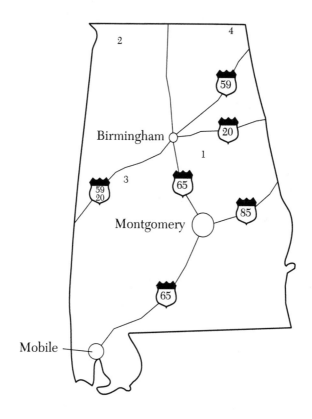

Alabama
1. De Soto Caverns Park
2. Florence Indian Mound and Museum
3. Moundville Archaeological Park
4. Russell Cave National Monument

ALABAMA

De Soto Caverns Park

Attraction: Cavern with prehistoric burial site
Hours: Guided tours daily from April through September and on weekends October through March
Admission fee: $8.99 adults; $5.50 children
For more information: De Soto Caverns Park, Childersburg, AL 35044; (205) 378-7252

Known to archaeologists as Kymulga Cave, after a Chickasaw village established nearby in 1760, this privately owned tourist attraction has served variously over the years as a saltpeter mine, a hideout for outlaws, and, during Prohibition, a speakeasy. According to Creek Indian legend, the cave was the place from which the spirit rose that created the Creek people. Hernando de Soto supposedly came across the immense cave during his month-long stay in the area in 1540, and an Indian trader, I. W. Wright, carved his name on the wall of the cave in 1723. Evidence of prehistoric occupancy came to light in 1964, when a human skeleton was unearthed on a ledge adjoining the main passageway, as the cave was about to open to the public.

Subsequent excavations by archaeologist Joseph Benthall of the University of Alabama uncovered a burial area containing the remains of four adults and one child as well as projectile points. Both the artifacts and the burial method indicated to Benthall that this was a Copena burial, the Copena being a Woodland people who settled farther north in the Tennessee Valley. They evidently had established an outpost in what is now central Alabama to mine or trade for greenstone and soapstone, which they used to produce burial objects. Today the archaeological site is one of many stops on the cavern tour.

How to get there: De Soto Caverns is located 5 miles east

3

of Childersburg, Alabama (36 miles east of Birmingham), on Highway 76.

Florence Indian Mound and Museum

Attraction: Large ceremonial mound and museum
Hours: Mound visible at all times; museum open Tuesday through Saturday, 10:00 A.M. to 4:00 P.M.
Admission fee: None
For more information: Indian Mound and Museum, South Court Street, Florence, AL 35630; (205) 760–6379

Although it bills itself as "the largest domiciliary mound on the Tennessee River," experts generally believe that the purpose of this riverside mound was ceremonial, not residential. Of its size, however, there is no question. This four-sided mound is 42 feet tall and 180 feet wide at the base, with a summit plateau that probably held a temple measuring 145 feet by 94 feet. The Mississippian peoples who built it, probably around A.D. 1200, lived on islands in the Tennessee River. When built, the mound was partially enclosed by a thick wall, between 12 and 15 feet high and 43 feet across at the top. The wall, although badly eroded, was still visible at the beginning of the nineteenth century.

Today the mound is wedged in between the river and the seedy industrial outskirts of Florence, but it is nonetheless well worth a visit. An excellent small museum has in its collection a variety of artifacts found in the Muscle Shoals area, including a fluted projectile point some 12,000 years old, a stone bowl from the Archaic period, and "transitional tools," such as knives and scrapers, from the Woodland and Mississippian periods.

How to get there: Pick up Court Street in the center of town and follow it southeast almost to the Tennessee River.

Moundville Archaeological Park

Attraction: Twenty preserved mounds, village and temple reconstructions, museum

Hours: Park grounds open daily 7:45 A.M. to 9:00 P.M.; museum hours 9:00 A.M. to 5:00 P.M. daily

Admission fee: $4.00 adults; $2.00 children; group rates available

For more information: Moundville Archaeological Park, P.O. Box 66, Moundville, AL 35474; (205) 371-2572

Known as Mound State Monument until its name was changed in 1991, Moundville Archaeological Park (also known by the acronym MAP) deserves its grander new name and its designation as the "best-preserved prehistoric Indian site east of the pueblos." The 317-acre park on the Black Warrior River contains twenty preserved ceremonial mounds, including the largest, Mound B, which is 60 feet tall and covers two acres at its base. Archaeologists have estimated that Mound B consists of more than four million cubic feet of earth.

Although late Woodland people began inhabiting the area about A.D. 1000, Moundville flourished as a major ceremonial center in the Mississippian period between A.D. 1200 and 1400. At its height it had a population of some 3,000, scientists believe; but it was a regional center for many more people, with perhaps as many as 10,000 living along the Black Warrior River valley, which stretches from present-day Tuscaloosa to Demopolis. Moundville apparently was abandoned before A.D. 1500. Some think that de Soto crossed the Black Warrior River south of Moundville in 1540, but there is no record that he ever came across the complex. "And he was beating the bushes big time around here," says Carey Oakley, chief archaeologist at the Alabama Museum of Natural History, the parent organization of MAP.

The Moundville inhabitants wore garments made of leather or woven vegetable fiber and practiced "head flattening," strapping infants to wooden cradle boards with leather thongs. They cultivated corn and beans and other vegetables such as pumpkins, they gathered native plants, and they hunted and fished. The remains of post holes indicate that the complex was protected by a wooden palisade. Although the people were not warriors, there is evidence of some hostility, probably border-type skirmishes.

As the population grew under these favorable circumstances, Oakley speculates that the leaders, fearing challenges to their authority, might have ordered the mounds built as a make-work

The temple mound at Moundville

project, a process that he describes as "keeping them busy, making them tired." The mounds were not all built at once. As many as ten distinct "building phases" are visible in some of them. The mounds were not generally used for burials, although some human remains, probably those of chiefs or priests, have been found in them. Commoners were buried throughout the site, some in a fetal position under the floors of their huts. Did the fetal burial position symbolize, as some believe, "a return to the womb of mother earth," or was it "just easier to dig a small round hole," Oakley wonders.

The Mississippians at Moundville were skilled potters. They used local clay mixed with crushed shells to produce quantities of both utlilitarian ware and highly decorated symbolic and ceremonial pieces. During the 1930s workers from the Civilian Conservation Corps (CCC), a government-run work program for unemployed young men, turned up more than 1,000 whole ceramic vessels and some 250,000 fragments of pottery. The famed rattlesnake disc, discovered about the turn of the century, was described by the early archaeologist Clarence B. Moore as an "incised design of two horned rattlesnakes knotted, forming a circle, within which is a representation of an open human hand bearing an eye upon it." The hand with the eyelike motif in the palm is common in Mississippian art, but the knotted rattlesnake is an image that has only been found at one other site. The disc is now displayed at the park museum.

Moundville was "rediscovered" by settlers in the early nineteenth century. Thomas Maxwell conducted the first excavation in 1840, digging into the largest mound and recording the stratification. In 1869 a team from the Smithsonian Institution under Nathaniel T. Lupton spent four days mapping and excavating the site, but the credit for the first systematic excavation at Moundville goes to Moore, a Philadelphia socialite turned archaeologist. (Today, Oakley and others at Moundville refer to Moore as "Steamboat Willie" because the wealthy archaeologist explored southern rivers, including Moundville's Black Warrior River, in his own steamboat, *The Gopher.*) Moore excavated many of the mounds with a twenty-man crew in 1905 and 1906. Moore's observation "that not one object . . . gave indication of influence of Europeans" helped lay to rest the speculation, widespread at one time, that the mounds were constructed by an unknown race of whites, probably European in origin, or that de Soto had them constructed.

Moore's work made Moundville known to the nation and this, unfortunately, attracted many pothunters and vandals to the site. In 1923 the Moundville Historical Society was founded as a first important step in protecting the mounds. In 1929 the Alabama Museum of Natural History, under its dedicated director, Walter B. Jones, purchased 175 acres, which included most of the mounds. (Jones mortgaged his home several times to acquire land for the site.) Mound State Park was established in 1933.

Despite the recognition it was receiving, the site had been badly damaged by farming and erosion. It was the work of the CCC that built the present Moundville museum, restored the mounds, dug drainage ditches, re-created the reservoirs that the original inhabitants had dug, and, according to records kept by Jones, recorded seventy-five structures, numerous burials, and more than 1,000 whole ceramic vessels. "If it had not been for the CCC," Jones said at the dedication of the museum on May 16, 1939, "there would be no Mound State Monument."

Six reconstructions of prehistoric buildings, with grass-thatched roofs and walls of woven cane plastered with mud, are presently on view at the site, including a reproduction of a temple atop Mound B. The museum contains exhibits explaining the way of life in a prehistoric village and examples of pottery and other artifacts excavated at Moundville and the surrounding area. A nature trail beginning behind Mound B and winding down through the woods to the river is a new addition to the park's recreational facilities.

Although the archaeological park is one of the most popular destinations in Alabama, it is probably best appreciated at quiet times (early morning or late afternoon) when what director Doug Jones has called "the pristine mystery of the place" is most keenly felt.

How to get there: The park is located off Route 69 just north of Moundville.

Russell Cave National Monument

Attraction: Large cave occupied by prehistoric hunters
Hours: Daily 8:00 A.M. to 5:00 P.M.
Admission fee: None
For more information: Russell Cave National Monument, Bridgeport, AL 35740; (205) 495–2572

This limestone cave in a hillside in northern Alabama was made habitable some 9,000 years ago when a rockfall diverted a stream to one side and raised the floor above the water. Measuring the radioactive carbon in the charcoal found some 12 feet below the present level of the cave indicates that a small group of fewer than twenty people first occupied the cave some time between 6550 and 6145 B.C. Probably these nomadic Indians from the Archaic period used the cave for shelter during the fall and winter, when they hunted game and gathered nuts. In addition to charcoal, they left tools such as needles and awls fashioned from bones, stone scrapers, and spear points chipped from chert found in the limestone.

Occupation of the cave fell off dramatically after the end of the Archaic period in 1000 B.C., when people began to practice farming more widely and society became more complex. During the Woodland period (1000 B.C. to A.D. 500) that followed, the cave was used as a winter hunting camp by Indians from nearby settlements. They made the first pottery found in the cave, as well as the smaller weapon points for the bow and arrow, which had replaced the more primitive spear and throwing stick, called an atlatl, used by the Archaic peoples. The cave was occupied even less frequently during the Mississippian period (after A.D. 700), by which time the Indians in the region were extensively engaged in agriculture.

In 1953 the cave was explored by a group of amateur diggers from Tennessee. They understood the importance of the site and notified the Smithsonian Institution, which began archaeological work in the cave with the National Geographic Society. Russell Cave was made a national monument in 1962 and the following year the National Park Service conducted more excavations.

The complex includes a visitor center and hiking trail. The archaeological site is part of an extensive cave system with about 7 miles of mapped but undeveloped passageways. The monument superintendent will issue free permits to properly equipped groups wishing to visit the undeveloped sections.

How to get there: Russell Cave is located 8 miles west of Bridgeport, Alabama. From U.S. 72 at Bridgeport, follow County Road 91 west to County Road 75.

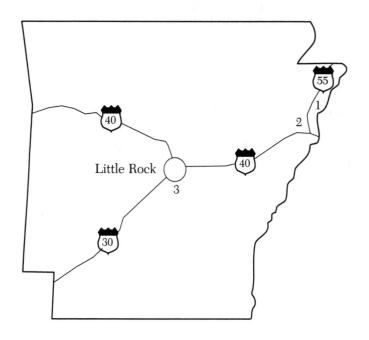

Arkansas
1. Hampson Museum State Park
2. Parkin Archeological State Park
3. Toltec Mounds Archaeological State Park

ARKANSAS

Hampson Museum State Park

Attraction: Small museum on important archaeological site
Hours: Tuesday through Saturday 9:00 A.M. to 5:00 P.M., Sunday
1:00 to 5:00 P.M.; closed on Mondays, on Sundays from November
1 to April 1, and on major holidays
Admission fee: None
For more information: Hampson Museum State Park, P.O. Box
156, Wilson, AR 72395; (501) 655–8622

In 1932 a local doctor, James Kelly Hampson (1877–1956),
began a successful second career as an amateur archaeologist by
studying prehistoric people of the Nodena culture who had once
lived on land occupied by his family's plantation (also named
Nodena). Hampson's extensive collection of artifacts, including
superb examples of a distinct pottery type, Nodena red and white,
has been preserved in an excellent small museum, now called the
Hampson Museum State Park.

The Nodena site was a palisaded village of about fifteen acres
that was inhabited by as many as 1,650 individuals for about one
hundred years sometime between A.D. 1400 and 1700. In addition
to providing protection for its inhabitants and neighboring vil-
lagers, Nodena was a ceremonial center with three major mounds.

Nodena red and white pottery, made from shell-tempered clay,
and the Nodena point, a small, teardrop-shaped point made from
different cherts, were both discovered here. The museum also
contains examples of head pots, similar in shape to the human
head but somewhat smaller, which are only found in this section of
northeast Arkansas between the St. Francis and Mississippi rivers.
Usually the face is painted white and the rest of the head red. The
closed eyes might indicate that the pots are likenesses of people
who had died.

The Nodena archaeological site, although a National Historic Landmark, is privately owned and not open to the public. After Hampson's death his collection was donated to the State of Arkansas and in 1961 was moved from his personal museum at the plantation to the present building in the town of Wilson.

How to get there: The site is located ¼ mile north of Wilson on U.S. 61.

Parkin Archeological State Park

Attraction: Large prehistoric mound and archaeological excavation site
Hours: Check in advance
Admission fee: None
For more information: Arkansas State Parks, One Capitol Mall, 4A–900, Little Rock, AR 72201; (501) 682–1191

The Parkin site is one of the newest archaeological sites open to the public in the country. While many such mounds once existed in this Mississippi Delta region of Arkansas, most have been destroyed by looting and farming. Archaeologists believe that the Parkin Mound was the ceremonial center of a seventeen-acre settlement that was occupied by Indians from A.D. 1350 to 1550. Nearly 1,000 people lived in the town, which was protected by a ditch and log palisade and, on one end, by the St. Francis River. The inhabitants farmed fields outside the ditch.

Parkin is also important because historians now believe that Hernando de Soto visited here in the summer of 1541 and that the Parkin settlement is the town he called Casqui, which appears in the chronicles of his travels. The de Soto expedition spent two years in Arkansas. One of the few friendly receptions the Indians gave the explorer occurred at Casqui. The chief, who personally greeted de Soto, and many of his subjects were baptized as Christians; they also helped the Spaniards erect a large cross on top of the mound. A small bead made of several layers of glass and a small brass bell found at Parkin are both probably evidence of the de Soto visit. "We know from archaeological work on other de Soto contact sites that this type of bead was carried by the expedition for giving or trading to the Indians," according to Jeffrey Mitchem, station archaeologist at Parkin.

The Arkansas Archaeological Survey has established a research station at Parkin to continue studying the site. Visitors will be able to watch archaeologists at work and see the results of excavations and laboratory analysis. The visitor information center, which opened in 1994, includes an exhibit area and audio-visual and other educational programs.

How to get there: Parkin Archeological State Park is located on Highway 75 about 12 miles north of I–40, on the north edge of the city of Parkin.

Toltec Mounds Archeological State Park

Attraction: Large mound site with visitor center museum and archaeological research station
Hours: Tuesday through Saturday, 8:00 A.M. to 5:00 P.M.; Sunday noon to 5:00 P.M.; closed Monday (except Labor Day and Memorial Day) and on Thanksgiving, Christmas Eve and Day, and New Year's Day
Admission fee: None; "nominal fee" charged for on-site tours
For more information: Toltec Mounds State Park, 1 Toltec Mounds Road, Scott, AR 72142–9502; (501) 961–9442

The name Toltec came from Gilbert Knapp, who owned this site during the latter half of the nineteenth century. Like many people at the time, Knapp believed that Indian mounds were built by people from Mexico, so he named the local community and railroad station Toltec after the great prehistoric Mexican culture. The mounds, however, were called the Knapp Mounds after their owner.

When it was developed between A.D. 750 and 950, Toltec consisted of eighteen mounds enclosed by an earthen embankment on three sides and by Mound Lake, an oxbow of Plum Bayou, on the other. The embankment—8 feet high and 5,298 feet long—had a ditch along the outside and was broken by four gaps. Only two short sections of it remain. It is not certain if the embankment was

Parkin archaeologist Jeffrey M. Mitchem with excavated vase

built for defense, to set a sacred area apart from the rest of the settlement, or for some other purpose. Archaeologists think that Toltec was a ceremonial center for a larger area and inhabited by only a few high-ranking religious and political figures.

The Knapp mounds were first investigated by Edward Palmer of the Smithsonian's Bureau of American Ethnology in 1882–1883 and described by Cyrus Thomas in the bureau's annual report for 1890–1891. Palmer excavated five mounds and mapped the site. Many more mounds were visible at the time; the principal ones, Mound A and Mound B, were 50 and 41 feet tall, respectively. Years of farming have diminished the mounds to the point where only a few are visible. (The locations of the others are indicated by markers.)

Eleven of the mound sites border a rectangular central plaza. Of the ones still visible, Mound A, 49 feet high and shaped like an elongated cone, is on the edge of Mound Pond on the west side of the plaza. It has never been scientifically studied and how it was used is unknown. The 41-foot-high Mound B is a flat-topped rectangular pyramid that, excavations have shown, consists of at least five separate layers of material. These indicate that the mound was used for human habitation, maybe for a chief or priest. Mound C is a burial mound, as excavations conducted by the Arkansas Archaeological Society and the University of Arkansas in 1966 proved. The complete lack of artifacts in the mass graves, such as the tools, pottery, or jewelry frequently found in prehistoric graves in the Lower Mississippi Valley, makes it difficult to date the mound.

The remnant of Mound G is on the east side of the plaza. This mound was apparently only 6 feet high but extraordinarily long and wide (300 feet by 150 feet). The location of Mound G, like many of the others, is the result of planning and forethought. For example, when viewed from Mound H, the equinox sunsets of both September 21 and March 21 are over Mound G. Indians used the mounds to keep track of the seasons.

The archaeological park has a wide range of activities, workshops, arts and crafts demonstrations, and other presentations. Guided tours of the park leave the visitor center at regular intervals and follow the ¾-mile-long Knapp Trail. Exhibits in the visitor center examine the archaeology of the site, the recent history of the site and park, and how archaeologists are researching the site. The Toltec Research Station of the Arkansas Archaeological Survey is housed at the park.

How to get there: The park is located between Scott and Keo, 16 miles southeast of North Little Rock and 9 miles northwest of England, off U.S. 165 on Route 386.

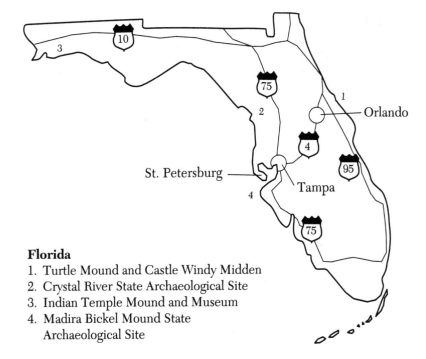

Florida
1. Turtle Mound and Castle Windy Midden
2. Crystal River State Archaeological Site
3. Indian Temple Mound and Museum
4. Madira Bickel Mound State
   Archaeological Site

FLORIDA

Turtle Mound and Castle Windy Midden

Attraction: Two shell mounds, visitor center
Hours: 6:00 A.M. to 6:00 P.M. in the winter and 6:00 A.M. to 8:00
P.M. during Daylight Savings Time
Admission fee: None
For more information: Canaveral National Seashore, P.O. Box
6447, Titusville, FL 32782; (305) 267–1110

Most of the ancient mounds made of shells in the New Smyrna
Beach area were destroyed and the material used for road work in
the early part of the twentieth century; however, Turtle Mound,
which has been called the "largest and most mysterious" of Florida's
prehistoric sites, was saved from such a fate in 1911, when it was
purchased by concerned citizens for $8,000. It became a state park
in the 1960s and part of the Canaveral National Seashore in 1975.

Turtle Mound has never been excavated by professional
archaeologists, so it is uncertain whether it is simply a pile of
debris—mostly oyster shells—or a ceremonial or burial mound.
The mound consists of two connected cones or peaks, which are
each about 35 feet high. At its base, Turtle Mound measures 180
feet by 360 feet (north to south) and covers one and a half acres.
Construction of the mound took about 700 years (between A.D. 690
and 1400) and required an estimated one and a half million
bushels of oyster shells. The mound towers over the flat terrain
and possibly was used as a lookout tower by the peoples of the late
St. Johns culture and their successors, the Timucuan Indians of
historic times.

Like the larger Turtle Mound just to the north, Castle Windy
Midden is composed of shells and overlooks the park's Mosquito
Lagoon. It extends for 275 feet along the lagoon and rises to a
height of about 17 feet. Radiocarbon dating indicates that the

17

mound was in use from about A.D. 1000 to 1350. Excavations here show that there is a layer of tiny coquina clam shells between two layers of oyster shells. This raises the possibility that the lagoon's oyster beds at one time ceased to produce for reasons unknown.

There is a visitor center and interpretive trails to both mounds.

How to get there: Take Route 44 off I–95 into New Smyrna Beach and A1A South to the seashore entrance.

Crystal River State Archaeological Site

Attraction: Temple, burial and midden mounds, museum
Hours: Site open daily 8:00 A.M. to sunset; museum hours are Thursday through Monday 9:00 A.M. to 5:00 P.M.
Admission fee: None
For more information: Crystal River State Archaeological Site, 3400 North Museum Point, Crystal River, FL 32629; (904) 795–3817

Two ceremonial stones, or stelae, were discovered here in the early part of the twentieth century during excavations conducted by archaeologist Clarence B. Moore. Today the stones, one of which has a likeness of a human head carved into its limestone surface, are central points of interest of this fourteen-acre archaeological park. The Crystal River site served as a ceremonial center from 200 B.C. to A.D. 1400. It was occupied even earlier by the Deptford culture, which existed from 500 B.C. to about A.D. 300 and was the first culture to build mounds at Crystal River. The Weedon Island culture, which developed more complex ceremonies and manufactured burial goods, existed here from A.D. 300 to 900. Beginning in A.D. 900, it was replaced by the corn-growing people of the Safety Harbor culture, who lived here into historic times.

Crystal River has two temple mounds, three burial mounds, and two midden or village mounds, which are the trash heaps of the various settlements and consist mostly of shells. Temple Mound A near the Crystal River was mostly destroyed by a previous owner of the site, but it is believed to have been 30 feet tall when it was built about A.D. 600. As its name indicates, it served as a high platform for a temple. Temple Mound H, built during the last 200 years that Crystal River was used as a ceremonial site, is completely intact. Unlike Temple Mound A, which is built of midden or refuse, Mound H is made of earth.

The largest of the three burial mounds, Burial Mound F, is 20 feet high with a base 70 feet in diameter surrounded by a 7-foot-high burial ridge. Clarence B. Moore excavated more than 400 burials here, although it is believed that as many as 1,000 persons were buried here from 200 B.C. to A.D. 400. The dead were buried with personal possessions such as jewelry, tools, and pottery. Copper earrings found in the graves indicate that there was trade with cultures in Ohio.

Artifacts excavated at the site are on display at the visitor center. There are also exhibits describing the various cultures that inhabited the site and a relief map of the area as it might have looked in prehistoric times. A half-mile paved walking trail leads through the mounds.

With ten days' notice, the park office will arrange guided tours for groups of at least ten persons.

How to get there: The site is located off Route 19, 5 miles northwest of Crystal River.

Indian Temple Mound and Museum

Attraction: Mound and museum with excellent collection of prehistoric ceramics
Hours: Mound is always open; museum hours are 11:00 A.M. to 4:00 P.M. Tuesday through Saturday, 1:00 to 4:00 P.M. Sunday; closed Mondays
Admission fee: None for mounds; museum is 50 cents
For more information: Indian Temple Mound Museum, Box 4009, Fort Walton Beach, FL 32549; (904) 243–6521

Members of an encamped Civil War artillery unit, the Fort Walton Guard, supposedly were the first whites to discover the existence of this temple mound, which is now known as the Fort Walton site. The site was occupied continuously from about 50 B.C.

Burial urn from Fort Walton area, on display at
Indian Temple Mound Museum

(Courtesy Indian Temple Mound Museum)

to A.D. 1700. The museum has an excellent collection of pottery
with particularly good examples from the Weedon Island culture
(A.D. 500 to 1000) and the Fort Walton period (A.D. 1200 to 1600).
The Fort Walton pottery was collected from five major Indian sites
in the Choctawhatchee Bay area of the Florida Panhandle. This
buff, sand-tempered ware was coiled and paddled into a variety of
shapes and then fired in an outdoor kiln.

The Temple Mound, which is located next to the museum, was
built in at least three different stages; some experts estimate that
construction started about A.D. 1300, others say building began at
least 200 years later in the Fort Walton period. The well-traveled
archaeologist Clarence B. Moore visited here in 1901 and reported

that the mound was about 12 feet high and some 200 feet square at its base. An estimated 200 graves have been found in the mound, the latest ones being what archaeologists call "intrusive burials," meaning that the graves were dug into the mound. In earlier burials, the bodies, usually a chief and his retinue, were placed on top of the mound and then covered. In this way the mounds gained height. There is a replica of a temple on top of the mound.

Known Fort Walton sites are usually located farther inland where the soil is better suited for agriculture. Indians living around the Temple Mound also subsisted on fish and shellfish; the shells, in fact, probably improved the quality of the soil.

In 1990 two unique burial urns from the Fort Walton culture were added to the museum's already notable ceramics collection. Both urns came from a private collection; one shows a male after death, his eyes closed and hands folded. The other is a more animated figure of a living person. Other important pieces include six-pointed ceremonial bowls with the points perhaps representing the solstice.

In addition to its collection of prehistoric ceramics, the Indian Temple Mound Museum, which is owned and operated by the City of Fort Walton Beach, has exhibits of artifacts that illustrate the early days of contact between Europeans and Indians.

How to get there: The site is located just off U.S. 98, less than ½ mile west of the bridge over Santa Rosa Sound.

Madira Bickel Mound State Archaeological Site

Attraction: Two mounds in an early archaeological site
Hours: Daily 8:00 A.M. to sunset
Admission fee: None
For more information: Manager, Gamble Plantation State Historic Site, 3708 Patten Avenue, Ellenton, FL 33532; (813) 722–1017

This ten-acre tract was Florida's first designated state archaeological site. It includes a large platform mound, the Madira Bickel or the Bickel Ceremonial Mound, which measures 20 feet high and 170 feet by about 110 feet at the base. There is a staircase on the west side where a wide ramp went up the mound. There is also a low burial mound built during the Weeden Island period (A.D. 700 to 1000). The Madira Bickel is from the more recent Safety Harbor period (A.D. 1300 to 1600 or later).

Archaeologist Ripley Bullen discovered parts of more than thirty burials in the burial mound during excavations in 1950. The burial mound is 18 feet tall and about 100 feet in diameter. The burial artifacts included exceptionally well made pottery.

How to get there: The site is located about 5 miles north of Brandenton. Take Bayshore Drive west off U.S. 19 for 1½ miles; the site is near the south shore of Terra Ceia Island.

GEORGIA

Etowah Indian Mounds State Historic Site

Attraction: Three large Mississippian mounds, visitor center
Hours: Closed Mondays except legal holidays; Tuesday through Saturday 9:00 A.M. to 5:00 P.M.; Sunday 2:00 to 5:30 P.M.
Admission fee: Adults $1.25; children and students 50 cents
For more information: Etowah Indian Mounds State Historic Site, 813 Indian Mounds Road SW, Cartersville, GA 30120; (404) 387–3747

The predominant feature of this once flourishing center of the Mississippian culture is the 63-foot-high Mound A, measuring almost three acres at its base and a half acre at its top. The mound stands at the western end of the large ceremonial plaza that was raised about a foot above the surrounding area by prehistoric workers who laboriously brought in red clay from outside the complex.

Mound A, like the neighboring Mound B, has never been excavated, so the best indication of life at the complex comes from Mound C, which was completely leveled in an excavation in 1953 and then rebuilt to a height of 19 feet. More than 350 burial sites were found within the mound. The rich assortment of goods found in the graves revealed that the Mississippian peoples who lived here between A.D. 1000 and 1500 traded far and wide, with copper coming from as far away as Lake Superior and shells from the Gulf of Mexico. Two lifelike marble figures, each about 2 feet tall, were found near the base of Mound C and are now on display at the site's museum. The male and female figures bear remnants of the original paint. The figures may be effigies of a man and a woman in the graves.

A tour of the site begins by taking a bridge across a moat, which is believed to have been built for defense of the settlement; to the right is a borrow pit from which dirt was carried in baskets to

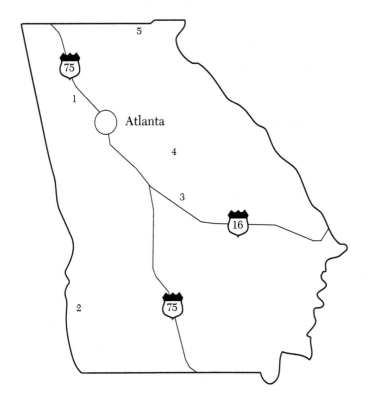

Georgia
1. Etowah Indian Mounds State Historic Site
2. Kolomoki Mounds Historic Park
3. Ocmulgee National Monument
4. The Rock Eagle Effigy
5. Track Rock Archaeological Area

build the mounds. A palisade of upright logs was located as a second line of defense just inside the moat.

The path leads directly to the steps leading up Mound A, which is about as tall as a six-story building and which has a splendid view of the Etowah River valley. Mound A was the platform for a great temple, from which the priest or chieftain reigned over the community. Mound A has never been excavated, but, in general, temple mounds at other Mississippian sites have yielded little of interest in the way of burial sites or interior structures.

The name Etowah is probably a corruption of the Indian Itawa, a word whose meaning has been lost. The name has also been Anglicized as Hightower and was recorded as Itaba in the chronicles of Hernando de Soto, who remained here six days during his exploration in 1543. The first published description of the mounds was written in 1817 by the Reverend Elias Cornelius, who was taken there by a group of Cherokee chiefs. They knew nothing about the origins of the mounds, he reported.

The site was excavated by John Rogan of the Smithsonian's Bureau of American Ethnology in 1887 and in 1925–1927 by Warren K. Moorehead, who directed the dig for Phillips Academy, Andover, Massachusetts. The last major exploration of the site, which included the final excavation of Mound C, occurred in 1953–1954 (A. R. Kelley, William Sears, and Lewis Larson) just after the Georgia Department of Natural Resources purchased the site.

A section of the site's trail follows the Etowah River, where cane used by the ancient Mississippians for arrows and roof thatching still grows. A rebuilt, V-shaped fish trap of piled stone is visible in the river. The Indians scooped up fish in woven baskets near the point of the V.

How to get there: Take I–75 to exit 124 (Cartersville) to Route 113 and 61; turn onto Etowah Mounds Road to site.

Kolomoki Mounds Historic Park

Attraction: Seven prehistoric mounds within large park
Hours: Park open daily 7:00 A.M. to 10:00 P.M.; museum hours are

Monday through Saturday 9:00 A.M. to 5:00 P.M., Sunday 2:00 to 5:30 P.M.

Admission fee: Museum is $1.50

For more information: Kolomoki Mounds Historic Park, Route 1, Blakely, GA 31723; (912) 723–5296

The location of this important historic park, which is on a spur of land isolated and protected by deep gullies and streams on three sides, helps explain why it was chosen as a settlement and ceremonial center by prehistoric peoples, who occupied it from about A.D. 400 to 1400. A description and a sketch of the mounds appear in an 1851 history of Alabama. In the Smithsonian Institution's annual report of 1872, William McKinley reported the existence of five mounds at the site. And in a book published in 1873, entitled *Antiquities of the Southern Indians*, Charles C. Jones, Jr., described the Mercier Mound (named for the property's original owner and now called Mound A) as one that "stands apart, prominent in size and marked in its physical peculiarities."

In the 1940s National Park Service archaeologist Charles H. Fairbanks reported seven mounds at the site, and the same seven are part of the interpretation of the park today. The site's second-largest mound, Mound D, was described by Sears as being 20 feet high and 100 feet in diameter. Mound G contained the Mercier family cemetery.

In 1948–1952 William Sears undertook extensive excavations of the area. He described Mound A as being a truncated rectangular pyramid about 60 feet tall and measuring 325 feet by 200 feet at its base. Mound A still dominates the site; today it is believed to have been part of a planned settlement that included a central plaza and residential and burial areas. Sears concluded that there were log or clay steps up the mound, not a ramp as earlier investigators believed. In the five years he excavated at Kolomoki, Sears retrieved more than 56,000 potsherds, 195 restorable vessels, 163 points, and numerous shell beads. The Kolomoki culture is believed to have developed out of the Weedon Island culture that flourished farther south. This transition is visible in the pottery, especially the elaborate work produced for burials.

Mound A was probably completed about A.D. 700. At its height Kolomoki was a sizeable population center, with perhaps 2,000 persons living there and as many living in villages within a 5-mile radius.

An exhibit at the mounds shows a completed excavation. The museum has representative artifacts found at the site and tells the story of prehistoric peoples in the region. The mounds are part of a 1,293-acre park with recreational facilities.

How to get there: The park is located about 6 miles north of Blakely, Georgia, off U.S. 27.

Ocmulgee National Monument

Attraction: Major prehistoric site, seven mounds, reconstructed temple, trails, visitor center and museum, discovery lab
Hours: Daily 9:00 A.M. to 5:00 P.M.; closed Christmas and New Year's Day
Admission fee: None
For more information: Ocmulgee National Monument, 1207 Emery Highway, Macon, GA 31201; (912) 752–8257

James Oglethorpe, founder of the colony of Georgia, provided the first description of Ocmulgee in 1739 when he wrote of "the three Mounts raised by the Indians over three of their Great Kings who were killed in the Wars." (Even early residents and travelers through Georgia realized that the mounds on the Ocmulgee River were the work of Indians and not, as the assumption went elsewhere at the time, the legacy of some ancient band of Europeans.) The early naturalist William Bartram in the late eighteenth century recognized the site as "ancient Indian fields," calling them "the wonderful remains of the power and the grandeur of the ancients in this part of America." The digging of a railroad cut across the site in 1843 turned up enough Indian artifacts to prove beyond doubt that the builders were prehistoric Indians.

Today a 683-acre national monument administered by the

National Park Service, Ocmulgee is a collection of seven mounds built between A.D. 900 and 1100 by Mississippians. In all, the site has been occupied by humans for about 10,000 years, beginning with the Archaic tribes of hunters and gatherers and ending in the Historic period when the Creek Indians lived here and traded with the English from about 1690 to 1715.

The end of the park known as the South Plateau is dominated by the Great Temple Mound, which is 45 feet high and 270 feet by 300 feet at its base. The adjacent Lesser Temple Mound is smaller but configured the same. Rectangular wooden structures were built on top during the period of Mississippian habitation and most likely used for important religious ceremonies. Railroad construction in the 1840s demolished part of Lesser Temple Mound.

In the 1930s the Smithsonian carried out large-scale excavations at Ocmulgee with several hundred workers provided by the Civil Works Administration. A 28-foot-deep shaft was dug from the top down into the Great Temple Mound. Before the shaft collapsed, it proved that this mound had been built in stages and not, as once thought, all at one time. Archaeological evidence indicates that the process involved burning the wooden temple on top of the mound— either as part of a ritual or when it rotted—and covering the remains with earth and constructing another temple on top. Similarly, the funeral mound, the third mound on the South Plateau, where more than one hundred burial sites have been uncovered, was found to have been constructed in at least seven stages.

On February 21, 1934, the remains of an earth lodge were discovered in such good condition that it was reconstructed and opened to the public in late 1937, and it remains one of the most interesting sights at Ocmulgee today. Forty-two feet in diameter, the earth lodge seated fifty people, probably chieftains and village leaders gathered for meetings and ceremonies. Three seats are on a clay platform shaped like a large bird, which is opposite the entrance; the rest are on a bench around the wall. There is a fire pit in the center.

Near both the earth lodge and the site of the original village is a small hump in the earth known as the Cornfield Mound. Originally about 8 feet high, the mound was excavated by the Smithsonian's James A. Ford, who found charred corn cobs in the area and an irregular surface under the mound, which he concluded was the contours of an ancient cornfield. Two lines of trenches near the village were probably dug either for defense against attack or to obtain fill for the mounds or some combination of the two.

The area, for unclear reasons, was unoccupied when William Bartram went there in 1773, although a band of Creek Indians had lived there for a period early in the eighteenth century.

Nearby Macon had long been interested in Ocmulgee and the preservation of the mounds. As early as 1828 the *Macon Telegraph* expressed the wish that the site, "long the favorite haunts of our village beaux and belles," might forever "remain as at present, sacred to solitude, to reflection and inspiration." In the 1930s local organizations purchased the land for the park and deeded it to the United States. President Franklin D. Roosevelt proclaimed Ocmulgee a national monument in December 1936.

Construction on Ocmulgee's handsome Art Moderne head-quarters, with its smooth walls and rounded corners, was interrupted by World War II and not completed until the early 1950s. Today the building houses the museum, visitor center, and administration facilities.

Visitors can tour the monument either by car or on foot along a network of paths that includes the well-marked Opelofa Nature Trail. The trail leads through the swampy lowlands near Walnut Creek, a tributary of the larger Ocmulgee River. The Dunlap Trail, named for Samuel Dunlap (who, at the time of the Civil War, owned the plantation that is now the monument), leads to the remains of a Confederate earthworks used during the Battle of Dunlap Hill on July 30, 1864.

School and other youth groups can make pottery; use reproduction Indian tools, weapons, and musical instuments; study the environment; and engage in other learning activities related to the site at the Charles Fairbanks Memorial Discovery Lab. Advance reservations are required for the lab.

How to get there: The site is located on the eastern edge of Macon on U.S. 80. From I–75, exit onto I–16 East. Take either the first or second exit and follow U.S. 80 a mile to the park.

(Courtesy University of Georgia Cooperative Extension Services)

Rock Eagle Effigy

The Rock Eagle Effigy

Attraction: Large bird effigy, viewing tower
Hours: Always open
Admission fee: None
For more information: Rock Eagle 4-H Center, 350 Rock Eagle Road NW, Eatonton, GA 31024–9599; (706) 485–2831

Made entirely of milky quartz rock and boulders, this huge likeness or effigy of a bird measures 102 feet from head to tail, has a wingspan of 120 feet, and rises about 10 feet from the ground. (A nearby companion effigy, not open to the public, is the same length but twelve feet longer in the wings.)

No evidence of human habitation, such as arrowheads or potsherds, has ever been found in the area, so the date of the effigy is unknown. Experts assume that it served ceremonial purposes. Georgia historian C. C. Jones made the first measured drawings of the effigy for the Smithsonian in 1877. A. R. Kelly, an archaeologist who did exploratory work on the effigy in 1937, speculated that the builders were related to later Adena and Hopewell peoples. Further excavations were conducted in the 1950s by Vincenzo Petrullo, who found fragments of human and animal bones close to the base of the tail and a small, ovate quartz tool. Archaeologist Charles H. Fairbanks has speculated that the effigy was a buzzard, not an eagle as is usually assumed. By carrying off carrion, he pointed out, buzzards performed an important function for prehistoric peoples.

The effigy, which was designated a National Historic Landmark in 1979, can be seen clearly from a granite observation tower.

How to get there: Take Rock Eagle Road west off Route 441, 7 miles north of Eatonton, and follow signs.

Track Rock Archaeological Area

Attraction: Rock art of uncertain date
Hours: Always open
Admission fee: None
For more information: Supervisor's Office, U.S. Forest Service, 508 Oak Street, Gainesville, GA 30501; (706) 745–6928

When asked for information about the mysterious petroglyphs that appear on six rocks in this section of the Chattahoochee National Forest, the U.S. Forest Service refers questioners to a work published in 1900: James Mooney's *Myths of the Cherokees*, which originally appeared in the annual report of the Smithsonian's Bureau of American Ethnology and has since been reprinted as a separate work. Scientists know no more about the rocks today than Mooney did back then, the Forest Service says.

The largest of the soapstone rocks is about 8 feet long and about 4 feet above the ground at its highest point. The petroglyphs have never been deciphered. Theories include speculation that the figures might be prehistoric graffiti. Or they might be connected with hunting rituals, since some of the markings resemble turkey tracks or deer antlers. It is often written that the "glyphs" date from 1500 B.C., but according to a Forest Service representative,

"They could be 3,000 or 500 years old. We have no idea." The rocks are protected from vandalism by steel grates.

How to get there: The site is located on Track Rock Road, 1½ miles south of U.S. 76, between the towns of Blairsville and Young Harris. A path leads from the parking lot to the rocks. There is a district ranger's office on Highway 19/129 South.

ILLINOIS

Cahokia Mounds State Historic Site

Attraction: Major prehistoric settlement, sixty-eight mounds, solar observatory, interpretive center, interpretive trails
Hours: Site open daily 8:00 A.M. to dusk and closed on New Year's Day, Thanksgiving, Christmas, and other major holidays; interpretive center open daily 9:00 A.M. to 5:00 P.M., closed Mondays and Tuesdays December through February
Admission fee: None; suggested donation $2.00 for adults, $1.00 for children
For more information: Cahokia Mounds State Historic Site, P.O. Box 681, Collinsville, IL 62234; (618) 346–5160

Located on the eastern floodplain of the Mississippi River, not far from the junction of the Illinois and Missouri rivers, Cahokia is a colossus among America's prehistoric settlements. It includes the largest Indian mound north of central Mexico and one of the largest man-made earthworks anywhere on earth. In its heyday, between A.D. 1100 and 1200, it might have had a population of 20,000 or more; some estimates are much higher.

Cahokia was also the cultural and population center of an expanse of fertile floodplains and alluvial terraces that make up the area known today as the American Bottom. This region might have had as great a population as Cahokia. Certainly it included a number of other prosperous settlements.

There were once more than 120 mounds in this prehistoric metropolis, which is named for an Indian tribe that inhabited the region shortly before the French settlers arrived in the late 1600s and early 1700s. Today sixty-eight earthen mounds—out of more than a hundred whose locations are known—have been preserved in the 2,200-acre state historic site.

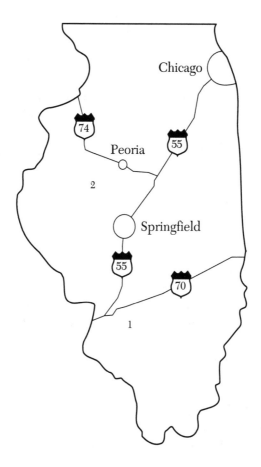

Illinois
1. Cahokia Mounds State Historic Site
2. Dickson Mounds

Monks Mound, the largest mound in the complex, is a platform mound that covers more than fourteen acres, rises 100 feet above the plain in four terraces, and contains some twenty-two million cubic feet of earth. Monks Mound was built in stages between A.D. 900 and 1200 and derives its name from a Trappist monastery that farmed on top of it in the early 1800s. It is believed that the Cahokia chief lived in and ruled from a large pole-and-thatch building on top of the mound. Monks Mound overlooks a central plaza covering thirty to forty acres. Although it took at least two centuries to build, probably in some fourteen stages, some experts have speculated that Monk's Mound was never finished and that the Cahokians abandoned it to work on a series of smaller mounds.

Excavations indicate that the site's other platform mounds and similar double platform mounds, which rise in steps, were also the sites for buildings, probably ceremonial structures and the residences of Cahokia's elite. Cahokia's so-called ridge-top mounds were built for burials and might mark the two major axes of the community. The site's seven conical mounds were used for the burial of important people.

Peoples of the late Woodland culture were the first to occupy Cahokia, probably about A.D. 600. Little or no mound building went on during this phase of occupation, which lasted about 300 years. It was at the end of this period that the emerging Mississippian culture, which was marked by mound building and elaborate burials, became dominant at Cahokia.

An early traveler, Henry Brackenridge, reported to Thomas Jefferson about Cahokia and other mound sites in 1818. "I have been sometimes induced to think that, at the period when these were constructed," he wrote, "there was a population as numerous as that which once animated the borders of the Nile, or of the Euphrates, or of Mexico." Albert Gallatin, Jefferson's Treasury secretary and the author of an 1836 book on American Indians, and Ephraim Squier, coauthor of the first (1848) comprehensive survey of the mounds, were two other prominent men who contemplated the mystery of the mounds at Cahokia. But serious work at the site didn't begin until the 1920s, a late date considering the size and obvious importance of the settlement.

In an excavation he conducted in the 1870s at Cahokia, William McAdams excavated more than a hundred pottery vessels, many of them effigies of birds and animals. In a book published in 1877, he wrote of digging "near the base of the great temple mound of Cahokia, whose towering height of over 100 feet gave a grateful shade for our labors" and of finding "in a crumbling tomb of earth and stone a great number of burial vases, over one hundred of which were perfect. It was a most singular collection, as if the mound builder, with patient and skillful hand, united with artistic taste in shaping the vessels, had endeavored to make a representation of the natural history of the country in ceramics."

In 1961 archaeologists excavating in advance of a highway crew first came across evidence that the Cahokians had developed and built sophisticated solar calendars. Called woodhenges because of their similarity to Stonehenge in England, the sun calendars were developed sometime after A.D. 900 and consisted of upright timbers arranged in a circle. Since the 1961 discovery, one of the woodhenges has been reconstructed; it consists of forty-eight large cedar posts arranged in a circle 410 feet in diameter around a central observation post. Today, the site conducts special programs for equinox and solstice sunrises.

Evidence of another wooden structure, a lengthy stockade that ran around Monks Mound and sixteen other mounds, was first detected with aerial photography. This wooden wall, a small part of which has been reconstructed, included bastions or towers spaced at regular intervals; therefore, experts have concluded that it was probably built for defense although it could have also served to separate the elite from the rest of the community.

The Cahokians dug the earth with tools made of chert, a type of silica. They probably also had wooden tools, although there is no evidence of this today, because the wood would have disintegrated over the centuries. The workers dug the earth out of the ground from what archaeologists call "borrow pits," the largest of which was 6 feet deep and covered seventeen acres.

In all, nine borrow pits have been discovered at Cahokia. One, uncovered during an excavation, had been filled in with trash; then a platform mound had been built on top of it. The earth taken from the borrow pits was transported in basket loads, each weighing fifty to sixty pounds, to the mound site. Like other prehistoric Americans, the Cahokians had neither the horse nor the wheel. Writing about Monk's Mound in his landmark 1894 study of the the mounds for the Smithsonian, Cyrus Thomas voiced a common sentiment when he wrote of Monk's Mound: "We can scarcely bring ourselves to believe it was built without some other means of collecting and conveying material than that possessed by the Indians."

One of the small ridge-top mounds, a mere 6 to 8 feet high and prosaically named Mound 72, was excavated in the late 1960s and early 1970s and turned out to be a rich depository of information about the structure of Cahokia's society as reflected in its burial practices. It also contained a treasure trove of burial artifacts and some very interesting skeletons. Mound 72, the archaeologists estimate, was built in six separate stages and contained the bodies of at least 280 individuals.

Mound 72 was apparently reserved for burial of elite members of the society. In one section, the remains of a male, obviously a person of considerable prominence, were found on a blanket made up of more than 20,000 shell beads. Nearby were the skeletons of four men whose hands and heads had been lopped off and the remains of fifty-three women between the ages of fifteen and twenty-five. Although there are no signs that the women were killed, "It is difficult to avoid the conclusion that, like the four mutilated men, the women were sacrificed, probably as a part of some kind of funeral ritual," wrote Melvin L. Fowler, one of the excavators of Mound 72, in *Scientific American* in 1975.

Grave goods found in Mound 72 are an indication of the considerable wealth of the Cahokian elite, the skill of their craftsmen, and the extent of their trading network. The tribute cache, with the prominent male placed on top of the graves of three men and three women, included a roll of sheet copper three feet long from Lake Superior, sheet mica from North Carolina, and hundreds of perfect, unused arrowheads made of cherts from Arkansas, Oklahoma, Wisconsin, Tennessee, Missouri, and Illinois.

Cahokia was well placed to thrive. It was situated near major waterways for trade and cultural exchange. The rich land of the American Bottom allowed the intensive cultivation of corn, squash, and sunflowers, although the Cahokians continued to hunt and gather wild foods to supplement their diets. The Cahokians also developed an efficient chert hoe with chert quarried in southern Illinois, and the woodhenges, or solar observatories, were aids in planning the agricultural cycle.

The reasons why Cahokia declined in importance and population after A.D. 1200 to 1250 are not so obvious. Experts have speculated that the Cahokians exhausted the supply of timber or game. Perhaps overfarming depleted the soil of its fertility, climate changes may have adversely affected crops, or other population centers in the region may have begun to compete successfully with Cahokia. For whatever reason, by the 1400s Cahokia was abandoned.

How to get there: Take Route 111 South off I–55/70 and go ¼ mile to Collinsville Road, then 2 miles east to site; or take exit 24 off I–255, then proceed west 2 miles on Collinsville Road.

Dickson Mounds

Attraction: Museum, mounds, village sites
Hours: 8:30 A.M. to 5:00 P.M. daily
Admission fee: None
For more information: Dickson Mounds Museum, Lewiston, IL 61542; (309) 547–3721

The state-run museum at Dickson Mounds focuses on the archaeological record left by people who lived along the Illinois River valley over a period of 12,000 years. The museum is also located on the site of several prehistoric settlements and includes a number of earthen mounds that were constructed between A.D. 1100 and 1350 by Mississippian and other Woodland people.

The main feature of the 162-acre site is a bluff-top mound used by Indians from about A.D. 900 to 1300. The mound is named for Don F. Dickson, a former owner of the mound, who began scholarly excavations there in 1927. A chiropractor, Dickson was interested in prehistoric diseases and he studied the site for two years, uncovering 237 individual burials. Unlike most researchers of the time, who removed burial remains for further study, Dickson conducted his research on site and left the burials in place. He operated the burial site as a private museum until he sold it to the State of Illinois in 1945.

Dickson's work attracted others to the area. While working in the vicinity in the 1930s, archaeologists from the University of Chicago established many of the methods used in archaeology today. Illinois's Fulton County, where Dickson Mounds is located, has more than 3,000 recorded prehistoric sites.

In 1972 Illinois built a museum on the site; one wing of the building covered the burial site. In the process, archaeologists discovered that the cemetery consisted of not one mound but ten burial mounds and one platform mound, which had merged together over the centuries. The exposed part of the cemetery in the museum consisted of part of two mounds or about 10 percent of the entire cemetery. The individuals buried at Dickson belonged to a local variant of the Mississippian culture; many were buried with pottery, shell spoons, chert knives, blades, and scrapers.

The cemetery was on view for twenty years. Then on April 3, 1992, the state closed the exhibit and re-entombed the remains. This action was taken in response to protests by American Indian groups who objected to public display of ancestral remains.

How to get there: Proceed 2 miles southeast of Lewiston, off Route 100 and County Road 9; the museum is 60 miles northwest of Springfield.

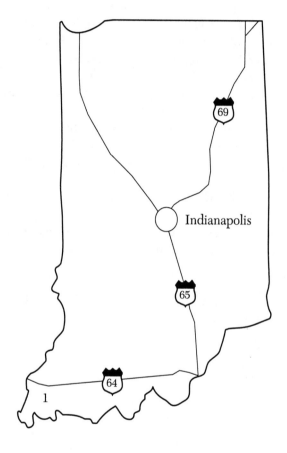

Indiana
1. Angel Mounds State Historic Site

INDIANA

Angel Mounds State Historic Site

Attraction: Prehistoric mounds and reconstructed buildings of the Mississippian period, interpretive center
Hours: Tuesday through Saturday 9:00 A.M. to 5:00 P.M.; Sunday 1:00 to 5:00 P.M.; closed Mondays and January 1 to March 15
Admission fee: None
For more information: Angel Mounds State Historic Site, 8215 Pollack Avenue, Evansville, IN 47715; (812) 853–3956

The central mound at Angel Mounds is one of the largest in the eastern United States; it is 644 feet long, 415 feet wide, and 44 feet high. Built as two terraces and a knoll, it covers four acres. Originally a 103-acre Mississippian village, Angel Mounds was occupied—and functioned as an important cultural, political, and economic center—from about A.D. 1300 to 1500. A population of 2,000 to 3,000 people lived in some 200 thatch-roofed houses. Today Angel Mounds is one of the best-preserved prehistoric sites in the country.

Named for its original owner, the Angel family, the site was purchased by the Indiana Historical Society in 1938 and transferred to the State of Indiana in 1947. Archaeological excavations under the direction of Glenn A. Black were carried out for twenty-four years with funding from the Lilly Endowment. Some 250 Works Progress Administration workers were involved in the project before that Depression-era program ended in the early 1940s.

The mounds at the Angel site were not for burial. Instead they were platforms for the residences of chiefs and other important figures or other buildings of political or religious significance. Archaeologists have uncovered evidence of eleven mounds. In addition to the large Mound A described above, there is a temple mound, called Mound B, which has been rounded off by years of plowing and erosion. Mound E, the only unplowed mound on the site, has retained its original shape—a truncated pyramid. It is assumed that the other mounds in the settlement originally had the same shape.

The town is bordered on the south by the Ohio River. A small portion of the defensive stockade that once stretched in an arc from the river around the settlement and back to the river again has been rebuilt. The stockade was 6,300 feet long and had bastions spaced every 120 feet.

A number of the site's square and rectangular structures, including the temple on top of Mound F, have been reconstructed with prehistoric methods—weaving twigs between upright logs set in a narrow trench. Clay mixed with grass was then applied to the walls. The roofs were covered with grass thatching.

The Mississippian people who lived at the Angel site were agriculturists who grew corn but also hunted, fished, and gathered nuts, fruit, and other plants to supplement their diet. They obtained salt by evaporating water from saline springs in large clay pots. Unlike other sites dating from this era, not much evidence of trade has been discovered.

There is an interpretive center at the site with exhibits of artifacts found at that location.

How to get there: Located just east of Evansville; take the Covert Avenue/Highway 662 exit off I–164 and follow the signs to Angel Mounds.

IOWA

Effigy Mounds National Monument

Attraction: 191 mounds, including twenty-nine effigy mounds; visitor center; self-guided trail; regular ranger-guided tours from Memorial Day to Labor Day
Hours: Visitor center open daily, 8:00 A.M. to 5:00 P.M. in winter, 8:00 A.M. to 7:00 P.M. in summer
Admission fee: None
For more information: Effigy Mounds National Monument, R.R. 1 Box 25A, Harpers Ferry, IA 52146; (319) 873–3491

Among the 191 mounds in this bluff-top monument is one that has been radiocarbon dated to about 2,500 years old. It is believed to have been built by peoples of the Red Ochre culture, the oldest mound builders in the Mississippi Valley. Named for the floor covering of red ochre on the floor of the burial pits, the mound contained such typical burial offerings as large chipped blades, spear or dart points, and round copper beads.

Several mounds in the monument, including three next to the visitor center, are associated with the Hopewell period from 100 B.C. to A.D. 600, but the monument is named for the twenty-nine mounds built in the shape of bears or birds, the so-called effigy mounds. These were built by the Effigy Mounds people who followed the Hopewellians and continued until about A.D. 1300 or 1400, when they, in turn, were supplanted by the Oneota Indians of historic times.

The monument's effigy mounds include the monumental Great Bear Mound, which is 70 feet wide at the shoulders, 137 feet long, and 3½ feet high. The Pleasant Ridge group of mounds includes a line of ten "Marching Bears." Each one is about 3 feet high and 80 to 100 feet long.

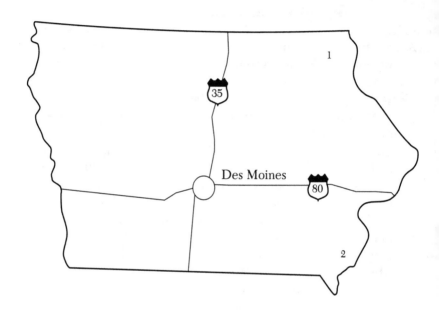

Iowa
1. Effigy Mounds National Monument
2. Toolesboro National Historic Landmark

The Effigy Mounds people were noted for using copper for tools (unlike the Hopewellians, who only used copper for ornaments). There is also little evidence that they buried their dead with valuable offerings.

The Effigy Mounds area first appeared in print in Jonathan Carver's *Travels Through the Interior Parts of North America in the Years 1766, 1767, 1768*. The mounds, however, received little further notice until 1881, when Theodore H. Lewis and Alfred J. Hill surveyed many mounds in the Mississippi River valley, including the Marching Bear Group. Effigy Mounds became a national monument in 1949. Since then, the addition of more than 400 acres to the original 1,000 has added ninety-nine mounds to the monument. Today the monument covers about two square miles.

How to get there: Travel 3 miles north of Marquette on Route 76.

Toolesboro National Historic Landmark

Attraction: Nine mounds on Mississippi River bluff, visitor center
Hours: Friday through Monday, Memorial Day through Labor Day, 1:00 to 4:00 P.M.; closed rest of the year
Admission fee: None
For more information: Toolesboro National Historic Landmark, 6932 Main Highway 99, Box 155A, Wapello, IA 52653

Between 200 B.C. and A.D. 400, the Hopewell people probably built nine burial mounds here on a bluff overlooking the Mississippi. Of these, six remain, preserved as part of this national historic landmark. The others, like so many prehistoric earthworks that were in the region when white settlers arrived in the early nineteenth century, have been destroyed by farming and development.

It is believed that the Hopewell people used the site, which is not far from the mouth of the Iowa River, for ceremonies and burials and that the Hopewell who built them lived elsewhere, either on the terraces below the mound site or at a farther distance. Several mounds were excavated by the Davenport Academy of Natural Sciences in the late 1880s. The findings indicated that the mounds often were the result of a series of burials in log tombs. When a tomb was filled, it was burned and a mound of earth was piled over it. Then another tomb was built until "there was no more space within the basic contour that had been chosen," a brochure on the site explains.

The excavations recovered human skeletons as well as a wide assortment of grave goods, including elaborate effigy pipes with representations of frogs, ducks, rabbits, and other animals carved on the bowls. Pottery, platform pipes, copper axes, mica ornaments, pearl beads, and bone and stone tools and weapons were also found in the excavations.

In an 1868 history of the region, William L. Toole, for whom the first village was renamed, wrote that the area "near the ancient mounds" was settled by 1835. The mounds became a national historic landmark site in 1966; three years later a visitor center with exhibits on Hopewell culture opened. The site also includes a half-acre Demonstration Prairie Plot that was originally planted with prairie grasses in 1974.

How to get there: Travel 8 miles east of Wapello on Route 99. The site is located east of the junction with Route 61.

KENTUCKY

Mammoth Cave National Park

Attraction: Immense cave with prehistoric sites
Hours: Park always open; visitor center open summer, 7:30 A.M. to
7:00 P.M.; fall through spring, 8:00 A.M. to 5:30 P.M.
Admission fee: Park is free; fees for cave tours range from $2.00
to $10.00
For more information: Mammoth Cave National Park, Mammoth Cave, KY 42259; (505) 758–2251

For the casual visitor, Mammoth Cave's extensive prehistoric
heritage is overshadowed by the natural beauty and spectacular
size of its many underground passages. A prehistoric person of the
late Archaic period first ventured into the dark depths of the cave
about forty centuries ago. Even earlier, Archaic peoples had been
using the entrance to the cave for shelter. The remains of a young
girl found buried in a grass-lined grave near the mouth of the cave
are estimated to be 3,000 years old.

The park covers 52,000 acres; the cave itself consists of more
than 300 miles of underground passages on five levels. Evidence of
prehistoric man within the cave includes footprints set in mud and
sand; aboriginal sandals woven of cattail, hemp, pawpaw inner
bark, or similar natural materials; and even mummies, their flesh
desiccated in the cool cave air. The most famous mummy, nicknamed "Lost John," died a full 2 miles inside the cave when a six-
and-a-half-ton rock fell on him. He was discovered by two guides
in 1935. Lost John was about 5 feet 3 inches tall, weighed about
145 pounds, and was about forty-five years old. The year of his
death is put at 17 B.C. His body was on display for forty years until
the Park Service forbade the exhibition of human remains.

It has been speculated that Lost John was mining gypsum or
other minerals such as epsomite or selenite when the boulder

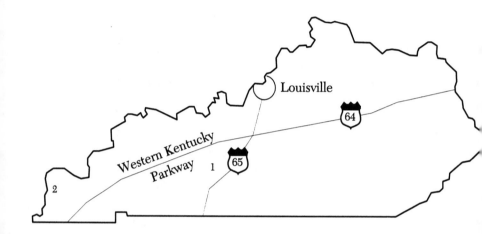

Kentucky
1. Mammoth Cave National Park
2. Wickliffe Mounds

crushed him. It is not certain why peoples of the Woodland period (1000 B.C. to A.D. 900) wanted such minerals—or how they used them—but there is ample evidence of their mining activity on the cave walls and in such leavings as stone hammers, mussel shell scrapers, and the bundles of reeds they used for torches.

Many prehistoric artifacts were taken from the cave in the nineteenth century. Even today looting remains a problem, both in the cave and at numerous unmarked prehistoric sites on the surface that are within the park's boundaries. Two tours led by park rangers—the Historic Tour and the Lantern Tour—include stops at prehistoric sites within the cave. For visitors with special interests in archaeology, the park sponsors an archaeology weekend each year, usually in November. Mammoth Cave was made a national park in 1941.

How to get there: The park entrance is 10 miles west of Cave City on Route 70 and 7 miles northwest of Park City on Route 255.

Wickliffe Mounds

Attraction: Mound site and archaeological research center
Hours: Daily, March through November, 9:00 A.M. to 4:00 P.M.
Admission fee: $3.00 adults
For more information: Wickliffe Mounds Research Center, P.O. Box 155, Wickliffe, KY 42087; (502) 335–3681

This site on the heights overlooking the Mississippi River, only a few miles below the mouth of the Ohio River, was occupied by Mississippian people starting about A.D. 1000. But why it was inhabited for only 300 years or so is an archaeological question that ongoing excavations might yet answer. There is a theory that, for unknown reasons, the entire region was emptied of people from 1450 to 1600.

Like similar small Mississippian towns that were once located all along the river, Wickliffe Mounds had a central plaza "framed" by platform mounds on the west and north and a burial mound on the east. The site was first mapped by Robert Loughridge in 1880.

In the 1930s a dealer and relic hunter named Colonel Fain White King purchased the site and began intensive excavations. He also opened the site, which he called an "ancient city," to tourists. In 1945 he donated the property to a local hospital, which, in turn, gave it to Murray State University in 1983. In addition to keeping the site open to the public, Murray State conducts excavations each summer, which visitors can observe.

A tour of the site includes visits to three buildings. The Lifeways Building includes displays from the earlier years of occupation. Artifacts on view include pottery for storage and cooking, grinding stones, gorgets, and the stone discs that were rolled along the ground in the game called chunkey. The object of chunkey was to throw a spear at the point at which the player thought the disc would stop rolling.

The Cemetery Building covers the excavation of the burial mound and includes reconstructions of grave sites. The Architecture Building is built over a platform mound where excavations have exposed the posthole patterns of the original structure. An exhibit in the building explains the wattle and daub method of construction, in which upright posts were interwoven with branches and vines (the wattle). Clay was then daubed, or smeared, on the wattle framework. When the structures burned, the clay was baked hard and became part of the mound itself. The Ceremonial Mound, the largest on the site, was probably built in six separate stages.

How to get there: Located ½ mile northwest of the town of Wickliffe on U.S. 51/60/62

LOUISIANA

Marksville State Commemorative Area

Attraction: Five prehistoric mounds within semicircular earthworks, museum/visitor center
Hours: Wednesday through Sunday 9:00 A.M. to 5:00 P.M.
Admission fee: None
For more information: Marksville State Commemorative Area, 700 Allen Street, Marksville, LA 71351; (318) 253–9546

There has been some scholarly speculation that this mound complex on a bluff overlooking Old River Lake was first inhabited at the same time (1700 to 700 B.C.) as Poverty Point, the immense earthworks and mound site in northern Louisiana. More often, however, it is regarded as a variation of the Hopewell culture of Ohio and Illinois. Like the Hopewell, the people of the Marksville culture (A.D. 1 through 400) built conical mounds, performed elaborate burial ceremonies, and traded over long distances.

A semicircular earthworks 3,300 feet long (and from 3 to 7 feet high) surrounds the site with the open end on a bluff overlooking the river. Although the purpose of the earthworks might have been defensive, several breaks or openings suggest it was constructed to mark a special ceremonial area.

There are five mounds within the earthworks. Near the center, 20-foot-high Mound 4, the tallest in the grouping, is a conical burial mound 100 feet across at its base. Mound 6 (there is no Mound 1) on the northernmost end of the site is a flat-topped mound 13 feet high and about 300 feet in diameter. It is not known how old it is or how it was used.

The Smithsonian Institution's Gerard Fowke conducted the first archaeological exploration and mapping of the site in 1926. During excavations of 1933, James A. Ford and F. M. Setzler, also of the Smithsonian, discovered evidence that linked Marksville to

51

Louisiana
1. Marksville State Commemorative Area
2. Poverty Point State Commemorative Area

the Hopewell culture, which until then was believed to be confined to the Ohio region. Among the artifacts found at Marksville is a ceremonial pipe in the shape of a dog. In 1938 and 1939, Robert S. Neitzel and Edwin B. Doran led a group sponsored by the Works Progress Administration and Louisiana State University in further excavations. Marksville became a state park in 1950 and a National Historic Landmark in 1964.

There is a nature trail, picnic area, and a museum/visitor center, built in 1952, which interprets the architecture of the Moundsville culture and displays prehistoric artifacts found in the area.

How to get there: The commemorative area is located just to the east of the town of Marksville, off Routes 1 and 452.

Poverty Point State Commemorative Area

Attraction: Prehistoric earthworks and mounds, trails, tram ride, viewing tower, museum/visitor center
Hours: Wednesday through Sunday 9:00 A.M. to 5:00 P.M.
Admission fee: $2.00
For more information: Poverty Point State Commemorative Area, P.O. Box 248, Epps, LA 71237; (318) 926–5492

Settlers who owned a plantation here in the mid-1800s and who undoubtedly had to struggle to survive gave Poverty Point its name; however, the relatively advanced culture that flourished here 1,000 years before the birth of Christ was hardly impoverished. It dominated an area stretching from the junction of the Arkansas and Mississippi rivers to the Gulf Coast and included ten major population centers that were connected by waterways.

Poverty Point dominated this area from about 1500 B.C. to 700 B.C. Other prehistoric societies north of Mexico at this time lived mostly in small groups as hunters and gatherers. The people of Poverty Point, however, lived together in large numbers—several thousand at Poverty Point itself. This society was complex enough and organized enough to be able to build large mounds and embankments. It also traded widely—some materials came from more than 1,000 miles away. Some experts believe the people of

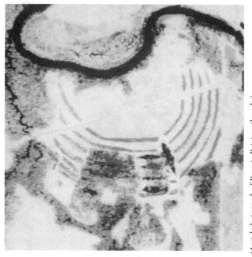

(Aerial photograph of Poverty Point earthworks)

Poverty Point

Poverty Point also grew corn, a development that didn't occur until much later in other cultures.

Given the size and complexity of the Poverty Point culture, it is logical to assume that the society was governed by a central authority—a chiefdom, perhaps—that governed and regulated trade in an area that extended far beyond Poverty Point itself. If this is true, writes archaeologist Jon L. Gibson, "It would have been one of the most complex developments in prehistoric America north of Mexico. This country would not see its like again until after A.D. 1000."

Samuel Lockett was the first to record the existence of Poverty Point in 1873, and Clarence B. Moore, the archaeologist who covered so much of the Southeast in his paddlewheeler, explored here in 1912. But the importance of the site was not understood until 1953, when aerial photographs revealed to James Ford and others that Poverty Point was a "giant earthworks" and that its mounds and ridges were man-made, not natural.

The nearly perfect symmetry of the layout of Poverty Point led some experts to conclude that the settlement was conceived and constructed according to a master plan in one concerted effort. Others, however, suspect that the complex developed in a more random fashion over a longer period of time.

The Ridges

The center of the Povery Point complex consists of six concentric arcs of earthen embankments that enclose a central plaza of about thirty-seven acres. The arcs are divided into five unequal segments by four aisles or corridors from 35 to 100 feet wide. The outside earthen arc is three-quarters of a mile long. There are two extra arcs in the northwest segment and one less (five) in the southern section. The ridges, which were between 50 and 150 feet apart, were once 10 to 15 feet tall. The ridges end at bluffs overlooking the Bayou Macon.

It was once thought that the ridges at Poverty Point formed an entire circle, half of which had been eroded away by the waterway. James Ford estimated in 1956 that the original arcs must have been octagonal in shape and more than 11 miles long. This conjecture was seriously undermined, however, when it was determined that the bluffs on the eastern edge of the site were formed thousands of years before prehistoric development began.

The Bird Mound

From the ground the giant Bird Mound, or Mound A—70 feet high at its head—looks like a natural part of the landscape. But, as aerial photography has shown, it clearly resembles a giant bird from the air: 710 feet from head to tail with a wingspan of 640 feet. The Bird Mound slopes off to 42 feet at its tail, which is just over half its head height.

Excavations at the mound have determined that it is manmade, using earth taken from nearby borrow pits (now low, swampy areas) and carried to the mound in woven split-cane baskets. Since there have been no burials or remnants of temples found in the mound, its purpose is unclear. An earthen ramp once connected the tail to the outermost ridge, or Ridge 6, but most of the earth was removed to be used as fill when a highway was built through Poverty Point many years ago.

Mound B and Other Mounds

Located 700 yards north of the Bird Mound, Mound B was probably once a burial mound. A partial excavation in 1955 revealed a layer of ash at the bottom along with one human bone fragment, which experts believe to be evidence of a cremation. Three horizontal layers of earth, each about 4 feet thick, were piled above the ashes. The remains of baskets and other containers were found on top of the third layer. This burial site is the only one ever found at Poverty Point.

About 1½ miles north of the embankments, but not on the walking tour of the area, is Motley Mound, which is smaller but also appears to be shaped like a bird. Square-shaped Lower Jackson Mound, which might be a natural formation that the Indians leveled off for some ceremonial or other purpose, is 1½ miles south of the Bird Mound.

Museum

The museum at the park displays a good sampling of the numerous artifacts that have been found at the site. These include the small, variously shaped lumps of baked clay, known as "Poverty Point objects," that Gibson calls "a distinguishing hallmark of Poverty Point culture." It is believed that these molded objects were used to heat the earth ovens made from holes in the ground and that their size and shape somehow controlled the intensity and duration of the heat.

Although many artifacts unearthed at Poverty Point were utilitarian—javelin points, atlatl weights, and plummets, which were probably bola weights for hunting—there are many other stone objects that were either decorative or ceremonial in function. These include stone pipes (maybe the first calumets used by Indians in the Southwest) and, in great numbers, stone beads made of red jasper. Figurative objects include tiny effigies, such as the charming fat-bellied owls, and figurines of women, mostly pregnant, with their heads missing.

The trail loop around Poverty Point is 2½ miles long and includes a steep climb to the top of the Bird Mound. Bird Mound and much of the park are also visible from an observation tower near the museum. There is a tram to take visitors to the mound and around the park.

How to get there: The site is located 15 miles north of Delhi, Louisiana, on Route 577.

MINNESOTA

Grand Mound Center

Attraction: Burial mound, history museum, trails
Hours: May through Labor Day, 10:00 A.M. to 5:00 P.M. daily; rest of year 10:00 A.M. to 4:00 P.M. Saturdays, noon to 4:00 P.M. Sundays; open other times for groups with reservations
Admission fee: None
For more information: Minnesota Historical Society, 345 Kellogg Blvd. West, St. Paul, MN 55102; (612) 296–6126

Constructed of 90,000 cubic feet of earth, Grand Mound is the largest surviving prehistoric earth structure in the upper Midwest. The surrounding region has produced archaeological evidence of

Reconstructions of Laurel culture pottery

(Courtesy Minnesota Historical Society)

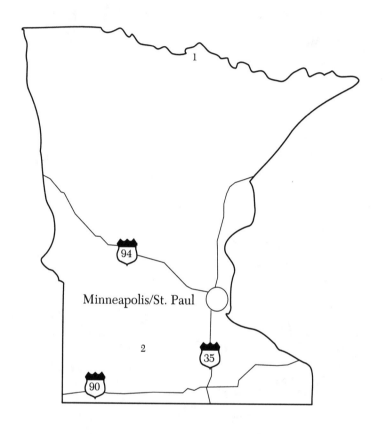

Minnesota
1. Grand Mound Center
2. Jeffers Petroglyphs

human habitation starting with the Archaic Indians, who camped here about 5000 B.C. and fished for sturgeon in the near-by Big Fork and Rainy rivers. The periodic flooding of the rivers deposited this evidence in chronological layers, which now extend to a depth of 7 feet below the surface.

People of the Laurel culture began arriving in the area about 500 B.C. Although the culture bears some similarities to the Hopewells in mound building, pottery, and projectile points, it is considered a distinct culture. Other aspects of the Laurel culture, such as the toggle-headed harpoon and a chisel made from a beaver's incisors, came from subarctic traditions.

The Laurel began building burial mounds in this region about 200 B.C. Today, Grand Mound—136 feet long, 98 feet wide, 25 feet high—is the largest of five known mounds surviving from this period.

Beginning about A.D. 800, the Blackduck culture began replacing the Laurel. These people were more dependent on wild rice in their diet than the Laurel, who were hunter-gatherers. The Blackduck also used the bow and arrow instead of the atlatl. They often buried their dead beneath the surfaces of the Laurel-built mounds.

Grand Mound is owned and administered by the Minnesota Historical Society. In the past, riverboats from Ontario brought tourists to dig for artifacts in the mound. Grand Mound's History Center offers an audiovisual program on the history of the mounds and the trails within the park.

How to get there: On Route 11, proceed 17 miles west of International Falls.

Jeffers Petroglyphs

Attraction: Prehistoric petroglyphs in prairie setting
Hours: May 1 through Labor Day, 10:00 A.M. to 5:00 P.M. daily; September, 10:00 A.M. to 5:00 P.M. weekends; closed rest of year
Admission fee: None
For more information: Jeffers Petroglyphs, Bingham Lake, MN 56118; (507) 877–3647 or (507) 697–6321

Located amid an expanse of virgin tall-grass prairie, this concentration of more than 2,000 prehistoric rock carvings tops a low quartzite ridge that extends from south-central Minnesota to southeastern South Dakota. Most of the carvings are located in areas of softer, rose-colored stone, a sloping outcrop about 700 feet long and 150 feet wide at its widest point.

The glyphs depict human figures, a variety of animals—deer, elk, buffalo, turtles, thunderbirds—and weapons such as atlatls and arrows. From these representations, experts have determined that most of the petroglyphs were done in the Archaic and early Woodland periods, 3000 B.C. to A.D. 500. Another group was carved by Siouan people, starting about A.D. 900 and extending into historic times, maybe as late as 1750.

Some twenty-five species of prairie grass and more than 125 species of wildflowers grow on the prairie surrounding the petroglyph site. There is a tepee-shaped visitor center with interpretive exhibits about the rock art and ecology of the prairie. An interpretive trail leads from the visitor center to the petroglyphs.

How to get there: From U.S. 71, take County Road 10 east 3 miles; then take County Road 2 south for 1 mile.

MISSISSIPPI

Grand Village of the Natchez

Attraction: Three prehistoric mounds, reconstructed dwellings, visitor center/museum
Hours: Monday through Saturday 9:00 A.M. to 5:00 P.M., Sunday 1:30 to 5:00 P.M.
Admission fee: None
For more information: The Grand Village of the Natchez, 400 Jefferson Davis Boulevard, Natchez, MS 39120; (601) 446–6502

This site on the banks of Mississippi's St. Catherine Creek was the home of the Natchez Indians, a culture that was at its peak in the mid-1500s; the Natchez occupied the site later, from 1682 to 1729. During this time of French colonization, the village was described in the journals of French travelers, and the current village is based upon these writings and archaeological evidence. In 1703 Jean Penicaut, a French ship's carpenter with the explorer Sieur d'Iberville, described the Natchez as "one of the most polite and affable nations on the Mississippi."

Penicaut went on to explain how the settlement "contained the dwelling of the Great Chief, whom they call the Sun, which means noble." This chief lived atop the Great Sun's Mound in the center of the village, which the French described as being about 8 feet high. When the Sun died, his wives and retainers were strangled and his house burned. The mound was then raised to cover over the debris, and the house of his successor was built on top. Burial ceremonies for a deceased chief were held in a temple on top of the Temple Mound. Here a fire, symbol of the royal family, kept burning. In addition to the two mounds, there is a third on the east side of the site that was abandoned by the time the French arrived at Grand Village.

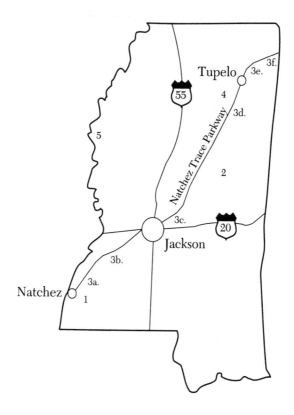

Mississippi
1. Grand Village of the Natchez
2. Nanih Waiya
3. Natchez Trace
   a. Emerald Mound
   b. Mangum Mound
   c. Boyd Mounds
   d. Bynum Mounds
   e. Pharr Mounds
   f. Bear Creek Mound
4. Owl Creek Mounds
5. Winterville Mounds State Park and Museum

Relations with the French began to deteriorate about 1716, and in 1729 the Natchez Indians massacred a large number of French at Fort Rosalie. A French siege trench, discovered in the course of an excavation in the 1970s, is evidence of French retaliation toward the Indians in 1730. The French victory destroyed the Natchez culture. The survivors were absorbed by other tribes, such as the Chickasaw, Creek, and Cherokee.

The site includes a reconstructed Natchez house and granary and a visitor center/museum.

How to get there: The site is located within the Natchez city limits. Turn off Highway 61 at Jefferson Davis Boulevard, which leads to the entrance gate.

Nanih Waiya

Attraction: Large prehistoric mound, legendary birthplace of Choctaw nation
Hours: Monday through Saturday 8:00 A.M. to 5:00 P.M., Sunday 1:00 to 5:00 P.M.
Admission fee: None
For more information: Nanih Waiya Historic Site, Route 3 Box 251A, Louisville, MS 39339; (601) 773–7988

Although this is a large mound of the Mississippian period, some 20 to 25 feet high and 218 feet by 140 feet at its base, Nanih Waiya is also significant as being the Choctaw Mother Mound, the legendary birthplace of the Choctaw nation. According to the story, two chiefs, the brothers Chata and Chickasaw, wandered with their followers for years in search of a homeland. Each night they planted a magic pole in the ground and the next morning proceeded on in the direction the pole leaned. When they reached this place, the pole stayed upright overnight, a sign that their quest had ended.

Yet another legend has the Choctaw people emerging from the ground at this place and drying themselves in the sun on the earthen rampart that once surrounded the site. When the Choctaw emigrated from Mississippi between 1830 and 1840, many members of the tribe refused to leave, saying they would never abandon the Mother Mound as long as it stood. And in later years, many Choctaw returned to this site, which is so important in their history.

James Adair was the first white man to record (in 1775) the existence of Nanih Waiya, which means something like sloping or leaning hill in Choctaw. Adair said there were two oblong mounds enclosed by a broad, deep ditch and a high breastwork. Adair believed the site to be a fortification. In 1843 the noted Mississippi naturalist, Gideon Lincecum, described the wall as being from 1½ to 2 miles in circumference. But by the time the site was studied by archaeologists in 1971, the wall had disappeared completely and there was only a trace of the second mound.

Nanih Waiya became part of the state park system in 1962. The site also includes the Nanih Waiya Cave Mound, a natural formation that also figures in the Choctaw birth legend. It is located about 1½ miles east of the large, flat-topped mound.

How to get there: Nanih Waiya is located 12 miles east of Noxapater off Route 490.

Natchez Trace

Attraction: Six prehistoric mound sites along a historic highway; visitor center with interpretive exhibits located near Tupelo, Mississippi (milepost 266)

Hours: Visitor center open daily 8:00 A.M. to 5:00 P.M., closed Christmas; mounds always open

Admission fee: None

For more information: Natchez Trace Parkway, R.R. 1, NT-143, Tupelo, MS 38801; (601) 680–4025

Although the Natchez Trace became a famed wilderness road after the arrival of the white man in historic times, it began as part of an intricate network of Indian trails linking the territories of such well-established tribes as the Natchez, Choctaw, and Chickasaw. Now a scenic and historic highway operated by the National Park Service, the Natchez Trace covers nearly 415 miles (in two segments) between a point a few miles north of Natchez, Mississippi, and Leiper's Fork, Tennessee, just south of Nashville. Along or near its route are seven prehistoric Indian mound locations, six of which are open to the public. They include Emerald Mound, the second-largest mound in the United States, not far from the Trace's start in Natchez.

An Indian trail running northeast from Natchez appeared on a French map as early as 1733. As European settlement and commerce increased, American settlers in the Ohio River valley, the famed "Kaintucks," would float crops and products down the river to Natchez or New Orleans and, having sold their flatboats for lumber, would return home overland via the Trace. By 1810 the Natchez Trace was one of the most heavily traveled roads in the Old Southwest, but soon thereafter it lost importance as steamboats began to ply the rivers. In the 1930s the National Park Service began building the parkway, which closely follows the route of the Trace. The mileposts given in the descriptions below indicate the distance from Natchez.

Emerald Mound

Located at the 10.3 milepost on the parkway near Natchez, the 35-foot-high Emerald Mound covers eight acres (770 feet by 435 feet at its base). It was built by Mississippian Indians, ancestors of the Natchez Indians, between A.D. 1250 and 1600. Two secondary mounds sit atop the primary mound; the larger one at the west end measures 190 feet by 160 feet at the base and is 30 feet high. Archaeologists believe that there were also six smaller mounds atop the main mound, although there is no longer any visual evidence of them.

Like Bear Creek Mound at the end of the Trace in northeast Mississippi, Emerald Mound was a ceremonial site, built to support temples and the houses of priests, chiefs, and other powerful citizens. The people who came to Emerald Mound to worship lived nearby and grew crops, mainly corn, beans, and pumpkins. To make their pottery, tools, and ornaments they brought materials from the Gulf coast and copper from the Lake Superior region.

Mangum Mound

At parkway milepost 45.7, Mangum Mound is a natural hill used as a burial mound by the Mississippian Indians, who lived here before de Soto passed through the region in 1540. Excavations in 1951 and 1963 turned up pottery, remains of clothing, ornaments, and weapons, all of which indicate that the people here had a close relationship with those at Emerald Mound. Archaeologists also found evidence of multiple burials, which might indicate that the natives practiced human sacrifice. The French who arrived in the early 1770s observed that the Natchez Indians, descendants of the Mississippians, sometimes sacrificed children when one of the parents died.

Boyd Mounds

Although this site (at milepost 106.9) was occupied at least 1,200 years ago by Woodland period Indians, the six burial mounds (only one of which is visible) were built during the Mississippian period, A.D. 1300 to 1500. The mounds grew in size as more bodies and earth were added to the top.

Bynum Mounds

The group of mounds at this Woodland period site was built between 100 B.C., when the site was first occupied, and A.D. 200. Two of the mounds can be seen from the visitor's path at this site, which is located at milepost 232.4. Archaeological work at Bynum revealed that the mounds grew through the practice of burning a temple or residence when a chief or important personage died, laying the corpse in the ashes, and then filling in the site with earth. The chiefs were often buried with such treasures as copper spool ornaments, polished stone axes, and flaked spear points. Common folk were buried in a fetal position in oval holes near the mound.

The site was continuously occupied for some 600 years after the mound building stopped. Then the village was abandoned until a band of Chickasaw, who were possibly related to the original Woodland Indians, reoccupied the site from the early 1800s to the 1830s.

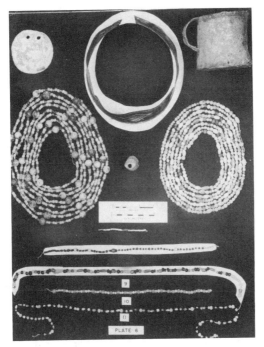

Bead necklaces and other artifacts from Bynum Mounds

Pharr Mounds

North of the Natchez Trace Visitor Center at Tupelo, Mississippi, Pharr Mounds (at milepost 286.7) is one of the largest and most important archaeological sites in Mississippi. It is also one of the oldest; it was occupied for nearly 4,000 years, from 2500 B.C. to A.D. 1400. The mounds, however, were built in the latter half of this period—A.D. 1 to 200. The eight large, dome-shaped burial mounds are scattered over an area of approximately ninety acres. After the primary mounds were completed, additional burials were made by placing bodies in shafts inside the primary mound.

Bear Creek Mound

This location at milepost 308.8 comes just before the Natchez Trace passes from Mississippi into the northwestern corner of Alabama. The site was occupied off and on from 7000 B.C. to A.D.

1300; the ceremonial mound was built in stages during the last 300 years the site was inhabited. As with other mounds of the period, its size increased when the temple on top was burned— often at the death of a ruler—and another layer of earth added to cover the debris.

The mound has been restored to its original size: 100 feet by 100 feet on each side and 10 to 12 feet tall. Intensive farming in the area had reduced the mound to less than half its height by the time archaeological excavations began in 1965.

How to get there: Sites are on Natchez Trace Parkway between Natchez and Tupelo. Mile markers for individual sites are mentioned in descriptions, above.

Owl Creek Mounds

Attraction: Five prehistoric mounds
Hours: Always open
Admission fee: None
For more information: U.S. Forest Service, 100 West Capitol Street, Suite 1141, Jackson, MS 39269; (601) 965–5518

There has been speculation that this collection of five flat-topped mounds was also the site of de Soto's 1540–1541 winter encampment; however, the evidence—a few Owl Creek artifacts that postdate the period of European contact—is far from conclusive. Archaeologists are certain that the mounds date from the Mississippian period (A.D. 1000 to 1300) because of their shape, which is typical of the period, and because of the shell-tempered pottery found there.

When the mounds were first described by Rush Nutt in 1805, there was a ditch or moat running around the entire mound group. The mounds surround an open plaza, which could have been part of a Mississippian village. (No evidence of a moat, even in aerial photographs, exists today.) Steep-sided Mound I, the largest in the group, is 81 by 111 feet at the base and 36 by 54 feet on the top. There was once a ramp on the middle of the south side. Excavations on smaller Mound II show that it was built in two stages, apparently with structures on top of each stage.

The mounds, also known as Shiloh Church Mounds, are owned and administered by the Forest Service. They are located near the Davis Lake Recreation Area in the 66,576-acre Tombigbee National Forest.

How to get there: From Tupelo, Mississippi, drive south 17 miles on the Natchez Trace Parkway to the Davis Lake exit at milepost 243. Turn west and drive 3 miles on the Davis Lake road. The site is on the right.

Winterville Mounds State Park and Museum

Attraction: Mound site, temple reconstruction, museum
Hours: Wednesday through Saturday 8:00 A.M. to 5:00 P.M., Sunday 1:00 to 5:00 P.M.
Admission fee: $1.00
For more information: Winterville Mounds State Park and Museum, Route 3 Box 600, Greenville, MS 38701; (601) 334–4684

The 55-foot-high central mound, the largest of the seventeen that have been recorded at this site, probably divided two plazas. A former bayou of the Mississippi River formed the straight, northwestern boundary of the D-shaped ceremonial center. On its other sides—the curve of the D—the site was mostly likely bounded by the forest, since no boundary embankment or moat has been found.

Winterville was founded about A.D. 1000 by Coles Creek people who had established a distinctive culture in the Lower Mississippi Valley by A.D. 700. (The Coles Creek culture was marked by the building of small groups of moderate-size mounds usually around a central plaza.) About A.D. 1200 Winterville came in contact with Mississippian peoples, whose cultural center was the great site at Cahokia in west-central Illinois. This contact transformed Winterville into one of the leading cultural centers of its day, "second only to Cahokia and a few other sites in the Southeast," according to a report on the site. For unknown reasons—perhaps the river bottom land became less fertile—the site was deserted by 1450.

Only a few of the mounds are visible today. Surprisingly, in view of its importance, only two major excavations have been carried out at Winterville. The first was conducted in 1907 by Clarence B. Moore of the Philadelphia Academy of Sciences. Moore dug more than 150 pits in fifteen mounds but turned up only a few skeletons and pottery sherds; after just six disappointing days, he abandoned the search. It wasn't until 1967–1968 that Jeffrey P. Brain of Yale University undertook a second excavation. Brain concentrated on the second- and third-largest mounds, 28 and 18 feet high respectively, and his findings established the link between the Coles Creek culture and the Mississippian peoples to the north.

A 30 foot by 60 foot replica of a temple has been built on top of the principal mound, which has also been restored. It is believed that a sacred fire burned perpetually in the center of the temple. A museum displays artifacts excavated on site.

How to get there: Take Mississippi Route 1 about 5 miles north of Greenville to site.

MISSOURI

Graham Cave State Park

Attraction: 10,000-year-old cave dwelling
Hours: Always open
Admission fee: None
For more information: Graham Cave State Park, Montgomery City, MO 63361; (314) 564–3476

When this sheltered bluff was excavated in the 1950s, archaeologists recovered deposits that extended 6 feet into the cave floor and that were radiocarbon dated to be at least 10,000 years old. The findings caused experts to revise their thinking on the arrival of humans in the region, since it was thought that man had not

Entrance of Graham Cave

(Courtesy Department of Natural Resources, Jefferson City, Missouri)

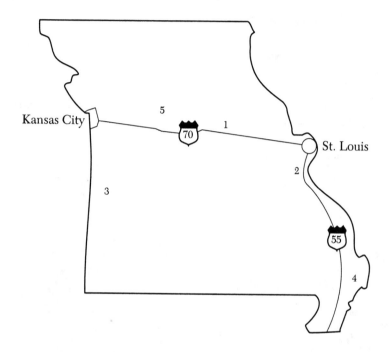

Missouri
1. Graham Cave State Park
2. Mastodon State Park
3. Osage Village State Historic Site
4. Towosahgy State Historic Site
5. Van Meter State Park

arrived until much later. Pieces of pottery found in the cave were from the later Woodland culture; the early Archaic period people had not developed the art of making pottery.

The cave is named after the first settler, Robert Graham, who purchased the property in 1816 from the son of Daniel Boone. Most of the 356-acre park was donated to the state in 1964. Because the 100-foot-long cave has not yet been completely excavated, it is not open to the public. But visitors can go into the cave entrance where there are interpretive signs.

How to get there: The park is located 2 miles west of Danville, off I–70 on Highway TT.

Mastodon State Park

Attraction: Pleistocene-era bone bed and archaeological site; visitor center/museum

Hours: Park open daily until one-half hour after sunset; visitor center open Monday through Saturday 9:00 A.M. to 4:30 P.M., Sunday noon to 4:30 P.M.

Admission fee: None

For more information: Mastodon State Park, 1551 Seckman Road, Imperial MO 63052; (314) 464–2976

Bones of the elephantlike mastodon were discovered here, in what is now called the Kimmswick Bone Bed, in the early 1800s. Further excavations in 1839 and the early 1900s turned up so many bones and fossils that the area became known as one of the most extensive Pleistocene bone beds in the country. During the last ice age, 35,000 to 10,000 years ago, mastodons and other animals such as giant ground sloths and peccaries were attracted to this then-swampy area by springs. Experts assume they were trapped by the mud, which also helped preserve their bones.

Bones from more than sixty mastodons were reportedly taken from the pit; one mastodon skeleton is at the British Museum of Natural History in London. Many other bones from the site were taken by looters or destroyed by a limestone-quarrying operation. In the 1970s the Missouri Department of Natural Resources, aided by citizens of Jefferson County who were concerned about the possible destruction of the bone bed, purchased the 425-acre site as a state park.

In 1979 archaeologists from the Illinois State Museum found a large stone spear point made by hunters of the Clovis period, 10,000 to 14,000 years ago. It was the first solid evidence archaeologists had that man and the mastodon existed at the same time in North America. Since the spear point was found between two layers of mastodon bones, it appeared that it had been used to hunt the huge beasts. This raises the possibility that man as well as environmental causes contributed to the extinction of the mastodon.

A short trail leads from the park's visitor center to the Kimmswick Bone Bed. A full-size replica of a mastodon is displayed in the visitor center with bones, tusks, teeth, and artifacts found at the site. There are also photographs of the past excavations and a walk-through area that depicts the region as it was more than 10,000 years ago.

How to get there: The site is located 20 miles south of St. Louis; take the Imperial exit off I-55.

Osage Village State Historic Site

Attraction: Site of early Osage Indian village
Hours: Always open
Admission fee: None
For more information: Harry S. Truman Birthplace State Historic Site, Lamar, MO 64759; (417) 682-2279

Located on a hill overlooking the Osage River, this is the earliest known Osage village in western Missouri. In 1719 the French fur trader Charles Claude du Tisne came across the village, which the Osage had apparently settled some fifty years earlier. Du Tisne reported that the village had 200 warriors and a hundred lodges; archaeologists have learned that the lodges were 30 to 50 feet long and 15 to 20 feet wide with east-facing doorways. According to contemporary accounts, by 1774 there were 2,000 to 3,000 people and about 200 lodges in the village.

A walking tour of the village area includes several historic locations, such as the site of Fort Carondolet, built by a family of traders in 1795; Indian-related sites such as the excavation area where two large houses were uncovered in 1962 and 1963; Blue Mound, where, according to Osage legend, important chiefs are buried; and several bedrock features where depressions made by mortars and grooves from sharpening bone tools and axes can be seen.

How to get there: Located near Walker, the site is reached by taking Highway C 6 miles north of U.S. 54 and going west 3 miles on a gravel road.

Towosahgy State Historic Site

Attraction: Remains of a fortified Mississippian village, including seven mounds
Hours: Daily during daylight hours
Admission fee: None
For more information: Big Oak Tree State Park, East Prairie, MO 63845; (314) 649–3149 or 649–9066

This sixty-four-acre site preserves the remnants of seven prehistoric mounds, once part of a fortified village and ceremonial center that existed here in the "Bootheel" section of southeastern Missouri from A.D. 1000 to 1400. The people who built the settlement were part of the Mississippian culture, which at the time was centered at the immense ceremonial site in Cahokia, Illinois. In the Osage language *Towosahgy* means "old town"; the Osage Indians lived in the region at a later period and were familiar with the earlier settlement.

Six of the seven mounds were located around a central plaza. The largest, located at the north end, is about 16 feet high and 180 by 250 feet at its base. Excavations show there were wooden structures plastered with clay built on top of the mounds. The mounds appear on a map of the site that the Smithsonian archaeologist Cyrus Thomas published in 1894. The map also shows about seventy-three house depressions and a well-defined wall around most of the village. Recent aerial photographs and excavations have shown that there were at least three log stockade fences as evidenced by trenches, postholes and other remains of the fortification.

Archaeologists from the Missouri Department of Natural Resources and the University of Missouri at Columbia have investigated the site since it was purchased by the state in 1967. In addition to the stockade, archaeologists have discovered evidence of a bastion that extended out from the fortification for about 17 feet. The bastion could have been a watchtower or blockhouse. A house built over a pit was also excavated just inside the stockade walls. The walls of the house were built of small posts placed in narrow trenches. Storage or garbage pits containing the charred remains of corn, beans, persimmons, and wild plums—staples of the inhabitants' diet—were excavated near the house.

How to get there: The site is located off Highway 77, 13 miles southeast of East Prairie.

Van Meter State Park

Attraction: Prehistoric "fort" and mounds
Hours: Always open
Admission fee: None
For more information: Van Meter State Park, Miami, MO 65344; (816) 886–7537

This area was once the site of a Missouri Indian settlement that might have had a population of 5,000 people. The village was located on top of the Pinnacles, a series of narrow ridges surrounded by deep glacial ravines. This flat area, encircled by a row of prehistoric parallel ditches, is now known as the Old Fort, although the original purpose of the earthworks is unknown. The Mound Field, north of Old Fort, is a large open area with several burial mounds.

Although the Missouri undoubtedly used the mounds for ceremonial purposes, they might have been constructed by an earlier group of prehistoric peoples. There is archaeological evidence that the area was occupied as early as 10,000 B.C. The Missouri Indians were living here when the first Europeans, the French explorers Jacques Marquette and Louis Joliet, came through the region in 1673. In the years that followed European contact, outbreaks of smallpox and other diseases decimated the tribe.

The park is named for the Van Meter family, who settled there in 1834. In 1932 the family deeded 506 acres, including the family cemetery, to the state. Trails lead to both the Old Fort and Mound Field. The visitor center has exhibits on the history of the park.

How to get there: Go 14 miles northwest of Marshall on Highway 122.

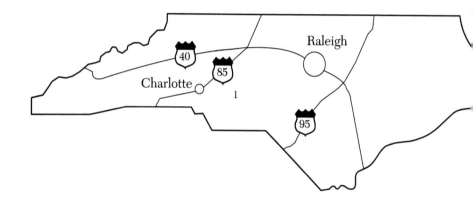

North Carolina
1. Town Creek Indian Mound

NORTH CAROLINA

Town Creek Indian Mound

Attraction: Large temple mound, temple and other reconstructions, visitor center/museum
Hours: April through October, Monday through Saturday 9:00 A.M. to 5:00 P.M., Sunday 1:00 to 5:00 p.m; November through March, Tuesday through Saturday 10:00 A.M. to 4:00 P.M., Sunday 1:00 to 4:00 P.M.
Admission fee: None
For more information: Town Creek Indian Mound, Route 3 Box 50, Mt. Gilead, NC 27306; (919) 439–6802

In 1937 the Town Creek Indian Mound was in danger of being leveled and plowed under to make way for a cotton field. Instead Joffre L. Coe of the University of North Carolina and others interested in its preservation convinced owner L. D. Frutchey of the importance of the site. Frutchey deeded the mound and two adjoining acres of land to the state and thereafter remained keenly interested in the archaeology of the area.

The mound at Town Creek was built by a group of Indians related to the Creeks, who lived in Alabama and Georgia, moved into this area of North Carolina about A.D. 1250, and settled along the Pee Dee River valley. The Creeks lived here for about 200 years and then left the area. At that time the same Siouan Indians whom the Creeks had originally displaced returned to the area. The highly religious Pee Dees, as they are now sometimes called, were sun worshipers. They kept a symbolic fire constantly burning in the ceremonial temple atop the mound. When the sacred fire was rekindled during the busk, or green corn, ceremony, the celebrants took embers from the fire back to their villages, which is why they called themselves "people of one fire."

Reconstructed temple on Town Creek Indian Mound

The mound was built in three stages; the original earth lodge was at ground level or slightly below. When it collapsed or burned, a mantle of earth about 5 or 6 feet high was placed over the remains. This mound became the foundation for what is now known as Temple I. Sometime later this temple burned, another mantle of earth was added, raising the mound to about 12 feet, and the last temple structure (Temple II) was added.

After the mound was excavated, it was rebuilt and the temple, with walls made of mud and a grass-thatched roof, was reconstructed. At the foot of the ramp leading to the mound were four sheds surrounding a small square where the Indians believed the Talwa, symbolic soul of the tribe, lived.

Across the plaza on the side by the river, a smaller "minor temple," surrounded by a log palisade, has also been rebuilt on its original site. Here the high priest lived, the center's only resident. Near one of the entrances to the ceremonial center there is a reconstructed burial hut or mortuary house. Inside, lifelike mannequins are shown performing a burial ceremony. Bodies were buried in shallow pits lined with cane matting or bark. Infants were buried in clay urns. Because they believed the urn also lived, the Indians ceremonially killed it by punching a hole in its base, so the child would not be trapped inside. Some of the urns discovered on the site are on display in the museum.

The entire complex is surrounded by a high palisade of upright logs interwoven with cane and small poles. Then as now, entrance to the site is through two towers that are part of the palisade. In the center of the plaza there is a 40-foot-high ball pole, topped by the skull of a bear, that was used for a variety of games in which young warriors were able to display their endurance, strength, and courage. Archaeologists were able to locate the position of the game pole and palisade posts by observing variations in the texture of the soil.

How to get there: Town Creek is located 5½ miles east of Mt. Gilead, between Routes 73 and 731.

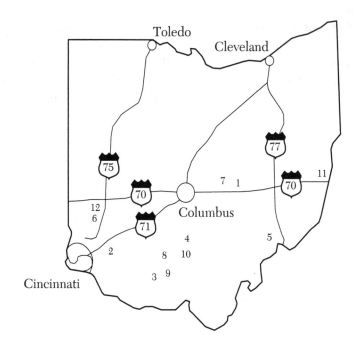

Ohio
1. Flint Ridge State Memorial
2. Fort Ancient
3. Fort Hill State Memorial
4. Hopewell Culture National Historic Park
   (Mound City)
5. Marietta Earthworks
6. Miamisburg Mound State Memorial
7. Newark Earthworks
8. Seip Mound
9. Serpent Mound State Memorial
10. Story Mound
11. Tiltonsville Cemetery Mound
12. Sunwatch

OHIO

Flint Ridge State Memorial

Attraction: Museum, nature preserve, trails
Hours: Memorial Day through Labor Day, 9:30 A.M. to 5:00 P.M. Wednesday through Saturday, noon to 5:00 P.M. Sundays and holidays; open weekends only Labor Day through October; closed November through Memorial Day
Admission fee: None
For more information: Ohio Historical Society, 1982 Velma Avenue, Columbus, OH 43211–2497; (800) 686–1545 (in Ohio) or (614) 297–2333

In 1933 the Ohio Historical Society established a 525-acre memorial to preserve this unusual flint quarry, which had been in use for about 10,000 years, from Paleo-Indian times well into historic times. In 1968 a modern museum was built over one of the original flint pits, where visitors can view Indian mannequins displayed as if working the quarry. Along the preserve's nature trails, the ponds with their abundant wildlife are actually abandoned pits that have filled with water.

The flint deposits, which cover about 5 square miles, are located in a series of irregular hills that extend for about 10 miles between Newark and Zanesville, Ohio. The stratum of hard, superior-quality flint began to elevate from the earth about 200 million years ago and was then exposed by erosion. Early Indians soon discovered that exposure to weather had rendered the surface flint flakey and unusable, but that a layer of hard, workable flint lay just below the surface. The first quarry workers used granite or quartzite boulders weighing up to twenty-five pounds to drive wooden or bone wedges into natural cracks in the flint.

The rectangular pieces of flint that were extracted in this way from the quarries were then "blocked out" by other workers into rough pieces measuring from 13 to 32 inches in length and from 2 to 5 inches wide. These blades were then finished at other nearby workshops or taken to villages where local craftsmen turned them into arrow and spear points, drills, knives, and scrapers.

The translucent flint of various colors is of a quality unmatched in the east. In prehistoric times it was a valuable trade item and samples have been found as far away as Louisiana, the Atlantic Coast, and Kansas City. Early settlers used the lower-grade, weathered flint from the western part of the ridge to make buhrstones for mills. In the early 1830s, discarded chips from the quarries were used to build the portion of the National Road that passed through Muskingum and Licking counties.

The museum on the site includes exhibits on flint-chipping techniques, flint objects, and trade routes for this valuable commodity.

How to get there: From Brownsville exit on I–70, take Route 668 North about 3¾ miles; the Memorial is on the east side of the road.

Fort Ancient

Attraction: Hilltop enclosure containing mounds and earthworks; museum, trails

Hours: Park open 10:00 A.M. to 8:00 P.M. Memorial Day through Labor Day, 10:00 A.M. to 5:00 P.M. rest of year; museum open 10:00 A.M. to 5:00 P.M.

Admission fee: $4.00 per car

For more information: Ohio Historical Society, 1982 Velma Avenue, Columbus, OH 43211; (513) 932–4421

This earthen enclosure located on a hilltop over the Little Miami River was named for the Fort Ancient people of the Mississippian period (A.D. 1000 to 1600), who, experts once believed, constructed it. Research has proved that this collection of earthworks and mounds was built by the Hopewell culture and that the

Fort Ancient peoples lived there long after the Hopewellians had abandoned it (about A.D. 500). Although the site has the appearance of a fort and was once thought to be a defensive complex, it is now believed that Fort Ancient was used for ceremonies and other gatherings.

Fort Ancient is divided into sections. The spacious North and South Forts are connected by the narrow Middle Fort. The earth and stone walls surrounding the hundred-acre enclosure have been restored; they range in height from 4 feet to 23 feet and are almost 4 miles long. Inside are mounds, crescent-shaped gateways, and stone pavements. Outside the gate to the North Fort are twin mounds; a pair of parallel earthworks extends across private property to another mound. The purpose or function of these structures is unknown.

Fort Ancient was made a state park—Ohio's first—in 1891. Now 764 acres, it includes a museum that contains a model of a Fort Ancient Indian village based on archaeological excavations at the nearby Anderson Village site. The park has nearly 2 miles of trails: the Earthworks Trail, with scenic overlooks and good views of the earthworks; the Terrace Trail, between the western side of the enclosure and the river; and the River Trail, which descends ¼ mile from the enclosure to the Little Miami Scenic Trail along the river.

How to get there: The site is 7 miles southeast of Lebanon, off Route 350.

Fort Hill State Memorial

Attraction: Hilltop enclosure, museum, nature trails, picnic area
Hours: Daily, dawn to dusk
Admission fee: None
For more information: Ohio Historical Society, 1982 Velma Avenue, Columbus, OH 43211–2497; (800) 686–1545 (in Ohio) or (614) 297–2333

It is likely that this walled, hilltop enclosure was built by Hopewell people, but why they constructed it is not known.

85

Because it is located on a steep slope, defense is one obvious explanation, although archaeologists have not found any evidence of warlike activity on the site. The discovery of a ceremonial arbor to the south of Fort Hill might be an indication that the enclosure was built and used for ceremonial purposes. The excavation of the arbor also turned up pottery fragments, spear points, flint knives, and other implements and ornaments belonging to the Hopewell Indians (300 B.C. to A.D. 600). From this evidence it can be deduced—but not proved—that the Hopewell people also built the enclosure.

The wall around the forty-eight-acre enclosure is just over 1½ miles long and ranges in height from 6 to 15 feet. The base, which is 40 feet wide, is set below the top of the hill so that in places the top of the wall is level with the top of the hill. There are thirty-three irregularly spaced openings in the wall that vary from 15 to 20 feet wide.

A museum at the site features models of Hopewell structures, including the arbor, found at the base of the hill. The Memorial has 10 miles of well-marked nature trails.

How to get there: Take Fort Hill Road about ¾ mile off Route 41.

Hopewell Culture National Historical Park (Mound City)

Attractions: Twenty-three Hopewell era burial mounds, interpretive trail, visitor center, audio stations
Hours: Visitor center open (except major holidays) daily 8:00 A.M. to 6:00 P.M., Memorial Day through Labor Day; 8:00 A.M. to 5:00 P.M. rest of year. Grounds are open daily during daylight hours.
Admission fee: $2.00
For more information: Hopewell Culture National Historical Park, 16062 Route 104, Chillicothe, OH 45601; (614) 774–1125

Historically known as the City of the Dead, the Mound City Group is one of the Ohio Valley's greatest concentrations of Hopewell Indian burial mounds; nowhere else in the region were there so many mounds in such a small area. In use from about 200

B.C. to A.D. 500, the site was used for several purposes, including the cremation and burial of people of high rank within the Hopewell society. Located on the banks of the Scioto River, the site is enclosed by a wall 2,050 feet long and from 2 to 3 feet high.

When the Ohio newspaper editor Ephraim Squier and E. H. Davis, a Chillicothe physician, first explored the complex they named Mound City in the 1840s, the thirteen-acre site contained twenty-three mounds. (At the time, the land was a farmer's woodlot and had remained undisturbed.) Twelve of these mounds were completely leveled after the woodlot was cleared for farming in the 1850s. The other mounds were damaged when the U.S. Army established a training camp and detention center there in 1917. After the facility was dismantled following World War I, excavations continued under the direction of the Ohio State Archaeological and Historical Society. Mound City was declared a national monument in 1923 and has since been restored to its original configuration.

Each mound at the site contains many burials. When they built a mound, the Hopewell Indians first cleared the land and laid down an earthen floor; then they built a crematorium or charnel house on the site. Bodies were cremated on a low clay platform. The ashes and various mortuary offerings were buried in the charnel house floor. When the site was full, the charnel house was dismantled or burned, and the site was covered with earth. One or two of the mounds were found to have been capped with cobbles from the river. Why the mounds are different shapes and sizes is unknown. "The Hopewell had specific reasons for the things they did," writes park ranger Robert Petersen. "What they lacked was a method of telling us about those reasons."

The burial sites at Mound City were rich in mortuary or ceremonial objects, which are indications of the deceased's rank, clan membership, or function in society. The wide variety of goods provides evidence that the Hopewells established a trading network that extended as far south as the Gulf of Mexico, where they obtained shark teeth and whelk shells used to make vessels, and as far west as the Rocky Mountains.

At the mound known as the Mica Grave, a portion of the structure has been cut away to reveal four mica-lined graves as well as details of the construction of the mound. In addition to the sheets of mica, which came from the Blue Ridge Mountains, archaeologists have also found buried at this same location a cache of 5,000 shell beads, elk and bear teeth, obsidian tools, raven and toad effigy pipes (perhaps representing clan membership), and two copper headdresses, one with antlers, the other representing a bear. In all, twenty grave sites have been discovered in the Mica Grave Mound. (The National Park Service no longer displays human burials.)

The mounds at Mound City are very dissimilar, both in size and in the type of artifact found buried there. The largest mound, the so-called Death Mask Mound, is the only one that was not damaged by the building of an army facility on the site during World War I. Thirteen individuals were buried in Death Mask Mound, which takes its name from a ceremonial headpiece made from fragments of human skull. The mound also contained an unusual subterranean charnel house.

The Mound of the Pipes, the third major structure at the site, "far exceeds any hitherto explored," Squier and Davis reported in their 1848 work, *Ancient Monuments of the Mississippi Valley*. The 200 stone pipes found here, which are now in the British Museum, have bowls "carved in miniature figures of animals, birds, reptiles, etc.," Squier and Davis wrote. "All of them are executed with strict fidelity to nature and with exquisite skill."

At the Mound of the Fossils, pieces of mastodon or mammoth tusk were found among the burials.

Many of the artifacts recovered from the mounds are displayed in the visitor center museum.

How to get there: The park is on Route 104, about 3 miles north of Chillicothe and 2 miles north of the U.S. 35 intersection.

Marietta Earthworks

Attraction: Prehistoric earthworks in a historic city
Hours: Visible at all times
Admission fee: None
For more information: Marietta Tourist and Convention Bureau, 316 Third Street, Marietta, OH 45750; (614) 373–5178

Mound Cemetery, Marietta

The first of Ohio's prehistoric earthworks to be mapped and surveyed were the earthworks in Marietta, Ohio's first settlement. They blend gracefully with the gracious small city that has grown up around them. The Revolutionary War general Rufus Putnam led the party of Ohio Company settlers that landed at the confluence of the Muskingum and Ohio rivers and founded the settlement in April 1788. Only a few months later, the directors of the Ohio Company took the first step toward the preservation of the earthworks by designating them a public square. At the same time they gave each a name, in Latin: Quadranaou, Capitolium, Sacra Via, and Conus.

Located high on the terraced slopes on which the city is built, the 30-foot-high conical mound, Conus, is surrounded by the city's Mound Cemetery, which was opened in 1801. Many of the original settlers, including General Putnam, are buried here, and it said that Mound Cemetery has more graves of officers of the American Revolution than any other burial ground in America. Conus Mound is ringed by a sizeable moat that separates it at the base from the historic cemetery.

The Washington County Public Library, on Fifth Street between Washington and Warren streets, sits on top of the remains of the square Capitolium Mound. The mound was excavated recently under the direction of Hopewell expert N'omi Greber of the Cleveland Museum of Natural History before the library broke ground for the construction of an exterior elevator. Artifacts recovered from the dig included pottery sherds and flint knives and indicate that the site is a Hopewell mound that might have been built about A.D. 500. Before this excavation, experts were uncertain who built the mound; some thought it might have been constructed much later, between A.D. 1300 and 1500.

Quadranaou, a large, square mound now called the Camp Tupper Earthworks, is a quiet park at the head of the Sacra Via, a 680-foot graded esplanade leading from the mound to the Muskingum River. The 150-foot-wide Sacra Via was once lined with walls about 20 feet high. Today the walls are gone and the Sacra Via is a parkway lined with some of Marietta's many elegant old houses.

How to get there: Mound Cemetery, the site of Conus Mound, is located on Fifth Street at the end of Scammel Street. The library situated on Capitolium Mound is also on Fifth Street, 3 blocks to the northwest. To reach the Camp Tupper Earthworks, turn left on Warren Street by the library and proceed 1 block.

Miamisburg Mound State Memorial

Attraction: Large Adena conical mound
Hours: During daylight hours
Admission fee: None
For more information: Ohio Historical Society, 1982 Velma Avenue, Columbus, OH 43211–2497; (800) 686–1545 (in Ohio) or (614) 297–2333

A pre–Civil War painting of the Miamisburg Mound, in the collection of the Ohio Historical Society, shows a high conical mound on the edge of a farm with a lone pine tree growing from its top. In the painting, the artist made the mound look higher and narrower than it ever was or is now. An excavation in 1869 reduced the height of the mound from more than 68 feet to its present 65 feet. Nonetheless, it is one of the largest conical mounds in the east, second only to Grave Creek Mound in West Virginia. Its circumference at its base is 877 feet.

Today the mound is located in a park within the city limits of Miamisburg. One hundred and sixteen stone steps lead to the top, which overlooks the city and the Miami River valley.

In the 1869 excavation a vertical shaft was sunk from the top to the base with two horizontal passageways leading off it. Two burial vaults were found in the excavation; one, 8 feet from the surface, contained a skeleton covered with bark. The second vault, 36 feet from the top, was surrounded by logs. The layers of ashes and stone indicated that the mound was built in stages, probably by Adena people (ca. 1000–100 B.C.), who, unlike the later Hopewell Indians, tended to build their mounds in the shape of cones.

In 1920 the industrialist Charles F. Kettering of Dayton, inventor of the automobile self-starter, purchased the mound and opened it to the public. He gave the mound to the Ohio Historical Society in 1929, which today leases it to the city of Miamisburg. Despite the mound's size and importance, it has never been scientifically excavated.

How to get there: Take the Route 725 exit off I–75 and proceed west for about 3 miles; following signs, turn south on South Sixth Street to Mound Avenue, which leads to Mound Park.

Newark Earthworks

Attractions: Two major and two minor Hopewell Indian sites; Ohio Museum of Indian Art (at Mound Builders State Memorial); observation platform (at Octagon State Memorial)

Hours: Grounds open daylight hours; museum hours Wednesday through Saturday 9:30 A.M. to 5:00 P.M., Sunday and holidays noon to 5:00 P.M.

Admission fee: Museum, $2.00

For more information: Newark Earthworks State Memorials, 99 Cooper Avenue, Newark, OH 43055; (614) 344–1920

Although they have been the subject of relatively little archaeological research, the Newark Earthworks are world famous for their size and complexity. Archaeologist Bradley T. Lepper, curator of the earthworks, has called the site, which once covered more than two square miles, "the largest complex of geometric earthworks in the world." Squier and Davis, the pioneering students of prehistoric mounds, said in their 1848 work: "These works are so complicated that it is impossible to give anything like a comprehensible description of them."

That task is even harder these days, since the city of Newark swallowed up and totally surrounded what remains of the earthworks. This process has been going on for over 150 years; in their writings, Squier and Davis deplored the destruction of the earthworks by urban development. In 1827 the Ohio Canal cut through the earthworks and eyewitnesses reported seeing skeletons dug up that had been buried with sheets of mica "of the finest quality in regard to transparency and size." In the early 1850s the Central Ohio Railroad came through. Later a rolling mill, an army camp, highways, a fairgrounds, and a golf course all contributed to the diminishing of the earthworks.

The earthworks gained considerable notoriety in the 1860s when a surveyor named David Wyrick claimed that he had excavated the so-called Newark Holy Stones from an enclosure at Newark. Wyrick claimed that the stones, which he said were engraved with Hebrew letters, were proof that the Lost Tribes of Israel built these and other earthworks in North America.

Wyrick's totally unsubstantiated claim attracted the attention of New York physician James Salisbury, an early proponent of the germ theory and the creator of the Salisbury steak, and his brother Charles. The Salisburys spent 1860 through 1862 surveying the Newark Earthworks and other sites in the region and produced a remarkably detailed map, which they gave to the American Antiquarian Society in 1862. Bradley Lepper rediscovered the map in 1989.

The Newark Earthworks are still attracting scholarly attention. Starting in 1975 two professors from Ohio's Earlham College, Ray Hively and Robert Horn, spent more than eight years studying the earthworks and concluded that they were constructed as a lunar

Bradley T. Lepper, curator of Newark Earthworks,
standing on Hopewell-built road

observatory that accurately marked the monthly rise and set point of the moon over its eighteen-and-a-half-year cycle. Such an achievement, the professors point out, would require mathematical and engineering skill far beyond what had previously been attributed to the Hopewell Indians.

More recently, in the early 1990s, Brad Lepper discovered traces of a Hopewell-built walled road that appears to run in an absolutely straight line from Newark to the Hopewell center in Chillecothe 60 miles away. The road is similar to the enclosed highways that the Anasazi built at a much later date from Chaco Canyon in present-day New Mexico to distant outlying communities. If further research confirms that the road did exist, it will prove that the Hopewell were better engineers—and more determined and better organized as a society—than previously thought.

Today what remains of the earthworks is preserved in two major sites and two smaller sites. The largest, the 120-acre Octagon State Memorial, includes a large earthen octagon covering fifty acres, inside of which are located a number of small mounds. This was the largest feature within the Newark Earthworks. The octagon is connected by parallel walls to a circular embankment of twenty acres. Today the Octagon State Memorial is owned by the Ohio Historical Society, which leases it to the private Mound Builders Country Club where it is maintained—and protected—as a golf course. There is an observation platform on the site with maps and information.

The other major site, the Mound Builders State Memorial, consists of the Great Circle Earthworks, a twenty-six-acre enclosure that once served as the racetrack for a country fairground in the mid-nineteenth century. The Great Circle is surrounded by an earthen wall from 8 to 14 feet high inside of which is a ditch. The first observers to study the Great Circle assumed, probably wrongly, that it was built for defense, although the unusual interior moat, one puzzled observer wrote in 1839, reflected "principles of military science now lost or inexplicable." Of course, the purpose of the moat inside the walls is no more clear to us today than it was a century and a half ago.

The Wright Earthworks, also a state memorial, is the remaining small section of what was once a large, important enclosure in the original Newark group. It is located approximately ¼ mile northeast of the Great Circle at the intersection of James and Waldo streets. The fourth part of the monument, the 6-foot-high conical Owen Mound, is visible from the entrance of the Newark High School's Evans Athletic Complex.

The Ohio Museum of Indian Art, the first museum in the country devoted exclusively to prehistoric American Indian art, was opened in 1971 at the Mound Builders State Memorial. In addition to its exhibits of Indian art, it includes a diorama of Indian artisans working flint and a bronze relief map inspired by the map published by Squier and Davis in 1848.

How to get there: The Moundbuilders State Memorial and the Ohio Museum of Indian Art are located on Route 79, 14 miles north of the intersection with I–70 and 1 mile southwest of

Route 16. Directions to the other locations may be obtained at the museum.

Seip Mound

Attraction: Large Hopewell burial mound
Hours: Open daily during daylight
Admission fee: None
For more information: Ohio Historical Society, 1982 Velma Avenue, Columbus, OH 43211–2497; (800) 686–1545 (in Ohio) or (614) 297–2333

Located at a roadside rest area 14 miles southwest of Chillicothe, the 30-foot-tall Seip Mound is the largest existing Hopewell mound. (Another Hopewell mound in the Chillicothe area was 33 feet tall, but was never rebuilt after it was excavated.) When Seip was excavated in the 1920s, Henry Clyde Shetrone of the Ohio Historical Society uncovered 122 burials with grave goods that included copper from Isle Royale on Lake Superior and some 15,000 freshwater pearls. Shetrone, a noted name in the history of archaeology in Ohio, was almost killed when part of an excavation collapsed on him, but he was pulled from the debris and recovered. The mound was rebuilt after the excavation was completed.

The oval-shaped Seip Mound (150 feet wide and 250 feet long) is the only remaining feature of what was once a 122-acre walled complex, which consisted of a twenty-seven-acre square and an eighteen-acre circle connected by an irregular circle of seventy-seven acres. Three connected mounds—Seip Mound and two other smaller mounds, now gone—were located within the large circle. Beyond the northern wall of the large circle are pits from which the Hopewell took earth to build the mounds and walls. An exhibit on Seip at the Ohio Historical Society in Columbus states that the walls of the complex might have been 50 feet wide at the base and at least 10 feet high.

Excavations in the 1970s uncovered the outlines of ten buildings that, it has been suggested, were workshops for craftsmen who produced the elaborate Hopewell burial goods.

How to get there: Take U.S. 50 southwest from Chillicothe for 14 miles. Seip Mound is part of a roadside rest area and park on the south side of the highway 3 miles east of Bainbridge.

Serpent Mound State Memorial

Attraction: Mound, museum

Hours: Park open daily 9:30 A.M. to 8:00 P.M. Memorial Day through Labor Day, 10:00 A.M. to 5:00 P.M. rest of year; museum open daily 9:30 A.M. to 5:00 P.M. Memorial Day through Labor Day, 10:00 A.M. to 5:00 P.M. rest of year

Admission fee: $4.00 per car

For more information: Serpent Mound State Memorial, 3850 State Route 73, Peebles, OH 45660; (513) 587–2796

When seen from the air, this mound, almost ¼ mile long, clearly resembles a snake: The seven curves represent its body, the coil its tail, and the oval embankment on the north end its open mouth ready to strike. No burials or artifacts have been found within the mound to indicate who built it. Several conical burial mounds in the vicinity have led many experts to believe that the serpent is the work of the Adena Indians who inhabited the region from about 800 B.C. to A.D. 100; however, the mound might also have been the work of the Fort Ancient people, who arrived here about A.D. 1000.

Ephraim Squier and Edwin Davis, the first to survey the mound, published their findings in their 1848 work, *Ancient Monuments of the Mississippi Valley.* Their book created widespread interest in the mound, but by the time Frederick Ward Putnam of Harvard's Peabody Museum visited there in 1885 he found that it was being destroyed by agriculture. Putnam spent three years excavating the mound and exhibited his findings at the 1893 World's Columbian Exposition in Chicago. Putnam also raised nearly $6,000 to purchase the mound in 1887 for the Peabody, which gave it to the Ohio Historical Society in 1900.

Although the serpent is a powerful symbol in many religions (its ability to shed its skin has come to symbolize a renewal of life), archaeologists have no knowledge of how the Serpent Mound fit into the beliefs of its builders. Whoever constructed it invested massive amounts of time and energy. After carefully constructing a base of rocks and clay, which averages about 20 feet wide, the builders then covered it with earth 4 or 5 feet high. To some, the oval at the end appears to be a snake swallowing an egg; others have speculated the the oval depicts a snake striking at a frog.

The Serpent Mound Museum, which opened in 1967, has exhibits based on various interpretations of the mound, the methods used in its construction, and the Adena culture. The museum also explains the unusual geology of the area. The mound is built in an area of faulted and folded bedrock, about 5 miles in diameter; the bedrock is an unstable formation possibly caused by gas explosions deep within the earth.

How to get there: Take Route 73 north from Locust Grove for 4 miles.

Story Mound

Attraction: Adena burial mound
Hours: Visible at all times, although the mound is fenced off
Admission fee: None
For more information: Ohio Historical Society, 1982 Velma Avenue, Columbus, OH 43211–2497; (800) 686–1545 (in Ohio) or (614) 297–2333

Located in a one-acre park in a residential center of Chillicothe, Story Mound was excavated in 1897 by Clarence Loveberry, who discovered a circular Adena building of timber. The building represents "a structural type now known as the norm in Adena ceremonial and domestic architecture," according to information provided by the Ohio Historical Society, owner of the mound. Erected by the prehistoric Adena Indians (800 B.C. to A.D. 100), the rounded, earthen burial mound is 19½ feet high and has a diameter at its base of 95 feet. The Story Mound is considered similar to the Adena Mound, which was located on the Chillicothe estate of Thomas Worthington, an early U.S. senator and governor of Ohio.

Artifacts recovered from Adena Mound about the turn of the century gave archaeologists the first indication that the Hopewell and Adena were separate cultures. Adena Mound was destroyed in 1901 by a combination of agriculture and archaeology.

How to get there: The site is located in northwestern Chillicothe on Delano Avenue, just south of Allen Avenue.

Tiltonsville Cemetery Mound

Attraction: Adena burial mound
Hours: Always visible, although the mound is fenced
Admission fee: None
For more information: Village of Tiltonsville, Tiltonsville, OH 43963

This 13-foot-high Adena burial mound with an oak tree growing out of the center of its summit is in the middle of one of the oldest historic cemeteries in Ohio. It was not at all unusual for early white settlers to establish a cemetery around a prehistoric Indian mound—Mound Cemetery in Marietta, Ohio, is probably the best example of this—and the cemeteries have often helped protect and preserve the mounds. The Tiltonsville mound is unusual in that it is located on a flood terrace only 1,000 feet or so from the west bank of the Ohio River, whereas most Adena mounds were located higher in the hills. Today Tiltonsville is a modest community located between large steel mills on the Ohio River.

The Tiltonsville Cemetery Mound was partially excavated in the 1890s, but no documentation from this time exists. Before the mound was restored in the 1960s, some parts of a human skeleton were discovered in a footpath worn across the mound. The skeleton had a deformed skull caused by the Adena practice of head binding. During the restoration, truckloads of earth were added to the badly eroded mound and the one-acre area was fenced.

The cemetery was laid out as an octagonal family cemetery by James Hodgens of Tiltonsville but was later deeded "to the public forever" by his family. There are eighty-eight known burials in the

Adena burial mound, Tiltonsville

cemetery, including town founder John Tilton, who died in 1810, and his son, John, who was killed by Indians in 1791.

How to get there: The mound is a short distance from the Tiltonsville exit off Route 7. After exiting, cross the railroad tracks and turn left on Walden Street; take the next right, Arn Avenue, to the mound.

Sunwatch

Attraction: Reconstructed Fort Ancient Village on original site
Hours: Monday through Saturday 9:00 A.M. to 5:00 P.M., Sunday noon to 5:00 P.M.; Sunday hours on holidays; last tour begins at 4:00 P.M.
Admission fee: Adults $5.00, children $4.00

For more information: Sunwatch, 2301 West River Road, Dayton, OH 45418; (513) 268–8199

Sunwatch Village is a reconstruction of a Fort Ancient village built along the banks of the Great Miami River only a few miles south of downtown Dayton. Abundant archaeological evidence, which includes such fragile items as crawdad pincers, egg shells from turkeys, and uncarbonized wood, indicates that the village was occupied continuously for about twenty years between the early- and mid-thirteenth century. The Fort Ancient people, the last prehistoric people in this region, occupied the Miami Valley from about A.D. 950 to the 1600s. They were named for an archaeological site in Warren County, Ohio.

Originally known as the Incinerator Site by archaeologists, the village is now called Sunwatch, a name derived from an arrangement of five posts in the plaza. The posts are believed to have served as a solar calendar, and, according to one study, they indicate that the inhabitants "were watchers of the sky." The site was first investigated by amateur archaeologists in the 1960s. Plans to build a sewage treatment plant on the site led to emergency excavations in 1971, which turned up evidence of a prehistoric settlement and eventually caused the city to scrap plans for the sewage facility. The site was placed on the National Register of Historic Places in 1974 and the village opened in 1988. The village is operated by the Dayton Society of Natural History.

A ¼-mile-long trail leads from the interpretive center through the partially reconstructed village, which includes gardens (the Fort Ancient people were sedentary farmers) outside the stockade and a section of reconstructed prairie. The oval-shaped village covers nearly three acres. As the reconstruction shows, it was arranged in concentric zones: the plaza in the center and other zones for burials, work, and housing extending outward. A stockade, part of which has been reconstructed, surrounded the village. The stockade posts, which were spaced about a foot apart, were apparently woven with branches.

Reconstructed buildings at Sunwatch include a wattle and daub house with a grass roof; the South House, which is believed to have housed from six to ten people; the Big House, probably the political and religious center of the community and the

Reconstructed building, Sunwatch

largest structure excavated so far in the village; and a house made of bark. Most buildings had basin-shaped hearths in the center and holes in the roof through which smoke escaped. Benches along the interior walls were used as seats and tables during the day and as beds at night. Arrangements of short cedar posts in the ground mark the location of prehistoric postholes that archaeologists have excavated and give a good visual idea of the arrangement of houses and stockade.

The complex of five poles in the plaza appears to have been arranged so that the shadow from the tall center pole lines up with the hearth of the Big House at sunrise in late April, at planting time, and mid-August, when corn is harvested. A shadow from the center pole falling between it and the center-most of the four smaller posts is thought to have signaled the winter solstice, the shortest day of the year. The height of the poles is based on the size of the excavated postholes; the hole for the 40-foot center pole was 4 feet deep.

In addition to exhibits and an audiovisual display in the interpretive center, Sunwatch has a wide range of lectures, demonstrations, workshops, and other educational activities, including a session on "atlatl shooting," where participants learn the art of spear throwing, and an Artifact Identification Day, on which visitors bring their prehistoric treasures for experts to identify.

How to get there: Just south of Dayton on I–75, take exit 51 and go west on Edwin C. Moses Boulevard. Following signs, cross South Broadway and turn left on West River Road; proceed 1 mile south to Sunwatch.

TENNESSEE

C. H. Nash Museum–Chucalissa

Attraction: Mounds, reconstructed prehistoric village, museum
Hours: Tuesday through Saturday 9:00 A.M. to 5:00 P.M., Sunday
1:00 to 5:00 P.M.; closed Mondays and most major holidays
Admission fee: Adults $3.00
For more information: C. H. Nash Museum–Chucalissa, Memphis State University, 1987 Indian Village Drive, Memphis, TN
38109; (901) 785–3160

This Indian village reconstruction is on the site of a Mississippian Indian settlement that was occupied and abandoned several times between A.D. 1000 and A.D. 1500. (Chucalissa is a Choctaw word meaning abandoned house.) The site, which was once occupied by nearly 1,000 people, is located on the edge of the Chickasaw bluff, from which the inhabitants probably descended to farm the rich bottomlands of the Mississippi River. Although de Soto might have passed near the village, its existence was not recorded by his expedition or other explorers or settlers. It wasn't until the 1930s, when a crew from the Civilian Conservation Corps discovered the abandoned village, that archaeological work began.

Chucalissa today is an interesting combination of reconstructions, large platform mounds, outdoor exhibits, and the C. H. Nash Museum, named for Charles H. Nash, who directed excavations at the village from 1955 until his death in 1968. In addition to an audiovisual presentation, the museum has exhibits on the prehistory of the region and examples of the highly developed pottery—polished bowls, bottles, and effigies, as well as common cooking pots—found at the village.

The site is dominated by a large platform mound that supported the chief's domicile, a building nearly 50 feet square. Excavations indicate that the building was burned when insect damage

103

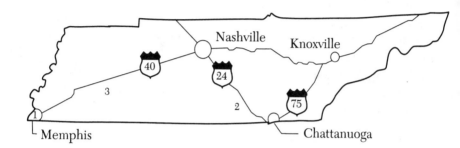

Tennessee
1. C. H. Nash Museum–Chucalissa
2. Old Stone Fort State Archaeological Area
3. Pinson Mounds State Archaeological Area

made it unsafe. A reconstruction includes the interior support posts and a central hearth.

The small mound on the west side of the central plaza was probably an earlier platform mound, built about A.D. 1200, for a temple or chief's home. During the last occupation of the village, about A.D. 1500, a section for burials was added. Most of the remains found here were dismembered and the skulls smashed into fragments. Experts speculate that these were either the remains of captives who had been tortured or the remains of members of the leader's retinue who were killed as part of the ceremony when he died.

Other reconstructions at Chucalissa include the hut of a shaman or medicine man; inside the hut mannequins are used to re-create a curing ceremony. There are also two reconstructed Mississippian shelters. The walls, plastered with mud mixed with grass, are made of posts interwoven with cane. The roofs consist of Johnson grass, from 16 to 20 inches thick, fastened to small poles.

There is a reconstructed corn crib, a dugout canoe, and an Indian garden, which is planted each summer with such staples of the Mississippian diet as corn, beans, squash, and sunflowers, as well as tobacco. The sunken passageway from the museum to the village passes through the Entrance Trench, which is actually one of the first excavations done at the site. There visitors can see the different soil levels that correspond to different periods of habitation at the village. Chucalissa is a facility of the Department of Anthropology of Memphis State University.

How to get there: Take U.S. 61 south of Memphis for 5 miles; turn west on Mitchell Road and proceed 4.5 miles west to site.

Old Stone Fort State Archaeological Area

Attraction: Middle Woodland ceremonial site on a high bluff, trails, visitor center
Hours: Daily 8:00 A.M. to sundown
Admission fee: None
For more information: Old Stone Fort State Archaeological Area, Route 7, Box 7400, Manchester, TN 37355; (615) 723–5073

Although it has no mounds or other eye-catching ruins, Old Stone Fort boasts a spectacular location high on the bluffs at the fork of the Duck and Little Duck rivers. It is also a location rich in folklore. Persistent stories attribute it to Norsemen in the tenth and eleventh centuries or to a band of Welshmen led by Prince Madoc in the twelfth century.

Archaeologists now agree that Indians of the Middle Woodland period began to build Old Stone Fort about the time of the birth of Christ and used it for the next 500 years. Why it was built and how it was used has never been determined. Early observers simply assumed the purpose of the fifty-acre enclosure high on the river bluffs was strategic, hence the name Old Stone Fort. In 1848 Squier and Davis described the site as "the citadels of a people having hostile neighbors or pressed by invaders."

But that interpretation has been challenged. Recent studies, including excavations conducted by the University of Tennessee in 1966, have convinced experts that the site was developed and used for ceremonial purposes. Archaeologists point out that the walls are too low to have been effective defenses, nor is there any indication that they were reinforced by wooden palisades.

Several trails lead through the area; one goes completely around the enclosure, now an open field, a distance of about 1¼ miles. The entrance is marked by a combination of walls, mounds, ditches, and angles. The "in-turned" entrance walls form a rectangle or box, with the actual passageway at the left rear. It was here that ceremonial processions probably made a dramatic entrance into the enclosure.

The wall surrounding the enclosure was not continuous; rather the sections, probably from 4 to 6 feet high, were built where the enclosure was not protected by steep bluffs. The walls consist of inner and outer sections built of stone and an earth and rubble fill. At the far, or south, end of the enclosure there is evidence of what was once thought to be a defensive moat linking the two forks of the river; however, it is now believed that this was a natural channel that Woodland Indians might have enlarged to increase the flow of water.

Old Stone Fort has a more recent history, too. During the Civil War, Federal troops camped here after the battle of Stone's River in 1863. The abundance of fast-flowing water at the site also made it an early industrial center. According to one account, a rope factory was built near the falls of Little Duck River in 1823. A variety of mills were built on the waterways, including an 1862 powder mill on the Duck River that provided the Confederate army with munitions. The last industry, built in 1879, was a paper mill that produced up to 10,000 pounds of newsprint a day from old rags. The state of Tennessee purchased the land for the archaeological area in 1966. During the summer of the same year, the University of Tennessee conducted the last major investigation of the area.

How to get there: Old Stone Fort is located off Highway 41 in Manchester, Tennessee. From I–24 take the Highway 53 exit and follow the signs 1½ miles to the entrance. There is a state-run campground, picnic area, and golf course next to the archaeological area.

Pinson Mounds State Archaeological Area

Attraction: Major mound site, visitor center/museum
Hours: Daily March through November, Monday through Saturday 8:00 A.M. to 4:30 P.M., Sunday, 1:00 to 5:00 P.M.; closed weekends, December through February
Admission fee: None
For more information: Pinson Mounds State Archaeological Area, 460 Ozier Road, Pinson, TN 38366; (901) 988–5614

In 1922 archaeologist William Myer of the Smithsonian Institution described Pinson Mounds on Tennessee's Forked Deer River as the "ruins of a great ancient walled city with outer defenses measuring fully six miles in length, with elaborate outer and inner citadels, with 35 mounds of various sizes." Subsequent investigations have shown that Myer was more fanciful than scientific in his assessment. There are actually no more than twelve mounds, and many of the features he saw in the site were natural, not made by prehistoric man. Still, Pinson ranks as the largest Middle Woodland period site in the country, with the second-tallest mound, and as one of the most important and interesting sites in the Southeast.

Today the 1,162-acre state park consists of three distinct areas. The Central Mound Group includes the 72-foot-high Sauls Mound (named for a former landowner, John Sauls), the Barrow Pit, where the dirt for Sauls Mound was dug, and the Duck's Nest, a rimmed circular depression with a large fire pit in the center that was used for ceremonies. The second area, the Eastern Citadel, has four mounds plus the Geometric Earthworks, a 900-foot remnant of the embankment that once surrounded this area. The third area, the Western Mound Group, includes Ozier Mound, the park's second tallest (32 feet), and the Twin Mounds, a burial area rich in ceramic sherds and other finds.

Radiocarbon dating indicates that the major construction at Pinson Mounds occurred from about 50 B.C. to A.D. 150, although Pinson apparently continued to function as a ceremonial center for another 150 years. Pinson is so large and complex that it was once mistakenly thought to have been built by the later Mississippian peoples. There is, however, one significant difference between sites of the two periods: large Mississippian centers like Moundville in Alabama had a year-round population dominated by a ruling class. Pinson, by contrast, was used only occasionally for ceremonial purposes by groups in the region. But precisely why Pinson was built or how the complex task was organized and managed is unknown.

Archaeologists have speculated that Pinson was built according to a master plan with Sauls Mound in the middle and four other platform mounds—numbers 5 (Ozier), 15, 28, and 29—marking the four corners. Since another platform mound, Mound 10, does not fit this pattern, it is believed that it was built one hundred or so years later by Indians who were unaware of the site's plan but still recognized it as a sacred place.

The site is named for Joel Pinson, an early surveyor of western Tennessee, who is credited with discovering the mounds in 1820. The mounds were explored and measured several times throughout the rest of the century, and in 1917 William Myer arranged to have the site mapped and surveyed. As Myer noted, few relics had been found at the site, which perhaps explains how Pinson managed to escape the ravages of pothunters and vandals.

The first systematic evaluation of Pinson Mounds by professional archaeologists was in 1961. At the same time local citizens began pressing the state to preserve the area, an effort that resulted in the establishment of the archaeological park.

The park has 6 miles of trails, including a nature trail, boardwalk, and picnic areas. The earth-covered museum building has been built to resemble an Indian mound (and, in fact, is often mistaken for one); it includes an archaeological library and a theater. The map that William Myers made of the site in the late 1910s is included among the exhibits.

How to get there: In Pinson, take Ozier Road off Highway 45 a short distance to the site.

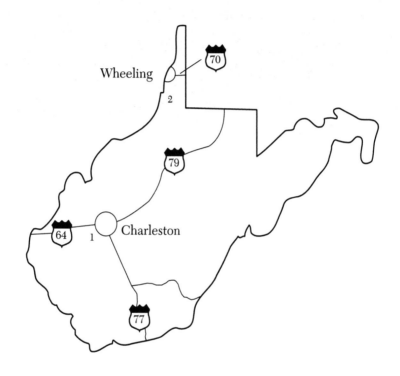

West Virginia
1. Criel Mound
2. Grave Creek Mound State Park

WEST VIRGINIA

Criel Mound

Attraction: Large Adena burial mound in a public park
Hours: Always open
Admission fee: None
For more information: South Charleston Chamber of Commerce, 607 D Street, South Charleston, WV 25303; (304) 744–0051

Also known as the South Charleston Mound, this Adena burial mound was originally 33 feet tall before the top of it was leveled off in the nineteenth century to accommodate a judges' stand for a racetrack that ran around the base. (Running a racetrack around the base

Criel Mound

of a prehistoric mound was a common practice in the nineteenth century, particularly in Ohio and West Virginia.) Still, despite this alteration, Criel is the second-largest mound in West Virginia after the immense Grave Creek Mound. It is also conveniently located just minutes off Interstate 64 and is pleasantly situated in a small public park. Steps wind around the mound to the summit.

When the mound was excavated in 1883 by the Smithsonian's Bureau of American Ethnology, archaeologists found eleven skeletons buried on a layer of bark near the base of the mound in what had once been a wooden building with a conical roof. One body, which had been buried with a copper headdress, was clearly at the center; the other bodies were arranged in two semicircles, their feet toward the central figure, on each side. Five of the bodies had been buried with new spearheads.

Criel Mound was one of a few remaining prehistoric sites in the Kanawha River valley, where Charleston, West Virginia, is located. In the nineteenth century nearly a hundred mounds and other earthworks were known; the archaeologist Cyrus Thomas reported on many of them after a twelve-year study of mounds by the Smithsonian Institution was published in 1894.

How to get there: Take Montrose Avenue exit off I–64, go north a few blocks, and turn left on MacCorkle Avenue. The mound is ½ mile on the left.

Grave Creek Mound State Park

Attraction: Large burial mound of the Adena period, museum
Hours: Monday through Saturday 10:00 A.M. to 4:30 P.M., Sunday 1:00 to 5:00 P.M.; closed major holidays
Admission fee: Museum, $1.50
For more information: Grave Creek Mound State Park, Box 527, Moundsville, WV 26041; (304) 843–1410

Located on the left bank of the Ohio River, Grave Creek Mound is the largest conical earth mound in America and one of the largest mortuary earth mounds in the world. In 1838, the same year the mound was first excavated, road engineers measured the

Grave Creek Mound

mound to be 69 feet high and 295 feet in diameter at the base. More recent measurements indicate that the mound is somewhat smaller: about 62 feet high and 240 feet in diameter.

The mound was built for burial by the Adena people, probably over a hundred-year period between 200 B.C. and 100 B.C. Excavations have shown that it was surrounded by a moat about 910 feet long, 4 to 5 feet deep, and 40 feet wide. Earth from the moat was used in building the mound. That the mound was a considerable organizational and engineering feat is obvious: Some three million basket loads of earth (the Adena had neither wheel nor horse) went into building the structure, which measures more than one million cubic feet in size.

Grave Creek Mound was the impressive centerpiece of a complex of smaller mounds that have disappeared since early visitors and settlers recorded their existence. In 1803 Captain Meriwether Lewis, an early visitor to the mound site, noted that "traces of old intrenchments are to be seen tho' they are so imperfect that they cannot be traced . . . for this enquire I had not leasure." Lewis also made note of the moat, although the traces must have been faint, for earlier the same year another visitor, Thaddeus Mason Harris, observed that "there are no excavations near the mound, and no hills or banks of earth . . . requisite to form such a stupendous mound."

Like other prehistoric mounds in the Ohio Valley and elsewhere in the country, the one at Grave Creek received its fair share of abuse. At one time a museum was built into the mound; at another a saloon was located on its summit; at yet another a racetrack for a county fair was built around its base. The mound was acquired by West Virginia in 1909 and maintained by a nearby penitentiary until the present state park was created in 1967.

The first excavation of Mammoth Mound (as it was then called to distinguish it from other earthworks in the complex) was undertaken by local amateurs in 1838. In the process of drilling two shafts, one horizontal and the other vertical, the excavators discovered two burial vaults, one above the other. Early in 1839 a Wheeling physician, Thomas Townsend, published the first account of the excavation in the weekly *Cincinnati Chronicle*. In his article he described the lower vault as being dug into "the natural earth about seven or eight feet deep [and] covered with timbers supported on the inside by logs . . . set on their ends at short intervals from each other."

This first excavation also produced what one modern archaeological report has called "the notorious Grave Creek tablet." This controversial find was a small, oval-shaped sandstone tablet, 1¾ inches long and engraved with some twenty-five hieroglyphic-type characters. There are many conflicting reports as to how it was found, but it apparently was discovered in a wheelbarrow of dirt taken from the mound.

Henry Rowe Schoolcraft, a pioneer of American archaeology, was one of the first to attest the tablet's authenticity. He believed that the characters came from different Old World alphabets. Other experts took the tablet as proof of their belief that the American Indians were not capable of building the mounds.

In his entertaining 1991 book, *Fantastic Archaeology, The Wild Side of North American Prehistory*, Stephen Williams of Harvard University gives examples of the "eccentric elegance" of some of the translations experts came up with. One, which Williams termed "a big message to get on a skipping stone," went as follows: "The Grave of one who was assassinated here. May God to avenge him strike his murderer, cutting off the hand of his existence." In an attempt to test the authenticity of the Grave Creek Stone, in 1874 one Ohio researcher asked four individuals at random to write twenty or so symbols using only straight lines. The results, he pointed out, could be interpreted as Phoenician, Cypriotic, Pelasgian, Coptic, Gothic, and Runic, just as the symbols on the tablet had been. Despite such convincing debunking of the tablet, belief in its authenticity persists. A new "translation" was published as recently as 1976, Williams reports.

A replica of the tablet is displayed at Grave Creek's Delf Norona Museum and Cultural Center. The museum, which includes an impressive array of Adena artifacts and a diorama showing the mound under construction, was named for Delf Norona (1895–1974), a founder of the West Virginia Archaeological Society and curator of the first museum at the site, which opened in 1952.

How to get there: Located at 801 Jefferson Street, the park is one block east of Route 2 in Moundsville and a fifteen-minute drive south of Wheeling and I–70.

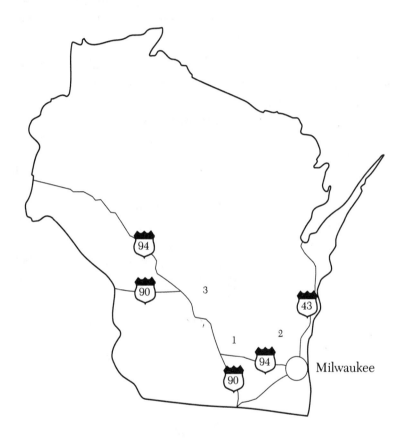

Wisconsin
1. Aztalan State Park
2. Lizard Mound County Park
3. Roche-a-Cri State Park

WISCONSIN

Aztalan State Park

Attraction: Restored mounds
Hours: May through December, 7:00 A.M. to 9:00 P.M.
Admission fee: None
For more information: Aztalan State Park, c/o Glacial Drumlin Trail, 1213 South Main Street, Lake Mills, WI 53551; (414) 648–8774

In 1835, when settlers first became aware of the ancient flat-topped mounds on the Crawfish River, they concluded that the earthen structures were built by peoples related to the Aztecs in Mexico. This was entirely in keeping with current scholarship of the day. Then in 1850 the scientist Increase A. Lapham, who was sponsored by the American Antiquarian Society in Worcester, Massachusetts, investigated the site and theorized that the mound builders were ancestors of modern Indians.

The larger of the two restored flat-topped mounds in the state park is a two-tier, truncated pyramid 40 feet wide and 25 feet high, on top of which was built a temple or chief's residence. Ten conical mounds also remain at the site. There was also a stockade around the site, a portion of which has been reconstructed. It is now believed that the site was settled by Missippian migrants from Cahokia, who lived at Aztalan for about 200 years beginning about A.D. 1100.

Although Lapham recognized the importance of the mounds in 1850 and urged that the site be protected (it had not yet been damaged by agriculture), it didn't become a state park for another century, in 1948. It was named a National Landmark in 1964. Today the 172-acre park is mostly open prairie.

How to get there: Take exit 259 South off I–94. Follow Highway 89 into Lake Mills. Take County Route B east 2½ miles and go south on County Route Q to the site.

Lizard Mound County Park

Attraction: Twenty-five effigy and other mounds
Hours: Daily during daylight hours, April through November
Admission fee: None
For more information: Washington County Land Use and Park Department, Courthouse Room 150, 432 East Washington Street, P.O. Box 1986, West Bend, WI 53095–7986; (414) 335–4445

This park is named for the spectacular lizard-shaped effigy mound in its southwestern corner, but it also contains twenty-four other mounds—eight panther effigy mounds, two bird effigy mounds, and the rest conical or cigar-shaped linear mounds. A self-guided, mile-long trail winds through the park, which was established in 1950. Some of the mounds are more than 3 feet high, but their exceptional length and width makes it difficult to discern or fully appreciate their shape from ground level. "One might ponder the significance of the fact that the best view of them is from above," anthropologist Robert Ritzenthaler has written.

(Photo by Daniel J. Smith, Graff and Associates)

Portion of Lizard Mound

118

The lizard mound is 258½ feet long, "of which 65 feet is represented by the body," according to a report published in the *Wisconsin Archaeologist* in 1942. Each of the lizard's legs was reported as being more than 30 feet long and its head 28 feet wide. The report put the height of the mound at 4⅓ feet at the shoulder and 2⅓ feet where the tail, which tapers off to only a few inches at the tip, joins the body.

The people of the Effigy Mounds culture constructed thousands of mounds in Wisconsin and nearby Iowa, Illinois, and Minnesota between about A.D. 400 and 1200. Many were in large groups, some of them numbering more than a hundred mounds. Why they built them is far from clear. It has been speculated that the mounds might have represented territory markers or seasonal meeting places. They might have been likenesses of clan totems or family symbols. Or they could have represented the guardian spirits, usually animals or birds, that the Woodland tribes worshiped. Unlike other Woodland people, the effigy mound builders did not usually bury their dead with durable artifacts that might have given modern archaeologists clues to their purpose.

How to get there: Go north of West Bend on Route 144, turn east on County Route A, and continue 1 mile to the site.

Roche-a-Cri State Park

Attraction: Large grouping of prehistoric rock carvings and some rock paintings
Hours: Daily 6:00 A.M. to 11:00 P.M.
Admission fee: None
For more information: Ranger Station, Box 100, Friendship, WI 53934; (608) 339–6881 (summer) or (608) 339–3385 (off season)

In the heart of Wisconsin's nearly flat central plain, Roche-a-Cri, a prominent sandstone outcropping, rises conspicuously about 300 feet from the surrounding terrain. Its south side, near the meandering Carter Creek, is covered with prehistoric Indian rock art that has been overlain with names, dates (the earliest being 1845), and other graffiti from historic times. The rock art has also been damaged by target shooting; here, as elsewhere, rock art has been an irresistible target to marksmen.

The most common rock carving, or petroglyph, is what experts call "geometric figures and nonrandom lines." A very common figure is the so-called turkey track, made by joining three lines of equal length at the lower end. (Although the meaning of virtually all prehistoric rock art found in the United States is unclear, archaeologist Victoria Dirst, in a 1989 report on Roche-a-Cri, made the interesting speculation that the turkey track could be a male stick figure inverted to indicate death.)

There are also at least seven X's, usually called thunderbirds, that cross below the midpoint and have additional lines at the top. These birdlike figures might have been inspired by the turkey vultures that nest today on top of the outcrop. Similarly, crescent figures amid the rock art have been interpreted as representing canoes, eclipses, or crescent moons.

Roche-a-Cri's rock paintings, or pictographs, are a prehistoric art form that is rare in Wisconsin. They include a group of three figures located high on the main face of the rock. The paintings, which appear to represent humans (one has a wavy line leading from the head to a large bird figure), were painted with red or reddish orange lines.

A government surveyor first reported on the rock art at Roche-a-Cri in 1851. An article in the *Wisconsin Archeologist* in 1919 makes this reference to the petroglyphs: "Their Indian origin is not questioned by residents of the vicinity but no explanation of their age, purpose or significance is available. The characters consist of crowfeet, arches and curved and straight lines. Above and about these vandals and thoughtless white visitors to this site have cut and scratched their names and initials."

How to get there: From Friendship take Route 13 north 2 miles.

THE WEST

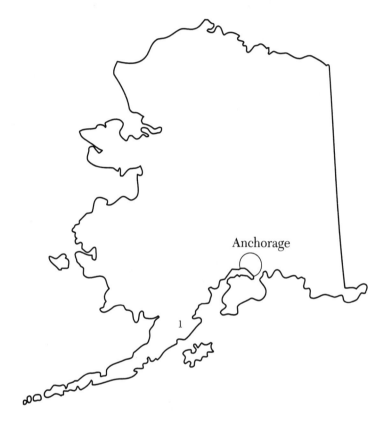

Alaska
1. Katmai National Park and Preserve

ALASKA

Katmai National Park and Preserve

Attraction: Reconstructed aboriginal pit house on original site
Hours: Always open
Admission Fee: None
For more information: Katmai National Park, P.O. Box 7, King Salmon, AK 99613; (907) 246–3305

Created in 1918 as a living laboratory to preserve the unusual ecosystem created after a cataclysmic volcanic eruption in 1912, Katmai National Park is still one of the world's principal centers of volcanic activity, with fifteen active volcanoes lining the Shelikof Strait on its southeastern border. The park, located on the base of the Alaska Peninsula, also has a rich prehistory. There are three archaeological areas within the park, all listed on the National Register of Historic Places.

(Courtesy Katmai National Park)

Reconstructed pit house at Katmai National Park

The first people came here about 5,000 years ago to hunt caribou during the peninsula's short summer. A thousand years later people began living on the Brooks River, today the site of both the park's main camp and a partially reconstructed subterranean dwelling. Archaeologists know of about sixty-five such dwellings, and there must have been a sizeable population of people living in this area. Bones found amid the excavations indicate that the salmon, for which the Brooks River is famous today, were running in abundance at least 4,000 years ago.

The pit house on view near Brooks Camp dates from about A.D. 1200 and represents a type of habitation that was found in southwestern Alaska from A.D. 1000 to the present century. The Brooks Camp pit house was excavated and reconstructed by the University of Oregon's D. E. Dumond in the summers of 1967 and 1968.

The excavated pit house was built from peeled and split cottonwood logs and covered with an insulating layer of clay and moss. Grasses and willows soon sprouted from this durable roof, adding to the protective layer. The original entrance to the pit house was a tunnel that was dug lower than the main floor in order to trap cold air and prevent it from entering into the dwelling. Smoke from a fire in the center of the single room escaped from a small hole in the ceiling that could be covered with translucent seal gut when the fire wasn't lit.

In the reconstruction, the roofing of split poles is unfinished, allowing for an unobstructed view of the interior from the outside. In one corner mud and moss cover the poles to indicate to visitors how the original roofing looked. When the framework of the pit house was complete, some of the material found in the excavation was put back in place, specifically stone hammers and anvils and sandstone slabs that were used for polishing and grinding. In addition, wood ashes and charcoal were placed where such debris was found in the original. As a result, Dumond wrote, "The floor looks roughly as it might have looked when the house was in use, and in that sense represents a violation of the unity of impression given by the rest of the structure, which is hopefully that of a house still being built."

In addition to the pit house, the public is welcome to visit the intermittent excavations that have taken place in recent years in the

Brooks Camp area. In the summers of 1992 to 1994, for example, park archaeologist Patricia McClenahan directed an excavation prior to the construction of a well house for Brooks Camp. The excavation produced a large quantity of prehistoric material, including thermally altered rock, burned caribou remains, hammer stones, charcoal flecks, and stone flakes and chunks. The excavation also showed the multicolored layers of volcanic ash that are the result of the various eruptions that have occurred at Katmai. This includes white ash at the surface that was deposited by the major eruption in 1912 and a gray-green layer left by an eruption about A.D. 1450. These layers aid archaeologists in the dating of material found in the excavations.

How to get there: The site is located 290 miles southwest of Anchorage. There are daily commercial flights from Anchorage to King Salmon, which is located about 6 miles from the park's western boundary. There are commercial float planes operating between King Salmon and Brooks Camp, a distance of about 35 miles. The pit house is within easy walking distance of Brooks Camp.

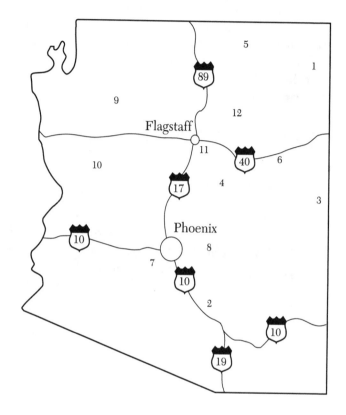

Arizona

1. Canyon de Chelly National Monument
2. Casa Grande National Monument
3. Casa Malpais
4. Montezuma Castle National Monument
5. Navajo National Monument
6. Petrified Forest National Park
7. Pueblo Grande Museum and Ruins
8. Tonto National Monument
9. Tusayan Ruin and Museum
10. Tuzigoot National Monument
11. Walnut Canyon National Monument
12. Wupatki National Monument

ARIZONA

Canyon de Chelly National Monument

Attraction: Major cliff dwelling site, tours, visitor center
Hours: Visitor center open daily October through April, 8:00 A.M. to 5:00 P.M.; open 8:00 A.M. to 6:00 P.M. rest of year
Admission fee: None
For more information: Canyon de Chelly National Monument, Box 588, Chinle AZ 86503; (602) 674–5436

The prehistoric people known as the Anasazi, or Ancient Ones, were the first Indians to seek shelter and livelihood on the riverbeds and amid the sheer limestone cliffs of Canyon de Chelly, today a national monument and one of the most extensive archaeological sites open to the public in the Southwest. When they arrived here about A.D. 200, these early Anasazi made their living as hunters and gatherers, although archaeologists today call them Basket Makers because of the excellent baskets and weaving they produced.

Gradually the Basket Makers, who at first lived in scattered subterranean habitations called pit houses, made the transition to farming and built villages of flat-roofed post and adobe structures. About A.D. 700 they moved from the riverbeds and began building multistoried pueblos and cliff dwellings perched on ledges and in crevices on the canyon wall. It was during this time, known as the Pueblo period, that kivas—underground rooms probably used for ceremonies—began to appear. It is not certain why the Anasazi moved to the cliff dwellings; perhaps for defense against their enemies, to protect themselves from flash floods, or to create more room on the canyon floor for farming. Experts speculate a twenty-five-year drought at the end of the twelfth century might have caused the Anasazi to abandon their pueblos by 1300. Afterwards the canyon was occupied, at least in the summer, first by the Hopi and then, after 1700, by the Navajo.

Mummy Cave, Canyon de Chelly

Canyon de Chelly was formed by the Rio de Chelly, which rises near the Arizona–New Mexico border and empties into the Chinle Wash just west of the monument. The name, Canyon de Chelly (d'SHAY), is probably a corruption of the Navajo *tsegi*, meaning "rocky canyon." The 131-square-mile monument also includes the adjoining Canyon del Muerto (Canyon of Death), which was so named when explorers found mummified bodies in one of its caves. It joins Canyon de Chelly about 4 miles east of the monument's visitor center.

The Navajo's defiant ways caused the Spanish, and later the Americans, to mount military expeditions to punish them. In 1805 a military column commanded by Antonio Narbona, who was to become governor of the province of New Mexico, fought a day-long battle with the Navajo in Canyon de Chelly. During the fighting twenty-five Navajo women and children were killed. The Navajo had taken refuge in a shelter, now called Massacre Cave, on the east near the top of Canyon del Muerto. The place from which the Spanish fired into the cave is now a viewpoint on the canyon rim.

After the American Civil War, Brigadier General James H. Carlton, military governor of New Mexico, dispatched Colonel Christopher "Kit" Carson and a force of 1,000 men against the Navajo. For the United States Army, the expedition was a success. Some 8,000 Indians surrendered and were marched 400 miles to Fort Sumner in New Mexico, a trek known as the Long Walk. They stayed in New Mexico under guard for four years before being returned to their homelands. Today Canyon de Chelly belongs to the Navajo Nation, which administers it with the National Park Service. In the summer Navajo families, whose hogans are scattered along the valley, farm and graze sheep on the bottomland.

There are more than 700 prehistoric sites in the monument; almost all the dwellings in the canyon are on the north side, where they would receive sunlight even in winter. The canyon dwellings were first recorded when Lieutenant James H. Simpson of the Corps of Topological Engineers accompanied a military expedition against the Navajo in 1849. Simpson named the canyon's best-known site Casa Blanca (White House) for the wall of white plaster across its upper portion. With sixty rooms and four kivas, White House Ruin is one of the largest in the monument and is accessible via a 1¼-mile trail that descends 500 feet down the canyon wall. This is the only trail visitors can take unaccompanied by a ranger or Navajo guide.

Ten to twelve families, or as many as sixty people, might have lived at White House, which probably had at least eighty rooms before stream erosion washed away part of the structure. At the far west end of the ruin there is part of a round kiva (a word meaning "room" in Hopi) that originally was covered with a log and mud roof. Since Pueblo Indians today use kivas for religious purposes, it is assumed that the Anasazi did the same.

Tree ring dating shows that the White House was built in stages between A.D. 1060 and 1275. The masonry on the White House is of a fine quality and more closely related to that found at the important Anasazi cultural and spiritual center Chaco Canyon (in present-day New Mexico) than elsewhere in Canyon de Chelly. The stones are carefully shaped and the mud mortar is reinforced with small, flat stones called spalls.

South Rim Drive

White House Ruin, located at mile point 6.4, is the principal stopping point along the 21.8-mile drive that follows the south rim of Canyon de Chelly. (Another drive of about the same distance covers the north rim of Canyon del Muerto and is described below.) At Junction Overlook (3.9 miles) there is a view to the left of First Ruin, the first Anasazi pueblo studied in the canyon, work done by archaeologist Cosmos Mindeleff in 1882. First Ruin has ten rooms and two kivas. The fifteen-room Junction Ruin is straight ahead on the far side of the canyon. It is located at the point Canyon del Muerto joins Canyon de Chelly.

Past White House Ruin, the principal stopping places are Sliding Rock Overlook (12.9 miles) where the Anasazi built a precariously situated cliff dwelling across the canyon on a sloping ledge, and, at the end of the drive, Spider Rock Overlook. Here a 200-yard path leads from the parking area to the canyon edge, where 800-foot-high Spider Rock rises from the canyon. According to Navajo legend, Spider Rock is the home of Spider Woman, who preys upon naughty children. The many ruins visible from this overlook are best seen with binoculars.

North Rim Drive

At 5.4 miles from the visitor center there is a turnoff to Ledge Ruin Viewpoint, where an Anasazi dwelling of some thirty rooms is located on a ledge about 100 feet above the canyon floor. At 10.2 miles is Canyon del Muerto's Antelope House, a forty- to fifty-room village that is known for the tan and white, half-scale antelopes painted high on a nearby cliff. The antelopes are possibly the work of a Navajo artist who lived in the canyon in the 1830s.

The Anasazi dwelling visible here consists of two major room blocks connected by a circular central plaza. A pit house dated A.D. 693 (late Basket Maker period) was found underneath Antelope House. In the 1920s the Tomb of the Weaver was found in an alcove across the wash from Antelope House; it contained the well-preserved body of an old man wrapped in a blanket of golden eagle feathers, a likely indication of his high rank in society. Antelope House was unoccupied by A.D. 1260, somewhat earlier than the rest of the canyon.

Mummy Cave (19.1 miles), actually two adjacent caves in Canyon del Muerto, is the largest ruin in the monument. The eastern cave contains fifty-five rooms and four kivas; the western cave contains twenty rooms. Mummy Cave is located about 300 feet up a talus slope. The traces of a hand-and-toe trail cut into the rock from the top of the slope to the ruin are still visible. A ledge connecting the two caves has fifteen rooms and a three-story tower house, which tree ring dating indicates was built about A.D. 1284. Since the masonry is of a type common at Mesa Verde in Colorado (another great center of Anasazi culture, like Chaco Canyon), archaeologists believe it was built by people who had migrated from that settlement. Whether the tower was defensive or ceremonial or both is not known.

Massacre Cave (described above) is the final stop, at mile 21, on the north rim drive.

Information on scheduled hikes and other programs is available at the visitor center. Lodging is available at the Navajo-owned Thunderbird Lodge, which is located within the monument, ½ mile south of the visitor center. There is also a cafeteria. Jeep tours of the canyon leave from the Thunderbird Lodge.

How to get there: Canyon de Chelly National Monument is located within the Navajo Indian Reservation 3 miles east of Chinle.

Casa Grande National Monument

Attraction: Four-story Hohokam tower
Hours: Daily 7:00 A.M. to 6:00 P.M.
Admission fee: $1.00
For more information: Casa Grande Ruins National Monument, 1100 Ruins Drive, Coolidge, AZ 85228; (602) 723–3172

The pueblo surrounding this towering desert landmark had been deserted for more than two centuries when, in November 1694, Father Eusebio Francisco Kino, the famous Jesuit missionary, came across "the Casa Grande—a four-story building as large as a castle and equal to the finest church in the lands of Sonora," while he was on an expedition down the Santa Cruz River. In

(Courtesy National Park Service)

Artifacts on display at Casa Grande

more recent times, the tower has been called "America's first skyscraper."

Casa Grande was built about 1350 by the Hohokam people, who had arrived in the region about 300 B.C. They lived in huts until they began building pueblos in the 1100s; the tower is part of such a pueblo. The Hohokam developed an extensive system of irrigation canals, and scientists have suggested that their disappearance about 1450 was the result of increased alkalinity of the soil caused by overwatering.

Archaeologists are not certain why Casa Grande was built. Perhaps it was the home of a chieftain, a temple, a large storage facility, or an astronomical observatory as indicated by holes in the wall that are aligned with equinoxes. Certainly the tower, which was constructed from caliche, a layer of hard desert soil, was the result of a prodigious effort. The structure was reinforced by more than 600 roof beams, which had to be carried (they had neither horse nor wheel) from 50 miles away. The walls of the tower are 4½ feet thick at the base and taper to a thickness of 1¾ feet at the top. The building consisted of a 5-foot-high foundation, a two-story building on top of that, and, finally, a tower.

Noted archaeologists such as J. Walter Fewkes, Adolph F. Bandelier, Frederick Webb Hodge, and Frank H. Cushing, leader of the privately sponsored Hemenway Southwestern Archaeological Expedition in 1887–1888, helped bring national attention to the rapidly deteriorating ruin. In 1892 it came under federal protection, and the first roof was built over it in 1903. It became a national monument in 1918.

There is a self-guided tour through the monument. The visitor center offers talks by rangers and exhibits, including a chart outlining the irrigation canals built by the Hohokam.

How to get there: The monument is located 1 mile north of Coolidge, Arizona, off Route 87.

Casa Malpais

Attraction: Ruins of pueblo and kiva of the Mogollon people; off-site museum devoted to Mogollon culture

Hours: Summer (May through September) tours at 9:00 A.M., 11:00 A.M., and 2:30 P.M.; winter (October through April) tours at 11:00 A.M. and 2:30 P.M.

Admission Fee: Adults $3.00, senior citizens $2.00, children under 12 free

For more information: Casa Malpais Foundation, P.O. Box 807, Springerville, AZ 85938; (602) 333–5375

It was the desire of the people of Springerville, Arizona (population 2,000), to turn a local Indian ruin into a revenue-producing park that led to the unexpected discovery that Casa Malpais had the potential to be among the most important prehistoric sites in the Southwest. The pueblo was built on a series of natural terraces, formed from collapsed volcanic basalt, overlooking Round Valley, the floodplain of the Little Colorado River. In the late 1880s Basque sheepherders settled in the valley and gave the abandoned pueblo its ominous name, Casa Malpais, or House of the Badlands.

To comply with a federal law that requires sites on federal land to be assessed and reviewed before they are developed, Springerville hired a team of professional archaeologists from Phoenix. They began work in 1990. The next year they announced at a meeting of professional archaeologists that their work had revealed the remains of a great kiva or ceremonial structure, an extensive pueblo of more than a hundred rooms, and, beneath the site, a series of caverns that the inhabitants had divided with stone walls into individual burial chambers, some of which were quite large, at least one being 50 feet high and 200 feet long. The announcement of the underground burial sites caused quite a stir—and some controversy—in the archaeological world, since these were the first prehistoric catacombs or tombs discovered in the region.

The pueblo was built and occupied by the Mogollon people, who lived in this area of southeastern Arizona and southwestern New Mexico from about A.D. 200 to 1450. Tree ring dating of roof beams in the pueblo shows that the pueblo was built between A.D. 1250 and 1300, with most of the work being done in two separate four-year periods. The size of the pueblo—over a hundred rooms have been discovered so far—plus the large number of rocks and logs, some of which had to be transported long distances, indicate "that a massive amount of human energy was involved" in its construction, according to an archaeologist on the project.

Experts are also weighing the possibility that Casa Malpais had special meaning for the Mogollon and that people from other settlements in the region contributed to its construction and then used the site for religious ceremonies. Archaeologists are uncertain what eventually happened to the Mogollon at Casa Malpais and elsewhere. A drought in much of the Southwest, crop failures, and warfare are possible explanations for their disappearance, if, indeed, they did disappear. The fact that present-day Hopi and Zuni people both claim the Mogollon as ancestors shows that they might have abandoned sites like Casa Malpais but remained in the region.

Many pottery sherds have been recovered from the ruins. Among the many styles are pieces of pottery with green designs painted over white slip; these closely resemble pottery that the Zuni produced in historic times and contribute to the theory that the Zuni and Mogollon are related. Many of these sherds, as well as other artifacts found by private collectors in the region, are displayed at the Casa Malpais Museum in Springerville. These include an exquisite stone bowl with a frog carved on its side and an intriguing piece of green soapstone resembling a golf tee that Zuni speculated might have been used by a medicine man to place small amounts of pollen on the body of an ailing person.

Arizona law requires that archaeologists notify all twenty Indian tribes in the state of the discovery of prehistoric burial sites. In accordance with the wishes of the Indian leaders, the burial sites at Casa Malpais have been closed to all outsiders. On tours of the site, visitors can see the restored wall of the kiva, the ruins of the pueblo, a number of petroglyphs, and, on a lower terrace, the remains of a large enclosure that might have been a dance plaza. A 30-foot-high rock pinnacle with hand-holds chipped into its sides might have been used for tethering sacred eagles. There are also a number of petroglyphs at the site, some of which apparently depict bighorn sheep, a centipede with immense pincers, and human beings.

At this writing, the site is still under development, and town leaders in Springerville hope that it will eventually be designated a National Historic Site or Park. Guided tours of the site take from an hour to an hour and a half. There are also plans eventually to open the site to self-guided tours.

How to get there: Stop first at the Casa Malpais Museum at 318 Main Street, near the stoplight in Springerville. Visitors follow the tour leader in their own cars to the site, 2 miles north of town.

Montezuma Castle National Monument

Attraction: Five-story cliff dwelling
Hours: Daily June through August, 8:00 A.M. to 7:00 P.M.; September through May, 8:00 A.M. to 5:00 P.M.
Admission fee: $1.00
For more information: Montezuma Castle National Monument, P.O. Box 219, Camp Verde, AZ 86322; (602) 567–3322

The Sinagua Indians, who lived at Montezuma and elsewhere in the high desert, were named by a zoologist, Harold Sellers Colton, who began a sixty-year study of the archaeology and natural history of the region in 1916 and who first recognized them as a distinct culture. Colton admired how well they adapted to the dry climate of the higher Colorado Plateau and named them Sinagua, from the Spanish, "without water."

Montezuma Castle, a five-story dwelling

(Courtesy National Park Service)

Montezuma Castle, on the other hand, is misnamed; the sixteenth-century Aztec ruler Montezuma was never anywhere near the ruin. In 1864 an Indian fighter, after a foray into the Verde Valley, told a newspaper in Prescott that his party had seen "an immense spring or well with walled caves in the cliffs surrounding it. They were probably built by the Aztec. We gave the name of Montezuma to the well." The name stuck.

The cliff dwellings were built by the Sinagua Indians in the thirteenth century after drought or other causes had driven them here from Wupatki and Walnut Canyon. The castle, a five-story structure of limestone blocks, is built into the cliffs about 100 feet above Beaver Creek. In places the walls of the twenty-room dwelling are curved to conform with the shape of the cliffs. Building materials, including large sycamore beams, had to be hauled up ladders or along a narrow path to the site. The Sinagua were not a warlike people, but it is likely that they had defense in mind when they picked this site.

In the 1880s Edgar Alexander Mearns, a surgeon stationed at nearby Fort Verde, extensively excavated the ruins, digging through a four-foot accumulation of bat guano to reach the floor of the dwellings. The first scientist to study the ruins, Mearns sent several thousand artifacts back east to museums, including "a handsomely wrought marlin-spike fashioned from the leg bone of a deer," as well as gourd cups and a stone ax that a "careless shot, aimed at the building by some passing hunter," had knocked out of a timber.

Mearns also noted an entrance—"a window of sub-Gothic form"—just slightly more than 3 feet high and 2 feet wide that inspired this passage in a magazine article he wrote in 1890: "The traveler in this region is quite certain of being entertained by exaggerated stories about gigantic human skeletons having been discovered in the ruined casas grandes; but if he be a good-sized man, and possessed of adipose tissue appertaining to the age of three-score years, he will become skeptical thereof when he comes to squeeze himself through the narrow portals of the ancient halls."

The castle can be viewed from a paved pathway behind the visitor center, but the public is not allowed to climb up to or enter it. The path leads on to the foundations of another ruin, Castle A, at the base of the cliff before it returns to the visitor center. Castle A was excavated in 1933–1934 by a young archaeologist, Earl Jackson, whose father was the monument's first custodian, and a Depression-era Civil Works Administration crew. Castle A collapsed after it was vacated, but, with five floors and two dozen or so rooms, it was once twice as big as Montezuma Castle.

Also part of the monument is Montezuma Well, a natural sinkhole 470 feet in diameter and 55 feet deep, located 11 miles northeast of Montezuma Castle. Its flow of more than 1,000 gallons a minute has been used to irrigate the land since the first permanent inhabitants, the prehistoric Hohokam, moved here in the seventh century. A trail leads to pueblo ruins around the well and there is a reconstructed pit house exhibited on the road leading to it.

How to get there: Montezuma Castle is located 5 miles north of Camp Verde off Route 17.

Navajo National Monument

Attraction: Two pueblo ruins within the Navajo Reservation
Hours: Visitor center open daily 8:00 A.M. to 5:00 P.M.
Admission fee: None
For more information: Navajo National Monument, HC 71 Box 2, Tonalea, AZ 86044–9704; (602) 672–2366

One of the enduring mysteries of American prehistory is why the inhabitants of Betatakin and Keet Seel, the principal ruins of this spectacular national monument, abandoned them at the end of the thirteenth century after having built them at a great expenditure of creativity and energy only a few decades before. Some experts believe that the same climate changes that earlier had driven the Anasazi from the valleys to the cliff dwellings eventually forced them out of the canyon altogether. The gentle winter rains that brought moisture to their fields ended midway through the thirteenth century, and the heavy summer thunderstorms that occurred thereafter caused erosion and arroyo cutting. The storms also lowered the water table and made crop growing difficult.

This valley was the home of the Kayenta Anasazi, and, along with Mesa Vede in Colorado and New Mexico's Chaco Canyon, it was a principal center of the Anasazi culture. Their cliff dwellings, although spectacularly situated and well preserved, and their pottery show that the Kayenta Anasazi were less sophisticated as craftsmen and builders than their counterparts in the other two locations.

In 1907 John Wetherill, a guide, interpreter, and Indian trader, and Byron Cummings, an archaeologist, came across the 135-room Betatakin cliff dwelling and, on the same expedition, discovered Inscription House with seventy-four rooms and granaries and one kiva. In 1895 Wetherill's brothers, Al and Richard, had discovered Keet Seel, the largest cliff dwelling in Arizona. John Wetherill was appointed the first custodian of the Navajo National Monument in 1907.

Located within the Navajo Reservation at 7,300 feet above sea level, the monument has two extensive ruins that the public can visit.

Betatakin

The sight of Betatakin from the overlook at the end of Sandal

(Courtesy National Park Service)

Betatakin, Navajo National Monument

Trail, only ½ mile from monument headquarters and visitor center, is one of the most spectacular and frequently photographed views in the country. Seen at a distance across the canyon, the 135-room cliff dwelling appears to be in a state of perfect preservation. And indeed, Betatakin, which means "Ledge House" in Navajo, is well protected by its location, a south-facing alcove that measures 452 feet high, 370 feet wide, and 135 feet deep.

Tree ring dating shows that the first families moved in about A.D. 1250. By 1269 they were cutting timbers to expand the village, probably in preparation for a large group that joined them in 1275. By the year 1300, the site was abandoned. Archaeologist Neil M. Judd excavated and stabilized a large part of the ruin in 1917. From what archaeologists can tell, Betatakin was built in well-planned stages, then occupied after the construction was complete.

To visit the ruin, visitors must take a guided tour with a park ranger on a strenuous 2½ mile trail that drops 700 feet.

Keet Seel

Located in a long, sheltering cave, the 160-room Keet Seel, which means "Broken Pottery" in Navajo, is so well preserved that some of the original roof beams are still in place. By dating their rings, archaeologists have determined that the Anasazi began building Keet Seel slightly before they started work on Betatakin. But unlike the carefully planned Betatakin, Keet Seel was constructed haphazardly, expanding to fit the needs of the moment. The site was occupied as early as A.D. 950 by small groups, and materials from their houses were used in the construction of the cliff dwelling.

A difficult 8-mile trail leads to Keet Seel, which can be reached either by foot or horseback. No more than twenty-five people per day are allowed to visit the archaeologically fragile site, so reservations for tours should be made within a two-month period before your trip. Check with the visitor center (see below) for schedules and reservations.

The monument also includes the seventy-four-room Inscription House, which was closed to the public in 1968. Because it is built partially from adobe and not protected by a cave or cliff overhang, it is badly eroded and in danger of further deterioration. It derives its name from a faint inscription scratched into the plaster bearing the date 1861, which was probably left by a party of Mormon settlers passing through. There is a film about the Anasazi and an exhibit of artifacts at the visitor center. There are thirty campsites in a nearby campground.

How to get there: The headquarters and visitor center of the Navajo National Monument are located 9 miles off Route 160 via Route 564.

Petrified Forest National Park

Attraction: Pueblo ruin and rock art within national park
Hours: Daily June through August, 7:00 A.M. to 8:00 P.M.; May and September, 8:00 A.M. to 6:00 P.M.; rest of year, 8:00 A.M. to 5:00 P.M.
Admission fee: $5.00 per car
For more information: Petrified Forest National Park, AZ 86028; (602) 524–6228

Petroglyphs at Petrified Forest National Park

(Courtesy National Park Service)

The petrified wood—some of it 225 million years old—that gives this forest its name is eons older than the earliest human habitation within park boundaries. Agate House, a small, eight-room pueblo at the southern end of the park, provides a link across the ages. The pueblo, which was reconstructed in 1934, is constructed of multicolored blocks of the ancient wood.

The earliest evidence of prehistoric man in the petrified forest is the remains of pit houses inhabited by Basket Maker people about A.D. 500. When these people consolidated their small, isolated homes into larger communities, they constructed a number of pueblos in the petrified forest. One of these, the 125-room Puerco Ruin, which is built as a rectangle around a central courtyard, was occupied intermittently from A.D. 1100 to 1400 by Anasazi, who farmed the arid area. Puerco Ruin is located 11 miles from the park's main entrance and is easily visited by the public.

Rock art, common throughout the park, can be seen at Puerco Ruin and at Newspaper Rock, located on a short side road a mile south of the Puerco River. The petroglyphs can be viewed from an overlook.

A traveler passing through the area in 1853 described the forest as a place "where trees have been converted to jasper." Not long afterwards the forest became a popular destination and, in 1906, President Theodore Roosevelt made it a national park to protect it from souvenir hunters and to head off a scheme to exploit the forest by grinding up the petrified wood for abrasives.

At the end of the nineteenth century, Jesse W. Fewkes of the Bureau of American Ethnology excavated and studied several archaeological sites within what is now the park and attempted to relate his findings to the traditional tales of the Hopi people. In the 1930s Henry P. Mera of the Laboratory of Anthropology in Santa Fe and a Civil Works Administration crew undertook an archaeological survey of the park; they also did work on Agate House and Puerco Ruin. In the summers of 1949 and 1950, Fred Wendorf excavated twenty-five pit houses at a pit house village known as the Flattop Site.

A 28-mile drive through the 93,533-acre park takes full advantage of the views and scenery—particularly of the Painted Desert—for which the park is famous.

How to get there: The site is located east of Holbrook between I–40 and Highway 80.

Pueblo Grande Museum and Ruins

Attraction: Hohokam excavation and museum
Hours: Monday through Saturday 9:00 A.M. to 4:45 P.M., Sunday 1:00 to 4:45 P.M.
Admission fee: 50 cents
For more information: Pueblo Grande Museum and Ruins, 4619 East Washington Street, Phoenix, AZ; (602) 495–0900

Despite its urban location near an airport, this excavation, which is connected to a municipal museum of archaeology, is one of the few Hohokam archaeological sites open to the public. The pueblo was built in the late 1100s on a large earthen mound that is held in place by a retaining wall, a type of construction that was common in prehistoric Mexico but unusual in the Southwest. A second wall around the pueblo was probably for defense.

Pueblo Grande was first excavated in 1897 by the anthropologist Frank Hamilton Cushing, and then in the 1930s by the WPA and CCC. The Hohokam flourished in this desert setting for two centuries; remains of their extensive canal network are visible from an observation tower. The canals were sometimes lined with clay to prevent leakage and were so efficient that experts suspect the area was eventually rendered uninhabitable by increased salinity and a rising water table resulting from centuries of irrigation. A ball court 85 feet long and 41 feet wide has been excavated and reconstructed. The museum displays Hohokam artifacts and cooking utensils in a reconstructed pueblo room.

How to get there: The site is located at 4619 East Washington Street near the airport.

Tonto National Monument

Attraction: Salado Indian cliff dwellings, visitor center
Hours: Daily 8:00 A.M. to 5:00 P.M., closed December 25; call the visitor center for tour schedules and reservations
Admission fee: $3.00 per car
For more information: Tonto National Monument, P.O. Box 707, Roosevelt, AZ 85545; (602) 467–2241

The Salado (Spanish for "salty") Indians began building these impregnable cliff dwellings above slopes covered with saguaro cactus in the early 1300s. Centuries earlier, when they first migrated from northeastern Arizona to this location near the headwaters of the Salt and Gila rivers, the Salado lived near their fields, close to the already settled Hohokam Indians, from whom they learned to irrigate the land and to raise corn, pumpkins, beans, cotton, and other crops. Why they moved to these cliffs, which are about 1,000 feet higher than their fields, is unknown, but the settlement apparently thrived throughout the century. The culture is noted for its black-and-white pottery, known as Gila Polychrome, and for its weaving. Excavations have turned up baskets, cotton textiles, plaited yucca baskets, spinning and weaving tools, and many other artifacts.

The monument and the Tonto Basin in which it is located are named for a band of nineteenth-century Apache Indians. When Adolph Bandelier came here in May 1883, he was able to see several cave dwellings with their roofs, which were covered with cactus ribs, reeds, and mud, still in place. The three major sites—Upper Ruin, Lower Ruin, and Lower Ruin Annex—were declared a national monument in 1907 to protect them from pothunters and population pressures resulting from the construction of Roosevelt Dam at the confluence of the Salt River and Tonto Creek. When the Lower Ruin was stabilized in 1937, many well-preserved fragments of cotton textiles were recovered. The Upper Ruin was stabilized in 1940.

A self-guided, half-mile trail leads from the visitor center to Lower Ruin, which has sixteen ground-floor rooms and a few in the upper story. The larger (forty-room) Upper Ruin can only be visited with a monument ranger.

How to get there: Located on Route 88 2 miles east of Roosevelt.

Tusayan Ruin and Museum

Attraction: Anasazi pueblo ruin and small museum
Hours: Daily 8:00 A.M. to 6:00 P.M. in summer, 9:00 A.M. to 5:00 P.M. in winter
Admission fee: Park fee is $10 per car; Tusayan Museum is free
For more information: Grand Canyon National Park, P.O. Box 1520, Grand Canyon, AZ 86023

The Grand Canyon's scenery—and contemplation of the immensity of geologic time that it inspires—is so overwhelming that it can disguise the fact that the canyon is a rich repository of human prehistory. There are some 2,000 known archaeological sites in the canyon, most of them Anasazi, but there is also evidence that the canyon was occupied at more or less the same time by more marginal prehistoric people who acquired traits of the Anasazi. The first permanent human habitation, a small Basket Maker population, probably started building pit house settlements about A.D. 500. The Anasazi began to grow in numbers in the A.D.

·1050s and they lived and farmed on both the rim and canyon floor for the next hundred years.

Members of an exploratory party from the 1540 Coronado expedition under the command of Garcia Lopez de Cardenas were the first Europeans to see the Grand Canyon. They traveled along the south rim but never found a way to reach the river. In two trips down the Colorado River in 1869 and 1871–1872, John Wesley Powell and his companions noted eight small ruins at the bottom of the canyon. In 1915 the Smithsonian's Bureau of American Ethnology's Neil M. Judd conducted the first archaeological survey of ruins in the park.

In 1933 Civilian Conservation Corps workers came across three small figures, made by bending split willow twigs, in a cave in the canyon. Since then hundreds of similar split-twig figurines, as they are now called, have been found in similar locations. These figurines, which seem to represent deer or elk or bighorn sheep, were probably created as effigies by ancient hunters to evoke the aid of their deities in assuring that game would be plentiful. Radiocarbon dating has determined that some of the figures are between 3,000 and 4,000 years old.

There are three archaeological sites in the park open to the public. One of these is a small Anasazi pueblo called Bright Angel, located on the canyon bottom and reachable only by foot or horseback. The other is a small four-room Anasazi settlement on the North Rim's Walhalla Plateau. Tusayan Ruin, described below, is the only easily accessible site interpreting the canyon's prehistory.

Tusayan Ruin and Museum

Located on the East Rim Drive, Tusayan Ruin was a U-shaped pueblo centered around a south-facing courtyard. From such invaluable archaeological evidence as the amount of refuse found at the site, archaeologists have determined that the pueblo was built about A.D. 1185 and was occupied by twenty people for about twenty-five years. Tusayan consisted of seven living rooms, eight storage rooms, and two kivas. When the first kiva burned, the second one was built on top of a trash heap. Some experts believe that the original pueblo was two stories high. In addition to the stone outlines of the pueblo rooms, there are also the remains of a circular

145

pit house dating from about A.D. 800. The remains of check dams that the Anasazi built to catch rain and melting snow can be seen along the trail to the northeast of the ruin. The pueblo was abandoned about the time the Anasazi left the Grand Canyon for good.

The site was excavated by the well-known archaeologist Emil Haury in 1930. The Tusayan Museum traces the development of Anasazi in the Grand Canyon.

How to get there: The site is off East Rim Drive, 22 miles east of Grand Canyon Village.

Tuzigoot National Monument

Attraction: Pueblo ruin, visitor center
Hours: Daily Memorial Day through Labor Day, 8:00 A.M. to 7:00 P.M.; rest of year, 8:00 A.M. to 5:00 P.M.
Admission fee: $1.00
For more information: Tuzigoot National Monument, P.O. Box 68, Clarkdale, AZ 86324; (602) 634–5564

This site, across the Verde River from the copper-smelting town of Clarkdale, was nameless when it was selected for excavation in 1933 by Byron Cummings of the University of Arizona and two graduate students, Louis Caywood and Edward Spicer. The dig was undertaken with funds provided by the Civil Works Administration, a government agency created during the Depression to provide jobs for the unemployed. One of the forty-eight men hired for the job, a member of the Apache tribe, suggested the ruin be called Tuzigoot (TOO-zee-goot), or Crooked Water, a name that actually describes the shape of a nearby lake.

The Sinagua, it is believed, arrived from the north in the early twelfth century, but the village didn't begin to expand for another one hundred years. Situated on a limestone ridge 120 feet above the plain, the two-story village had ninety-two rooms housing 250 or more people and extended for 500 feet along the ridge. Some of the rooms had second and perhaps third stories. The first rooms at Tuzigoot were constructed from round boulders from the river; later additions to the complex were built from soft limestone taken from old lake beds. The building materials were mortared with clay.

Southern view of Tuzigoot ruin

During the first week of the excavation, Caywood and Spicer uncovered a male body that was buried in a stone cist and covered with sandstone slabs. The jewelry buried with him, the archaeologists wrote, "tells a story of infinite skill, infinite patience, a passionate love of ornament and a very fine and true taste for beauty." The articles included a 12½-foot-long necklace that was made up of 3,295 small stone and shell beads. In contrast with the necklace, Tuzigoot pottery is plain, unadorned, and often crudely crafted. Most of the more than 400 tombs uncovered at Tuzigoot contained only a few plain red bowls, called Tuzigoot Red.

As part of the excavation, the archaeologists dug an 11-foot-deep trench across the west slope of the hill, which was used as a trash heap while the site was occupied. At the bottom of the trench, they found black-on-white pottery produced near Flagstaff about A.D. 950.

In time, scientists believe, overpopulation in the Verde Valley caused drought, famine, and possibly warfare. About A.D. 1425, the Sinagua people left the settlement. Where they went is unknown, although similarities in their pottery have led experts to suspect that some Sinagua joined the Hopi to the north.

A ¼-mile trail leads through the ruin, and visitors may climb to the top of the lookout tower for a sweeping view of the Verde Valley. The visitor center has an excellent collection of prehistoric jewelry, tools, baskets, textiles, and religious objects. There is also a reconstruction of a pueblo room.

How to get there: The monument is located off Alternate 89 between Cottonwood and Clarkdale.

Walnut Canyon National Monument

Attraction: Cliff dwellings in deep canyon, trails, visitor center
Hours: Daily Memorial Day through Labor Day, 7:00 A.M. to 6:00 P.M.; rest of year, 8:00 A.M. to 5:00 P.M.
Admission fee: $3.00 per car
For more information: Walnut Canyon National Monument, Walnut Canyon Road, Flagstaff, AZ 86004; (602) 526–3367

Lieutenant Edward F. "Ned" Beale, the adventuresome commander of the famous Army Camel Corps (an experiment in using the desert beasts for military transportation in the American West), explored this picturesque canyon in 1858, but its existence didn't become widely known until the transcontinental railroad reached Flagstaff in the 1880s. Looting and pot hunting soon became popular pastimes despite the efforts of concerned local citizens, including a Catholic priest from Flagstaff who preached that it was a desecration to vandalize the ruins. Their efforts finally paid off in 1915 when the canyon was made a national monument.

The Sinagua lived in this dramatic canyon, which was formed by Walnut Creek cutting through the limestone ledges, from about A.D. 1150 to 1250. A steep trail descending 200 feet from the canyon rim leads past some eighty cliff dwellings, which are wedged under natural overhangs and closed off with walls made of stones and clay used as mortar. The canyon itself is 20 miles long and 400 feet deep. A pinnacle, called Third Fort Island, rises from a bend in the creek just below the visitor center. It was formed

(Courtesy National Park Service)

Sinagua dwelling at Walnut Canyon

when a prehistoric earthquake blocked the creek and forced the water to cut another path, thereby forming an island. A walled compound on top of the island might have been for defense.

The Sinagua, who lived in clusters of family groups, farmed land around the rim of the canyon. They also cultivated terraces they built within the canyon and sunny patches along the river. To survive in the high altitude (nearly 7,000 feet) and chilly climate, they also hunted and harvested edible wild plants such as wild grape, elderberry, and yucca, which still grow there. Why the Sinagua abandoned Walnut Canyon is uncertain; war, drought, depleted soil, and disease are all possibilities. It is also believed that the Sinagua mingled with the Hopi, whose earliest villages date from about A.D. 1300. Some Hopi clans claim the Sinagua sites as their ancestral homes.

James Stevenson of the Smithsonian Institution was the first archaeologist to study the ruins, starting in 1883. From the burial sites he excavated, he recovered shell and turquoise necklaces, clay animal figurines, and a cap made of 3,600 beads that were so small that no modern needle could fit through their holes.

In 1920 Harold Colton of the Museum of Northern Arizona undertook an extensive survey of the region. In 1930 an important burial site filled with more than 600 burial offerings was discovered in the canyon. The Hopi were able not only to identify certain ceremonial objects from this find, but also to identify the clan within the tribe to which the objects belonged. The discovery provided important evidence supporting the link between the Sinagua and the Hopi.

In addition to the Island Trail, which descends into the canyon, the cliff dwellings are visible from the Rim Trail, a level, half-mile loop that also passes two reconstructed surface dwellings. Sinagua pottery and artifacts are on display in the visitor center. The exhibit includes split twig figures, probable representations of sheep or deer, that are nearly 4,000 years old. They were presumably left there by the earliest inhabitants of the region.

How to get there: The monument is located 7 miles east of Flagstaff; go 3 miles south of exit 204 off I–40.

Wupatki National Monument

Attraction: Large park with many prehistoric ruins; self-guided trails; guided tours for groups on request
Hours: Park open during daylight hours; visitor center open daily 8:00 A.M. to 5:00 P.M.
Admission fee: $3.00 per car
For more information: Wupatki National Monument, 2717 North Steves Boulevard, Suite 3, Flagstaff, AZ 86004; (602) 527–7040

The Sinagua Indians had been living in the area of this 35,693-acre national monument for 400 years when the volcano known as Sunset Crater erupted in A.D. 1064, covering their farmland with lava, cinders, and rock and forcing them to evacuate. The Sinagua, together with some Kayenta Anasazi from the northeast and Cohonina from the west, returned a few decades later, after they discovered that the layer of volcanic ash absorbed moisture and conserved heat, thereby making the land more productive than it was before.

Wutpatki was abandoned permanently between A.D. 1215 and 1225. Why the Indians, who had intermarried and shared farming techniques, left this time is unknown; disease, overfarming, and drought have all been suggested as causes. Pottery found in the excavations indicate that small groups of Hopi Indians, who today claim the ruin as the ancestral home of their Parrot Clan, may have lived in Wupatki after the Sinagua left. In 1896 the archaeologist Jesse W. Fewkes photographed, mapped, and described the ruins. He also gave them their intriguing Hopi names: Wupatki ("Tall House"), Wukoki ("Big and Wide House"), and Lomaki ("House Standing Alone").

There are at least 2,500 prehistoric sites within the monument, although only the four major ones are open to the public and accessible by self-guided trails. There is also a short trail leading up the crater known as Doney Mountain. Its namesake, the colorful prospector and pothunter Ben Doney, guided Fewkes and other archaeologists in the late nineteenth century. From Doney Mountain there is a splendid view of the Painted Desert and the San Francisco Range. The Wupatki National Monument, located on the southwestern part of the Colorado Plateau to the west of the Little Colorado River, was established by President Calvin Coolidge in 1924.

Wupatki Ruin

Reached by a short trail behind the visitor center, Wupatki, the largest ruin in the monument, was built between A.D. 1120 and 1170. Wupatki Ruin is believed to be located on an important prehistoric trade route extending from Mexico to areas north and east of the ruins.

Typically the stones for the wall were put together with a clay mortar; the roofs consisted of wooden support beams and poles covered by shakes, grass and clay, or adobe. Rooms were added as they were needed until the dwelling was four stories tall and had nearly a hundred rooms and a population of several hundred people.

Here visitors can see the layout of a typical pueblo room: a small storage bin in the rear, firepit in the center, and a T-shaped doorway. The top of the T was probably covered with a rug or animal skin in the winter and the bottom left open for ventilation. Because the rooms are small and dark, it is believed that the inhabitants mostly lived outdoors. In one room, the remains of seven infants were found in slab-lined burial pits. Like the Hopi who came later, the prehistoric residents might have believed that the spirit of a deceased child would be reborn in the next offspring; therefore parents often buried children right in their homes to keep their spirits close by.

To the right of the self-guided trail that leads through the ruin, visitors can look down on an amphitheater, now a circular depression surrounded by a low stone wall. Experts aren't sure why it was built or how it was used. It is constructed like a kiva, but, unlike other Sinagua ceremonial chambers, it never had a roof. Farther down the trail, there is an oval ball court that is similar to ones found in Mexico and Central America. (The ball court has been completely restored, unlike the rest of the monument, which is simply stabilized.) The game as played by the Aztecs and Maya was highly ritualized. The goal was to knock a rubber ball through a stone ring.

Near the ball court is a fissure in the ground known as the blow hole. Atmospheric conditions cause air to rush either in or out. Blow holes seem to have had special meaning for the inhabitants of prehistoric pueblos; they often built their pueblos near them.

Wukoki

The elegantly constructed walls of this three-story pueblo were once covered inside and out with plaster. "The prehistoric Indians seem to have been expressing an attitude that the unseen was as important to them as the seen," a booklet on the site speculates. The ruin, which is perched dramatically on an outcropping of Moenkopi sandstone, is surrounded by a wash of black cinders.

Citadel Ruin

This solidly built, thirty-room Sinagua pueblo was two stories tall when built (A.D. 1125–1200) and may have housed sixty people. It looks like a fortress, but from what is known today, the Sinagua were a peaceful people. Perhaps it was built on the narrow butte (located 9 miles by road northwest of the visitor center) to give the inhabitants a view of their fields. The remains of terraced gardens are visible at the foot of the citadel.

The short footpath to the citadel passes the ten-room excavation called Nalakihu Ruin; the name means "House Standing Alone" in

Hopi. Large storage jars made near present-day Prescott (150 miles away) were discovered here when the site was excavated in 1933. How they got here—by trade or by migration—is unknown.

Lomaki Ruin

This nine-room pueblo probably housed two to four families when it was built about A.D. 1192. Its exquisite masonry inspired its Hopi name, which means "Beautiful House." Nearby, a collapsed fissure in the earth might have had religious or spiritual meaning for the Sinagua. The ¼-mile trail to the ruin passes the mouth of Box Canyon, which contains smaller ruins, probably the homes of one extended family.

How to get there: Wupatki National Monument is located off Highway 89 between Flagstaff and Cameron. A loop road that connects with Highway 89 at both ends runs through the monument and the Sunset Crater National Monument to the south. The visitor center is 14 miles from the northern end of the road and 24 miles from the southern end.

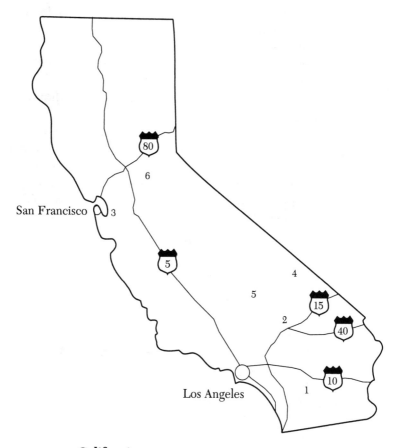

California

1. Anza-Borrego State Park
2. Calico Early Man Site
3. Coyote Hills Regional Park
4. Death Valley National Monument
5. Indian Grinding Rock State Historic Park
6. Little Petroglyph Canyon

CALIFORNIA

Anza-Borrego State Park

Attraction: Pictograph site within large state park
Hours: Park always open; visitor center open June through September 10:00 A.M. to 3:00 P.M. Saturday and Sunday, October through May 9:00 A.M. to 5:00 P.M. daily
Admission fee: None
For more information: (619) 767–4684

This 600,000-acre park is named for the explorer Juan Bautista de Anza, who passed through this arid and mountainous region in the eighteenth century, and for the *borrego* (Spanish for "yearling lamb") that he found here. Of the many prehistoric sites within the park, the most accessible—and the only one interpreted for the public—is at the end of a 1-mile trail and consists of red and yellow sunbursts and animated stick figures painted on boulders. Off another trail, there are a number of *morteros*, or grinding holes for crushing seeds and pods with pestles. There are also smooth surfaces, called slicks, where Indian women could grind fine seeds into flour.

How to get there: The park is located 90 miles east of San Diego; the visitor center is 2 miles northwest of Borrego Springs.

Calico Early Man Site

Attraction: Excavation site and visitor center
Hours: Wednesday noon to 4:30 P.M. Thursday through Sunday 8:00 A.M. to 4:30 P.M.; call for tour times
Admission fee: None
For more information: Bureau of Land Management, California

Desert Information Center, 831 Barstow Road, Barstow, CA 92311; (619) 256–8617

Some believe this site in the Calico Mountains of Southern California could be 200,000 years old, making it the earliest known prehistoric site in America; however, since there is no other evidence of human activity in the region before 12,000 years ago, controversy has surrounded it ever since excavations began here in the early 1960s.

Some 12,000 artifacts, mostly pieces of flaked chert and chalcedony, have been recovered here—some on the surface, but most from pits 6 to 9 feet deep. (A circle of rocks around a shallow basin, one of which showed signs of being fired, was interpreted as a hearth.) Most experts believe they are "geofacts," or pieces of stone created by geological forces, while others have interpreted them as tools and debris from the tool-making process.

The paleontologist Louis S. B. Leakey, famed for his discovery of early human fossils in Africa, first saw the site in 1963 and pronounced it "a great plain which must have been verdant green, with animals and plants suitable for food." Leakey urged that the site be excavated, and on trips back to California he would examine the material recovered from it. Leakey remained Calico Project Director until his death in 1972.

In 1968 the L. S. B. Leakey Foundation invited scores of archaeologists and geologists to visit the site and evaluate the evidence. Most remained "highly skeptical that the site gave evidence of human occupation," wrote anthropologist Jesse D. Jennings. The skepticism was based on the fact that no other evidence of human occupation was found there, such as charcoal, hearths, or "recognizable artifacts"; nor have any comparable sites ever been found in the Americas. "On the face of it, every form of archaeological logic is against the site," writes archaeologist Brian Fagan in *The Great Journey: The Peopling of Ancient America*.

In 1980 material taken from the site was determined to be about 200,000 years old by uranium-thorium dating. Of course this determination of age does not prove that the material is man-made. The site is operated jointly by the Bureau of Land Management and the Friends of Calico Early Man Site (P.O. Box 535, Yermo, CA 92398), a nonprofit, public-benefit corporation established to support the excavation and interpretation of the site.

How to get there: The site is located 15 miles northeast of Barstow on I–15. Take the Minneola Road exit and follow the signs north 2½ miles along graded dirt roads to the site.

Coyote Hills Regional Park

Attraction: Four prehistoric mounds, reconstructed village, museum
Hours: Visitor center and museum open daily 9:30 A.M. to 5:00 P.M.; park open daily 8:00 A.M. to dusk
Admission fee: Cars $2.50
For more information: Coyote Hills Regional Park, 8000 Patterson Ranch Road, Fremont, CA 94536; (510) 795–9385

Four low mounds are preserved within the park. They are the few surviving remains of a prehistoric culture that might have existed for 3,500 years, until historic times when the Indians were largely destroyed by European disease such as measles and

(Courtesy East Bay Regional Parks District)

Reconstructed hut at Coyote Hills Regional Park

157

smallpox. The mounds, which were used for burials as well as the foundations of dwellings, are made of shell, animal bones, and ashes. The largest is 10 feet high and 300 feet in diameter at the base.

The aboriginal inhabitants of this region around San Francisco were called Costanoans, or "Coast People," by the first Spaniards to settle here. The group was split up into many small tribes and spoke a dialect of the Penutian tongue. Excavations have uncovered entire skeletons and a wide assortment of grave goods, including bird-bone whistles, obsidian projectile points, elk antler wedges, and a wide assortment of abalone pendants, olivella beads, and fragments of mortars and pestles. The remains of hearths and house floors have also been found.

The composition of the mounds reveals how important shellfish were to the diet of these people. They harvested oysters, clams, mussels, horn snails, cockles, and abalone from the mud flats west of the hills in which they lived. Some of their dwellings, including a sweat house, have been reconstructed in the park. These huts, of mud-covered tule thatch over a willow sapling framework, were built over a shallow depression in the earth.

How to get there: Go north on Newark Boulevard and turn left on Patterson Ranch Road, which leads to the park.

Death Valley National Monument

Attraction: Prehistoric petroglyphs at several locations within a desert park
Hours: Park always open; visitor center open daily mid-April to mid-October 8:00 A.M. to 5:00 P.M.; rest of year 8:00 A.M. to 8:00 P.M.
Admission fee: $5.00 per car for seven-day permit
For more information: Death Valley National Monument, Death Valley, CA 92328; (619) 786–2331

This 120-mile-long valley is known more for harsh, unforgiving, and incredibly beautiful terrain than for any aspect of prehistoric culture, but as exhibits at the Furnace Creek Visitor Center show, humans have survived in the valley for nearly 9,000 years. This would certainly come as a surprise to the parties of prospectors and settlers who cut across here as a shortcut in 1849 and, after much suffering and hardship, gave the valley its name.

Today petroglyphs, probably carved by ancestors of the Shoshone Indians some 4,000 years ago, are visible in several accessible places within the park: Titus Canyon, Klare Spring, Greenwater Canyon, and Emigrant Canyon. Recent vandalism has made the park reluctant to release information on prehistoric sites, however, so visitors should make their interest in the subject known to National Park Service employees on duty at the visitor center.

How to get there: The monument is located off Route 190, 110 miles north of Ridgecrest.

Indian Grinding Rock State Historic Park

Attraction: Reconstructed Miwok Indian village with prehistoric grinding pits, petroglyphs, regional Indian museum
Hours: Park always open except during heavy snowfalls; museum open 11:00 A.M. to 3:00 P.M. Monday through Friday, 10:00 A.M. to 4:00 P.M. Saturday and Sunday
Admission fee: $5.00 per vehicle
For more information: Indian Grinding Rock State Historic Park, 14881 Pine Grove–Volcano Road, Pine Grove, CA 95665; (209) 296–7488

This 135-acre park includes a reconstructed village of the northern Miwok, a regional Indian museum, and, located on a huge bedrock of limestone, nearly 1,200 circular mortar cups, or *chaw' se*, from which the park takes its name. Here Miwok women ground up acorns and other seeds with pestles. There are also many petroglyphs carved into the limestone.

The main group of the Miwok was living in this region, on the western slopes of the Sierra Nevada, when the Spanish first arrived in California. At the dedication ceremony for the village, a member of the present-day Miwok made the following comments on the site: "For them [the Miwok] this was an ideal home. The large flat-topped rocks were here and the acorns were much better and less bitter than those that grew in the valley. The acorn meal

(Courtesy Indian Grinding Rock State Historic Park)

Depressions in limestone bedrock where Miwok Indians ground acorns

was an essential part of their diet. They used it as food and drink and made bread with it." The nutritious acorns had to be leached with water to remove the bitter tannin.

The centerpiece of the reconstructed village is the traditional round house, or *hungé*, 60 feet across and 20 feet tall with a door opening to the east. The roof is supported by four oak posts and large oak beams. A foot drum, made of a hollowed-out log over a pit dug in the ground, is located near the back of the round house. The log was beaten with a pole to keep time for dancers. There is a granary, which is lined with wormwood as protection against rodents and insects and is large enough to store more than 1,000 pounds of acorns. A reconstructed shelter or bark house made of cedar poles interwoven with grape vines or willow and covered with cedar bark is also on site. There is a hole at the top for smoke from heating and cooking fires to escape.

The Chaw'se Regional Indian Museum contains a collection of basketry, dance regalia, and tools crafted by the Miwok as well as other California peoples, including the Miadu, Monache, Washo, and Foothill Yokut.

How to get there: Take Highway 88 from Jackson to Pine Grove; take Pine Grove–Volcano Road northeast to the park.

Little Petroglyph Canyon

Attraction: Large concentration of rock art
Hours: Weekend tours in spring and fall
Admission fee: $1.00
For more information: Maturango Museum of Indian Wells Valley, 100 East Las Flores, Ridgecrest, CA 93555; (619) 375–6900

These ancient basalt cliffs of the Coso Range in the extreme northwestern corner of the Mojave Desert are the canvas for the largest concentration of petrogylphs, or rock art, in the Western Hemisphere. The more than 100,000 individual examples of rock art represent at least 6,000 years of prehistory; the earliest examples may be more than 11,000 years old. Some experts believe that the rock art was created by ancestors of the Panamint Shoshone Indians, who were living in the Cosmo Mountains when the first white explorers and miners arrived. Others believe that the Shoshone and other groups with similar languages arrived in the area well after most of the rock art was created.

The Coso Range is located on the China Lake Naval Air Weapons Station. Driving tours conducted by the Maturango Museum of Indian Wells Valley are offered on weekends in the spring and fall provided they do not conflict with missions on the weapons range. The hike through the entire canyon is a 3-mile round trip.

The rock art consists of both representational and abstract figures. Bighorn sheep are the most common petroglyph design; in some examples spears and arrows are lodged in the animals. (The bow and arrow replaced the spear in this region about A.D. 500.) The human figures, called anthropomorphs, range from simple stick figures to likenesses of men wearing elaborate clothing and headdresses.

At the entrance to the canyon, near the bronze tablet identifying it as a National Historic Site, is a boulder with many examples of rock art, including a figure of a man that was reworked by a later artist. Other representations found elsewhere in the canyon include four shaman figures who, it has been speculated, are likenesses of participants in rituals held in the canyon.

Experts believe that the deep grooves in some of the figures are the result of repeated cutting, probably as they were incorporated again and again into ceremonies; therefore, the more deeply carved figures are believed to be the oldest in the canyon. A likeness of a bighorn sheep, for example, is estimated to be 5,000 years old.

The carved symbols in the canyon include many variations of the sun symbol and realistic likenesses of snakes, which are common figures in the mythology of many historic Indian groups.

How to get there: Tour participants drive their own vehicles from the main gate of the China Lake Naval Air Weapons Station; the trip to the parking lot of the canyon is 40 miles one way.

COLORADO

Anasazi Heritage Center

Attraction: Museum with Anasazi artifacts, adjacent ruins
Hours: Museum open daily March through November 9:00 A.M.
to 5:00 P.M.; December through February 9:00 A.M. to 4:00 P.M.
Ruins open daily 8:00 A.M. to 5:00 P.M.
Admission fee: None
For more information: Anasazi Heritage Center, 27501 Highway 184, Dolores, CO 81323; (303) 882–4811

This attractive museum housing nearly two million prehistoric artifacts, samples, and documents from the Four Corners region (where Colorado, Utah, Arizona, and New Mexico meet) was created to salvage the record of Anasazi culture along the Dolores River, which was dammed in 1984 to create the McPhee Reservoir. The reservoir flooded some 1,600 archaeological sites but not before archaeologists working for the Bureau of Land Management, which operates the museum and the adjacent ruins, excavated or sampled at least 125 of them.

Anasazi artifacts, a replica Anasazi dwelling, and other exhibits relating to their culture are displayed in the museum's exhibit hall. The discovery area has a variety of hands-on exhibits—a loom, a grinding bin, microscopes for examining seeds, and computer games designed to teach how the Anasazi lived. The center's facilities also include research laboratories, storage areas for the vast collection, a library, theater, and museum shop. A short trail leads from the center to the Escalante and Dominguez Ruins.

Escalante and Dominguez Ruins

These two ruins, located just a short walk from the Anasazi Heritage Center, are named for the Spanish explorers and Franciscan

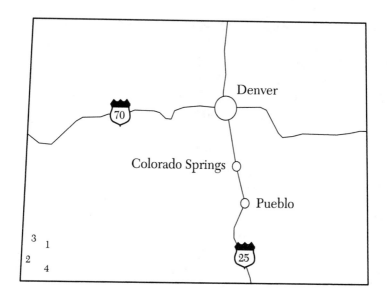

Colorado
1. Anasazi Heritage Center
2. Hovenweep National Monument
3. Lowry Pueblo Ruins
4. Mesa Verde National Park

fathers Escalante and Dominguez, who stopped here on a hill overlooking the Dolores River in 1776, sixteen days into their unsuccessful attempt to find a trail from Santa Fe to California. In his journal Escalante referred to the ruins as "a small settlement of the same type as those of the Indians of New Mexico." Archaeologists can tell from the masonry that the rectangular, twenty-five-room Escalante Ruin was built by Anasazi from Chaco Canyon in the early twelfth century. The settlement, measuring 82 by 63 feet, has a kiva at its center. Anthropologists speculate that the Chacoan men who built the habitation intermarried with women from nearby Mesa Verde; as a result the pottery produced here shows the influence of that other important cultural center.

Dominguez Ruin at the base of the hill is a small, four-room habitation with a kiva that probably housed an extended family. In excavating this site, archaeologists uncovered the grave of a person buried with a considerable amount of jewelry, an indication, perhaps, that the person was a high-ranking member of society. This in itself is interesting; most burial sites excavated in the Southwest have revealed no indication of the deceased's status.

How to get there: The site is located on Route 184, 10 miles north of Cortez and 3 miles west of Dolores. The ruins are a short walk from the Anasazi Heritage Center.

Hovenweep National Monument

Attraction: Six groups of masonry towers and pueblos
Hours: Daily 8:00 A.M. to 4:30 P.M.
Admission fee: None
For more information: Mesa Verde National Park, CO 81330; (303) 529–4461

W. D. Huntington, leader of a Mormon mission to southeastern Utah in 1854, was the first white settler to report seeing the wondrous towers of Hovenweep. These unusual structures—their sturdy construction, their gracious lines, the mystery surrounding their use and purpose—intrigued and stimulated the imaginations of a long succession of later visitors. The photographer William

Henry Jackson passed through the area in 1874 and named the site Hovenweep, a Ute word meaning "Deserted Valley." Archaeologist William H. Holmes, the rancher Richard Wetherill, who brought the wonders of Mesa Verde to public attention, and archaeologist Jesse Walter Fewkes of the Smithsonian, who published a report on Hovenweep in 1923, were other early visitors to the site.

The Anasazi lived at Hovenweep in gradually increasing numbers since A.D. 1, although they didn't establish settlements or begin to farm until about A.D. 550. Then, starting about A.D. 1150, they moved from mesa-top villages to the heads of the many canyons that cut into Cajon Mesa, on which the settlement is located.

The reasons why they moved are unknown; perhaps they moved for defense, although no archaeological evidence has been found to indicate that they were under attack. Perhaps a drought made dry farming on the mesa tops impossible, so they moved to the canyons where water was more abundant and could be controlled and conserved with check dams and reservoirs. Whatever the reasons, the move to a more protected location was similar to a migration that occurred at Mesa Verde at the same time.

The towers, hundreds of which have been found throughout the area, present other unanswered questions, such as: Why were they built? How were they used? Certain ones, like a number of those at Mesa Verde, are connected by tunnels to nearby kiva or ceremonial chambers—an indication, perhaps, that the towers were constructed for ceremonial purposes. Some, especially those with narrow peepholes, were apparently used as lookouts, whereas others may have served as solar calendars, a function that would be important to an agricultural people. Sunlight beaming through doorways and portholes accurately marks the change of seasons—the winter and summer solstices and the spring and autumn equinoxes. The towers may have served a number of different purposes simultaneously, including food storage.

This small but archaeologically and historically rich national monument located on the Utah-Colorado line comprise six groups of masonry towers and pueblos. There is a small visitor center and ranger center at the Square Tower Ruin. From the ranger station there are three self-guided trails around the Square Tower Group.

The ⅓-mile-long Square Tower Loop passes the well-preserved Hovenweep Castle, consisting of two wings, several towers, and ceremonial kivas. The thick walls are made of double-and triple-coursed stone; only a ground-level doorway opens into the canyon. Nearby Hovenweep House was one of the largest pueblos in the Square Tower group. Other stops on the trail include a ruin called Square Tower, one of the few cliff dwellings at Hovenweep; a depression indicating the location of a kiva; and the debris that marks the site of the appropriately named Talus Pueblo, which archaeologists think once reached up to the base of Hovenweep Castle.

The trail loops back to a point near Hovenweep Castle. From here the visitor can continue on Tower Point Trail (½ mile). The clear view up and down the canyon from the tower ruins and the peepholes in the canyon wall indicate that the structure was built for defensive purposes.

Near the ranger station the Tower Point Trail connects with the 1-mile-long, "moderately strenuous" Twin Towers Trail. This path, after passing the remains of an Anasazi storehouse and a group of petroglyphs, leads to Round Tower, a ruin that was once probably two stories tall and entered by ladder through the roof. Farther on, the trail passes Eroded Boulder House, a dwelling built under the overhang of a huge boulder, and Twin Towers, which are actually two large dwellings (sixteen rooms in all) built on separate boulders. The walls of the north tower are sandstone slabs mixed with larger blocks, a distinctive mixture that gives the structure a layered look. The south tower is similar to other Hovenweep structures in that it is built of same-sized, bread loaf–shaped blocks.

On the return to the visitor center, the trail passed Rimrock House, a two-story rectangular structure with an abundance of peepholes that might have been for ventilation as well as viewing, and Stronghold House and Tower, a solidly constructed, fortresslike building that was the top story of a huge pueblo that once stood on the slope below. The final stop is at Unit-Type House, which dates from an earlier period (A.D. 900 to 1100) than other Hovenweep structures. The small complex, so named because it was probably inhabited by a single family unit, has a kiva with fine masonry.

At the visitor center there are trail maps to the other groups—
Cajon Ruins, also in Utah, and Holly Ruins, Hackberry Canyon,
Cutthroat Castle, and Goodman Point in Colorado.

There is a park ranger on duty, an information center, and a
campground at the Square Tower Group. The monument is open
year-round, although the graded dirt roads leading into it might be
impassable during bad weather. The monument is administered by
the superintendent of Mesa Verde National Park.

How to get there: The monument spans the Colorado-Utah
border. From Utah take Route 262 to Hatch Trading Post, then go 16
miles on graded dirt road to the monument. From Colorado take the
marked road that turns off Highway 666, 18 miles north of Cortez.

Lowry Pueblo Ruins

Attraction: Forty-room Anasazi pueblo and Great Kiva
Hours: Always open
Admission fee: None
For more information: Bureau of Land Management, San Juan
Resource Area, 701 Camino del Rio, Durango, CO 81301; (303)
247–4082

This secluded, out-of-the-way ruin, 9 miles down a farm road
away from the main highway, is a pleasant refuge from the crowds
at nearby Mesa Verde National Park and an outstanding example
of Anasazi architecture. Although only the first floor remains,
Lowry Pueblo once had buildings two or even three stories high
and was home to perhaps a hundred people. The Anasazi began
constructing the pueblo about A.D. 1060 and abandoned it about
1170. At the time the Anasazi left, the dwelling had about forty
rooms, eight kivas, and a Great Kiva located a short distance from
the main building.

It is believed that the pueblo was remodeled and expanded at
least four or five times during the time it was occupied. The original part of the structure appears to have been built by peoples
from Chaco Canyon; the layering of the narrow sandstone slabs is
typical of the high-quality masonry construction found at that

Ruins at Lowry Pueblo

important settlement. Later stonework at Lowry is less refined. A panel in one kiva illustrates the fragile paintings that were found on the interior plaster when the kiva was excavated.

Lowry's Great Kiva, some 40 feet in diameter, is the largest such chamber found in the area and indicates that the pueblo might have been a ceremonial center for the region. The kiva apparently had an entrance cut into the side wall as well as the traditional entrance by ladder through the smoke hole in the roof. Masonry platforms inside the kiva probably held support beams for the roof.

The pueblo is named for George Lowry, a local homesteader. It was first excavated in the 1930s by Paul S. Martin of the Chicago Field Museum of Natural History. In 1965 the Bureau of Land Management, which administers the site, undertook another excavation and stabilization of the project. Lowry Pueblo was made a National Historic Landmark in 1967.

There is a picnic area at the site but camping is not allowed.

How to get there: The site is located near Pleasant View, Colorado, 9 miles off Highway 666. The road to the site is not maintained in winter.

Mesa Verde National Park

Attraction: Largest cliff dwelling in the United States, other Anasazi sites, visitor center and museum, self-guided and guided tours
Hours: Park open daily year round but on limited basis in winter; Far View Visitor Center open Memorial Day through Labor Day 8:00 A.M. to 5:00 P.M.; Mesa Verde Museum on Chapin Mesa open mid-June through Labor Day 8:00 A.M. to 6:30 P.M.
Admission fee: $5.00 for a seven-day permit
For more information: Mesa Verde National Park, CO 81330; (303) 529–4465

Mesa Verde National Park is one of the premier archaeological sites in the country and the only one accorded national park status. The park, 15 by 20 miles in area, is located in southwestern Colorado on a high table land, which rises 2,000 feet above the valley on the north and is broken up into fingerlike mesas on the south by canyons leading to Mancos River valley. There are more than 3,000 prehistoric sites in the park, only a fraction of them excavated and viewable by the public. One of these, Cliff Palace, the largest cliff dwelling in North America, is the architectural pinnacle of the Anasazi civilization, which developed here beginning about A.D. 550 and then disappeared without a trace by the year 1300.

How two ranchers unexpectedly came across Cliff Palace and Spruce Tree House, Mesa Verde's third-largest ruin, while they were looking for stray cattle in December 1888 is one of the most frequently told stories in the annals of American archaeology. One of them, Richard Wetherill, dedicated himself to excavating Mesa Verde, despite his lack of scientific knowledge and archaeological expertise. At the time he was criticized for selling artifacts in great numbers from the site, but he is also responsible for bringing the ruins to public view.

The photographer William Henry Jackson was one of the first to record the existence of cliff dwellings in the region when he explored the Mancos River valley with a U.S. Geological Survey party in 1874. A Swedish nobleman, Gustaf Nordenskiold, made the first scientific excavation at Mesa Verde in 1891 and published a book, *The Cliff Dwellers of Mesa Verde,* two years later.

In 1906 Mesa Verde was made a national park; soon afterwards Jesse Walter Fewkes of the Smithsonian Bureau of American Ethnology began extensive excavations that opened many ruins to public view for the first time. The excavation and stabilization of Cliff Palace in 1909 was one of his most important undertakings at Mesa Verde. In 1924 John D. Rockefeller, Jr., donated money for an archaeological museum. Many ruins were stablilized in the 1930s through the efforts of the Civilian Conservation Corps, whose members also put up buildings, constructed roads, and cut trails throughout the park. Both the cliff and mesa-top ruins on Wetherill Mesa were excavated beginning in the late 1950s, after which that part of the park was open to the public.

Through the scientific studies conducted at Mesa Verde, we have learned that the first Anasazi moved up to the mesa about A.D. 550. From that time on, the Anasazi developed in distinct phases (as illustrated by dioramas in the Mesa Verde Museum, described below). The Anasazi who occupied the mesa from A.D. 550 to A.D. 750, which archaeologists call the Modified Basket Maker period, built pit houses, permanent dwellings dug into the earth and covered with roofs of poles and mud. In this period pottery began to replace the skillfully crafted baskets that had given the period its name. The Anasazi also began to adopt the bow and arrow, which eventually replaced the less efficient spear and throwing stick known as the atlatl.

From A.D. 750 to 1100 (the Developmental Pueblo period), the Anasazi developed more advanced masonry techniques and began building connected, vertical-walled dwellings. It was during this period that pit houses began to be used as ceremonial kivas rather than dwellings. The final period, known as Classic Pueblo (A.D. 1100 to A.D. 1300), had two phases. First, the Anasazi built compact villages on the mesa tops; then, after A.D. 1200, they moved to caves and alcoves in the canyons and built the now-famous cliff dwellings from shaped sandstone blocks and mud mortar with roofs made of poles and mud. The superb Anasazi black-on-white pottery was produced during this period. Although several hundred people might have lived in the largest cliff dwellings, most Anasazi remained in relatively small groups. In fact, 75 percent of the nearly 600 cliff dwellings within park boundaries have five rooms or fewer.

Why the Anasazi moved from the mesa-top communities and began to build dwellings on the cliff is not known. The towers they constructed at the larger dwellings appear to have been built more for ceremonies than defense. Nor do we know why the Anasazi abandoned Mesa Verde, although their disappearance appears to have coincided with the beginning of a drought that lasted from A.D. 1276 to the end of the century. At any rate, by A.D. 1300 Mesa Verde appears to have been completely abandoned.

Mesa Verde is a large and complex park, and a visitor who wants to see it all at leisure could easily spend several days there. The Far View Visitor Center, 15 miles from the park entrance, has information that will help visitors get their bearings. The road to the visitor center passes Park Point, the highest spot on the mesa at 8,571 feet. A short walk to the summit from the parking lot provides a 360-degree panoramic view of the Four Corners area where Colorado, Utah, Arizona, and New Mexico come together.

At the visitor center the road splits, one fork leading to Wetherill Mesa, open only during summer months, and the other to Chapin Mesa.

Chapin Mesa

Far View Ruins, the complex nearest the visitor center, is on the Chapin Mesa Road. This mesa-top area was densely populated from A.D. 900 to 1300. It includes Far View House, with about fifty rooms and five kivas; Pipe Shrine House, 100 feet to the south, with twenty rooms, a large kiva, and a tower, named for the twelve decorated pottery pipes found in the kiva; and the remarkable Mummy Lake, a circular structure 90 feet in diameter and 12 feet deep, lined with stone masonry. It may have been designed to catch runoff from rain and snow.

Farther on, 6 miles from the visitor center, the Chapin Mesa road brings the visitor to the loop leading to Spruce Tree House and the Mesa Verde Museum (both described below) and park headquarters. At headquarters visitors must register if they wish to hike the 3-mile loop called Petroglyph Trail. The narrow path, a good introduction to the vegetation and geology of the mesa, leads to the Petroglyph Point, the largest group of petroglyphs in the park.

Spruce Tree House

When Wetherill and Mason came upon this cliff dwelling in 1888, a Douglas spruce was growing from the plaza in front to the top of the mesa above. The two men supposedly reached the dwelling by climbing down the tree, and so this ruin got its name.

With about 114 rooms and eight kivas, Spruce Tree House is the third-largest cliff dwelling within the park. Probably a hundred or so people lived here when it was fully constructed. The overhanging cliff, which protects the dwelling from the elements and accounts for its remarkable state of preservation, forms a cave 216 feet wide and 89 feet deep at its deepest point. The cave's ceiling is covered by soot from fires, which must have burned day and night during winter months. Unlike the kivas with their efficient shafts that brought in and circulated fresh air, the Anasazi dwellings were poorly ventilated.

Spruce Tree House, Mesa Verde

The deepest part of the cave contains a roofless kiva in the foreground, three rows of rooms behind it, and a large refuse area. The slope in front of the ruin was another trash heap, where the Anasazi often buried their dead. Bodies have been found here and also in sealed rooms at the rear of the cave, but these burials do not equal the number of people who must have lived here from A.D. 1200 to A.D. 1276 when the cave was occupied. How other bodies were disposed of is one of the many mysteries connected with this and other Mesa Verde sites.

Another mystery at Spruce Tree House concerns the function of a cylindrical room, which is located above a large boulder on which the inhabitants sharpened stone tools. Similar rooms found elsewhere in the park were either connected to kivas by tunnels, and probably served some ceremonial function, or they were located on overlooks to serve as probable lookout towers. At Spruce Tree House, however, the round room has neither view nor tunnel.

Mesa Verde Museum

The park museum contains extensive displays interpreting the development of the Anasazi culture at Mesa Verde. Near the entrance are four dioramas illustrating developmental periods: Basket Maker, Modified Basket Maker, Developmental Pueblo, and Classic Pueblo.

The museum has displays of Basket Maker weaving, including woven baskets, sandals, cradle boards, and yucca-fiber rope. Also on view is Anasazi pottery, including early cooking jars Indians made by shaping the base in a basket or bowl and adding wide bands of clay. The corrugated pottery used for cooking and holding water and the beautiful Mesa Verde black-on-white pottery (intricate black geometric designs on a grayish white background) were produced during the last stage of development, and they are also displayed.

There are exhibits on clothing, tools, religion, and food. Notable are a collection of decorative sashes spun from dog hair by people of the Modified Basket Maker period in northwestern Arizona and a sampling of Basket Maker jewelry, including a necklace made of 1,242 juniper berries.

Leaving the Headquarters and Spruce Tree House area, the road leads on to the Mesa Top Loop, which passes a variety of dwellings, including a Modified Basket Maker pit house (circa A.D. 575) that is the earliest-known permanent dwelling in Mesa Verde. Also on this loop is picturesque Square Tower House (circa A.D. 1200 to 1300). Sixty of its original eighty or so rooms, seven kivas, and a four-story tower still stand. Also on the loop is Sun Temple, which appears to have been under construction when the site was abandoned in 1276. There are excellent views of Cliff Palace (described below), the largest cliff dwelling in North America, from Sun Point Overlook and Sun Temple.

The Cliff Palace Loop road includes several interesting overlooks as well as the important dwellings, Cliff Palace and Balcony House. The latter can also be viewed from the end of Soda Canyon Trail, which begins near the end of the loop. Balcony House is a dwelling of about forty rooms and two kivas. Visitors must take a ranger-guided tour along a ½-mile trail, climb a 32-foot ladder and crawl through a 12-foot long tunnel to leave the site, and, finally, climb 60 vertical feet on ladders and stone steps carved into the cliff face.

Cliff Palace

The 217-room Cliff Palace, built on four terraced levels in a cave that reaches a depth of 89 feet and a height of 59 feet, is the largest cliff dwelling in North America. In addition there are twenty-three kivas, or underground ceremonial rooms. Most of these kivas have six pilasters, or masonry columns, on the inside wall to support the roof beams. They also have in common a recess on the south side (use unknown), a fire pit, a fire deflector wall, a ventilator opening, and a *sipapu*, or spirit hole, which, it is believed, the Anasazi regarded as a symbolic opening to the under-world. The original roofs were used as small courtyards; it is also believed that weaving was done inside the kiva.

On the south end of the site, a tunnel connects two kivas. It is believed that priests might have used such tunnels for sudden and dramatic appearances during ceremonies. Sometimes tunnels connected kivas with towers, which might indicate that the towers were also built for ceremonial purposes. The tower on the southern end is four stories tall, the tallest structure in the complex. When Wetherill came across Cliff Palace in 1888, one of the corners had collapsed. It has since been reconstructed, and some of

Cliff Palace, Mesa Verde

the paintings on the plaster covering parts of the inside walls have been preserved.

Cliff Palace was probably inhabited by 200 to 250 people. It was built with sandstone blocks held together with a mud mortar, into which small chinking stones were inserted. Remnants of the plaster that once covered the stonework are still visible in a few places. Fourteen of the rooms, wedged between the upper ledge and the roof of the huge cave, were storage rooms no more than 42 inches high.

Because the cave floor sloped downward, the Anasazi built retaining walls and filled the area behind them with rubble. The depth of the fill ranges from a few feet to almost 25 feet. The Anasazi also buried their dead in the refuse they discarded on the talus slope in front of the dwellings. Usually the dead were buried in a fetal position and covered with a yucca fiber mat or a fur or feather blanket. Jewelry, pottery, and tools were also buried with the individuals. Broken pottery, tools, and the remains of food and clothing have also been found in these archaeological trash heaps.

The wooden support beams protruding from the base of the wall are among the few original timbers found on this site. Tree ring dating of the beams indicates that construction of Cliff Palace took place from A.D. 1209 through 1270, not too long before the dwelling was abandoned for unknown reasons.

Wetherill Mesa

A 12-mile road leads from the Far View Visitor Center to Wetherill Mesa. Here Step House (described below) is accessible by self-guided trail. Visitors must take a mini-tram to visit Long House (described below) and other sites such as Badger House Community, which is actually two villages, one built on the foundations of the other. The tower of the second, or later, village is connected to a kiva by a 41-foot tunnel, the longest such tunnel in the park. There are also two early pueblo villages and some pit houses (circa A.D. 650) along the route.

Step House Cave

In 1891 the Swedish archaeologist Gustaf Nordenskiold found two pots that he suspected were "the work of a people who inhabited

Step House Cave, Mesa Verde

177

Step House Cave before the erection of the cliff village." It was one of the first indications that Mesa Verde had been the home of a people older than the the cliff-dwelling peoples of the Classic Pueblo period. Since then, four semisubterranean pit houses of the Modified Basket Maker period (circa A.D. 600) have been excavated at Step House. (They are visible on the left side of the site near the prehistoric stone staircase leading into the village.) With their roofs of poles and adobe, a ventilator shaft for fresh air, fire pits, and storage cists, pit houses were a great improvement over the caves that the Anasazi inhabited before. Kivas, which the Anasazi of the Pueblo period probably used ceremonially, developed from pit houses.

A ladder leads to the small masonry pueblo under the cliff overhang above. Thirty to forty Indians lived here from about A.D. 1100 to 1276. There is a kiva by the top of the ladder. Its roof, supported by six columns, was level with the ground and probably was used as a small courtyard or work area. This kiva, one of three in the small village, has a sipapu, or spirit hole, in the wall rather than on the floor.

Long House

The second-largest cliff dwelling in the park—with some 150 rooms and twenty-one kivas—Long House also has a central dance plaza. The recessed areas near the large rectangular fire pit might have been covered to serve as a foot drum during ceremonies, in order to amplify the beat of a dancer's foot. (The only other plaza like this in Mesa Verde is at Fire Temple on Chapin Mesa.) The remnants of storage rooms can be seen in the ledges above the main part of the ruin; there are water basins, fed by a seep spring system, at the rear of the cave. Twenty-eight burials were found in the talus slope in front of the dwelling. It is estimated that 150 to 175 people lived at Long House.

The only lodging within the park is at Far View Lodge near the visitor center, open May 1 to mid-October. There are campfire programs during the summer season at Morefield Campground, located 4 miles from the park entrance and open mid-April through October.

How to get there: Mesa Verde National Park is located 10 miles east of Cortez on Route 160.

MONTANA

Madison Buffalo Jump State Monument

Attraction: Site of prehistoric *pishkun,* or buffalo jump
Hours: Daylight hours
Admission fee: None
For more information: Department of Fish, Wildlife, and Parks, Parks Division, 1420 East Sixth Avenue, Helena, MT 59620; (406) 444–3950

Located in south-central Montana near Bozeman, the Madison Buffalo Jump, or Pishkun, is a bluff with a cliff more than 30 feet high, over which Blackfeet Indians on foot drove herds of buffalo to their death. Archaeologists believe that the Madison Pishkun was used over a period of more than 2,000 years, including the early years of the historic period. The Indians depended on the buffalo for survival, using different parts of the huge animal for food, shelter, and clothing. After the Indians acquired the horse in the early to mid-1700s and adopted horses to hunt buffalo, this pishkun and others like it became less important to their livelihood. In the Blackfeet language, pishkun means "deep blood kettle."

The Madison Buffalo Jump has all the components the hunters needed: a grazing area nearby that attracted the animals; an area of broken terrain over which the buffalo could be skillfully "herded" or driven; a precipice; and a long slope at the foot of the precipice down which the dead and injured animals could roll. The grazing animals were driven into V-shaped funnels or drive lanes formed by long rows of low rock piles and, it is believed, brush. At the foot of the precipice, hunters waited with spears, clubs, and arrows to finish off animals that had been injured but not killed by the fall.

Less than ¼ mile from the base of the jump is a village site, marked by abandoned hearths and numerous rings of rocks, called

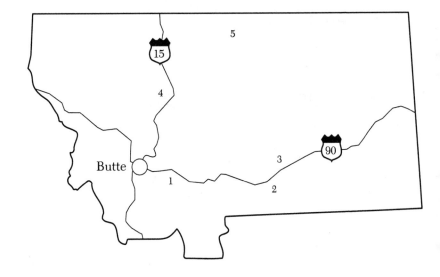

Montana
1. Madison Buffalo Jump State Monument
2. Pictograph Caves State Park
3. Pompey's Pillar National Historic Landmark
4. Ulm Pishkun State Monument
5. Wahkpa Chu'gn Buffalo Jump and
   Archaeological Site

tepee rings, that the Indians used to hold down the edges of their shelters. By the site's parking area, an open-air shelter houses an interpretive exhibit on the jump. On the ridge north of the shelter are the ruins of other tepee rings as well as two circular rock piles about 6 feet in diameter. The purpose of the latter is unknown; perhaps they were pits to which the Indians lured eagles and other birds with bait to capture them. Or the circles could have been vision questing sites, fortifications, or pits to contain fires that the Indians used to send smoke signals.

How to get there: Turn off I–90 at the Logan interchange (5 miles east of Three Forks) and follow the gravel road 7 miles south to the monument.

Pictograph Caves State Park

Attraction: Two caves with prehistoric rock paintings
Hours: May 1 to October 1, 8:00 A.M. to sundown
Admission fee: None
For more information: Department of Fish, Wildlife, and Parks, 1125 Lake Elmo Drive, Billings, MT 59105; (406) 252–4654.

Archaeological excavations at two of the three caves that make up Pictograph Caves State Park have produced nearly 30,000 artifacts from prehistoric and early historic times, among them spear and arrow points, gaming sticks, hafted knives, bone scrapers, stone tablets, potsherds, and bison and human bones. In Pictograph Cave, a recess 160 feet wide and 85 feet deep, the artifacts represent four distinct cultural periods, the earliest dating back to 7100 B.C.

Remains of the hundreds of rock paintings or pictographs that once adorned the walls of Pictograph Cave are the only visible evidence of prehistoric occupation. Many of these have been destroyed or damaged by vandalism and erosion. The most visible paintings are those that were done with a red pigment probably made from a mixture of red ochre, animal fat, and plant resins, but there are also drawings done in black as well as white pigment. Many of the paintings are of large shields, heart-arrow motifs, animals, and costumed individuals. Experts believe that most of the pictographs date from the late Prehistoric and Protohistoric periods (A.D. 500 to 1800).

Pictograph Cave was excavated between 1937 and 1939 by H. Melville Sayre of the Montana School of Mines and between 1940 and 1941 by William Mulloy of the University of Chicago. Although they never reached the floor of the cave, they found artifacts down to a depth of 23 feet.

Over the years, the site has been greatly damaged by vandals. A small museum constructed on the site in 1939 was vandalized and burned. Steps toward protecting the site were taken in 1964 when it was declared a National Historic Landmark. Montana's Department of Fish, Wildlife, and Parks took over the caves in 1969 and, since then, has added landscaping, trails, interpretive panels, toilets, and a small picnic area.

How to get there: The site is located 7 miles southeast of Billings, with access from I–90 at the Lockwood exit.

Pompey's Pillar National Historic Landmark

Attraction: Sandstone outcropping with Indian petroglyphs and historic signature
Hours: June 1 to September 1, 8:00 A.M. to 6:00 P.M.
Admission fee: None
For more information: Bureau of Land Management, Billings Resource Area, 810 East Main, Billings, MT 59105

This 100-foot-high sandstone tower, which rises abruptly from the level plain, is best known for the carved signature, "Wm Clark July 25, 1806," the only physical evidence of its journey left behind by the Lewis and Clark party. Because of the rock's prominence, the fame of its signature, and the fact that it is located near the intersection of the forty-sixth parallel and the 108th meridian, making it handy for pioneer navigators, Pompey's Pillar was often called "Montana's first landmark."

On the rock face, just southeast of the Clark signature, are the faint remnants of prehistoric rock paintings and carvings. One painting shows an animal with an arrow in its back. How old these are and who may have drawn them is still unknown, but a series of stick figures is believed to have been carved by the Shoshone between A.D. 1200 and 1800. Although the rock surface is now covered with hundreds of more recent scribblings and signatures, the Indian art work was noticeable to William Clark, who wrote in his diary: "The natives have ingraved on the face of this rock the figures of animals &c. near which I marked my name and the day of the month & year."

Clark originally named the landmark Pompy's Tower for Sacajawea's infant son, Baptiste Charboneau. (Clark nicknamed the baby Pomp, the Shoshone Indian word for chief.) Later recorders changed the tower's name to Pompey's Pillar after the famed Roman column. The signature has been modified slightly several times over the years; in 1926, a local chapter of the Daughters of the American Revolution reported it had the signature cut more deeply into the rock. There is no doubt of its authenticity, however, and today the signature is protected by shatter-proof glass set in bronze.

The site was privately owned until 1991 when the Bureau of Land Management purchased 366 surrounding acres along the Yellowstone River. Since it acquired the landmark, the bureau has built a boardwalk leading past the signature to the top of the pillar and a small visitor center.

How to get there: Pompey's Pillar is located 28 miles east of Billings. Take the Pompey's Pillar exit from I–94 and go 1 mile north on Route 312.

Ulm Pishkun State Monument

Attraction: Mile-long buffalo jump
Hours: Daylight hours, April 15 through October 15
Admission fee: None
For more information: Great Falls Chamber of Commerce, 926 Central Avenue, Great Falls, MT 59403; (406) 761–4434

Experts believe that this mile-long precipice might be the largest buffalo jump ever discovered. The pishkun, a Blackfeet Indian word for a buffalo kill site, is located on a plateau in the valley formed by the confluence of the Sun and Missouri rivers. The rimrock cliff forms the edge of the plateau and varies in height from 15 to 30 feet. The main jump area faces south, although the buffalo were first driven east and then turned to the cliff. The piles of rock used to funnel the animals to the cliff extend back from the edge ½ mile.

In addition to extensive deposits of buffalo bone, which were mined after World War II to make fertilizer, excavations at the site have turned up numerous prehistoric artifacts, including pottery made from local clay, side-notched arrowheads of the late Prehistoric period, knives, hide scrapers, and similar objects. At least one pictograph, or rock painting, on the far eastern end of the cliff depicts a warrior with a shield lying on his back.

It is believed that Indians began regularly using the site at least by A.D. 500 and that buffalo kills increased in frequency until the Indians began using their newly acquired horses to kill buffalo in the 1700s. A scientist studying the teeth of the buffalo killed here has determined that the hunts were most often held in the fall as the Indians prepared for winter.

The park is about 170 acres and includes only a small portion of the actual jump. In March 1992 the cable television magnate Ted Turner purchased the adjoining 1,080 acres of privately owned land that includes the rest of the jump. Although he owns a bison ranch nearby, it is believed that he made the purchase to preserve the land and may eventually trade it to the state for its future management and protection.

How to get there: The site is located 4 miles northwest of Ulm. Take I–15 to the Ulm exit and follow signs north and west to the site.

Wahkpa Chu'gn Buffalo Jump and Archaeological Site

Attraction: Bison kill site
Hours: Guided tour from the H. Earl Clack Memorial Museum offered Tuesdays and Thursdays, July and August, at 7:00 P.M.
Admission fee: $2.00; $25.00 for guided tours at other times

For more information: H. Earl Clack Memorial Museum, Havre, MT; (406) 395–4282

This significant buffalo jump, or kill site, was undisturbed when it was discovered by a local archaeological society in 1961. The name Wahkpa Chu'gn means "Little River" in the Assiniboine language and is the Indian name for the Milk River, which passes by the site. The jump, over which Indians drove the buffalo, consists of the 30- to 72-foot-high bluffs of a dry coulee. There was also a campsite near the pishkun, and excavations have turned up evidence of an impoundment or corral into which buffalo were also driven and then killed.

Radiocarbon dating of the buffalo bones indicates that the site was used repeatedly from about 50 B.C. to A.D. 1850. In the excavations large numbers of small, side-notched projectile points characteristic of the late Prehistoric period in the Northwestern Plains have been found. A few glass beads, metal finger rings, and other trade items indicate that the site area was also used in historic times, possibly by the Gros Ventre, Assiniboine, Blackfeet, and Cree peoples.

How to get there: Tours leave from the museum, which is located 1 mile west of Havre on Highway 2.

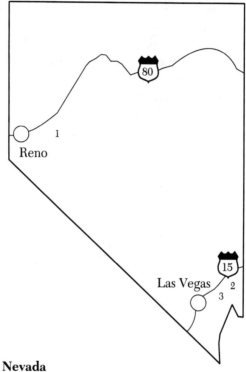

Nevada
1. Hidden Cave
2. Lost City Museum
3. Valley of Fire State Park

NEVADA

Hidden Cave

Attraction: Prehistoric cave
Hours: Guided tours on the second and fourth Saturday of each month begin at the Churchill County Museum in Fallon at 9:30 A.M.
Admission fee: None
For more information: Churchill County Museum, 1050 South Maine Street, Fallon, NV 89406, (702) 423–3677; or Bureau of Land Management, Carson City District Office, 21535 Hot Springs Road, Suite 300, Carson City, NV 89706, (702) 882–1631

The narrow, almost impassable entrance to Hidden Cave was first discovered in historic times—1926 or 1927—by four boys who were exploring caves at Grimes Point in hope of finding loot from a stagecoach robbery that, so legend had it, was hidden there. A draft of cold air coming from the narrow entrance alerted the boys to its existence; otherwise Hidden Cave might have stayed hidden for many more years. In the early 1930s Hidden Cave was mined for bat guano, but its archaeological significance was overlooked until a miner was heard to remark that the mining operation would go more smoothly if it weren't for "all that Indian junk" lying about.

When archaeologists first entered the cave about 1935, they found it to be more than 150 feet deep and at least half as wide. Ancient Indian artifacts lay scattered about, including well-preserved basketry, wood, and leather. The blinding dust that was kicked up by human feet made working in the cave extremely difficult. Nevertheless, the cave has been excavated on three different occasions: in 1940, 1951, and 1979–1980.

The difficult working conditions led the leader of the last expedition, David Hurst Thomas of the American Museum of Natural History in New York City, to conclude that "Whatever people did at Hidden Cave four thousand years ago, they obviously never

187

lived there. . . . Then, as now, exterior light barely penetrated the central alcove. Anyone who crawls 15 feet inside the cave is engulfed in disorientating darkness. Breathing the dust of Hidden Cave is difficult enough without adding the noxious fumes and smoke of torches or open fires."

The impossible living conditions, the presence of two dozen storage pits, and the absence of evidence of food being consumed in the cave led Thomas to conclude that the cave had been used for storage, not living. In an article on the cave, Thomas observed that more than 80 percent of the hundreds of projectile points found at Hidden Cave "were unbroken and fully serviceable," an indication that these items were being stockpiled here for future use.

There were also indications that food was stored in the cave; dessicated feces called coprolites were found to contain seeds of plants harvested in different seasons, a sure indication that the individual had eaten food from storage. In an article on the cave, Thomas also discusses the likelihood that feces containing undigested seeds were deliberately deposited inside the cave, so that the seeds could be reused in times of famine. This so-called second harvesting has been observed among other prehistoric people.

Hidden Cave is located on a mile-long interpretive trail that includes several other caves and some prehistoric rock art sites. The cave, however, is only open for tours. There is also an exhibit on the archaeology of Hidden Cave at the Churchill County Museum in Fallon.

How to get there: The site is located at Grimes Point, 12 miles east of Fallon on Highway 50.

Lost City Museum

Attraction: Museum of prehistoric culture, reconstructed village structures on original foundations
Hours: Daily
Admission fee: $1.00
For more information: Lost City Museum, Box 807, Overton, NV 89040; (702) 397–2193

At the entrance to this museum of prehistoric archaeology, there is a Bastket Maker pit house that was reconstructed on the site of an actual pit house dating from A.D. 655. The museum, which was built by the Civilian Conservation Corps in 1935, houses artifacts taken from Pueblo Grande de Nevada, also known as the Lost City, an extensive Anasazi settlement that stretched along the Moapa Valley from Warm Springs to the Virgin River. The fate of the ruins became a matter of national concern when it was realized that a large part would soon be flooded by the waters of Lake Mead rising behind Hoover Dam, which was called Boulder Dam when Franklin Delano Roosevelt dedicated it in September 1935.

Behind the museum there are several more replicas of pueblo-type houses of wattle and daub construction that have been built on original foundations. The museum itself houses a collection of artifacts, including baskets, pottery, and weapons, from peoples who lived in the region from the time of the Desert culture 10,000 years ago through the Basket Maker cultures, which lasted until about A.D. 500; the Pueblo Anasazi, who lived here from about A.D. 500 to 1150; and finally the Paiutes, who arrived about A.D. 1000 and whose descendants still live in the region. The museum also displays a reconstruction of a pueblo living and storage structure.

How to get there: Take Route 169 off I–15 and go south to the museum, which is just south of Overton.

Valley of Fire State Park

Attraction: Petroglyphs visible from trail through canyon
Hours: Visitor center open daily 8:30 A.M. to 4:30 P.M.; summer weekend hours are 8:30 A.M. to 6:30 P.M.
Admission fee: None
For more information: Valley of Fire State Park, P.O. Box 515, Overton NV 89040; (702) 397–2088

Valley of Fire, dedicated in 1935, is Nevada's oldest state park. It is named for the spectacular formations of red sandstone that were created some 600 million years ago and sculpted into their present shapes by later erosion. Basket Maker people and

Atlatl Rock at Valley of Fire State Park

later Anasazi farmers from the fertile Moapa Valley nearby frequented the area from 300 B.C. to A.D. 1150, probably to hunt or gather food. Or perhaps the eerily beautiful rock formations, which glow with particular intensity at sunset, had spiritual meaning for prehistoric man. Prehistoric petroglyphs chipped into the desert varnish coating the rocks can be seen in several places, but they are particularly numerous along a short, self-guided trail leading into Petroglyph Canyon. The rock art is neither dated nor interpreted, but human and animal figures as well as hunting scenes are among the drawings. Similar petroglyphs can be seen at the towering landmark called Atlatl Rock, where a staircase brings the visitor close to the vivid rock art high on the rock face.

A spacious visitor center with exhibits on the plant and animal life in the park is located about midway between the east and west entrances.

How to get there: The east entrance of the state park is located 15 miles from Overton on Route 169.

NEW MEXICO

Aztec Ruins National Monument

Attraction: Large Anasazi pueblo, visitor center
Hours: September through May 8:00 A.M. to 5:00 P.M.; June through August 8:00 A.M. to 6:30 P.M.
Admission fee: $3.00 per car
For more information: Aztec Ruins National Monument, Aztec, NM 87410; (505) 334–6174

This large and well-preserved Anasazi pueblo had two lives. Anasazi Indians, who emigrated from Chaco Canyon 60 miles to the south, began construction about A.D. 1110 and lived here until the end of the twelfth century. The availability of water in the nearby Animas River probably drew them to the site, but why they left is unknown. Twenty-five years after the pueblo was deserted, people from Mesa Verde, 40 miles to the northwest in present-day Colorado, moved in and rebuilt it. The reasons for their departure some seventy-five years later are also a mystery. As a result of this dual occupancy, both a Chacoan style of masonry (alternating bands of large and small stones) and a Mesa Verdean style (same size stones) are visible at Aztec.

The ruins received the name Aztec from white settlers who incorrectly assumed that the settlement must have been built by Indians from Mexico. (The ruins are on the edge of the small, attractive community of Aztec, settled in 1890.)

Aztec was a satellite or "outlier" community for both the Chaco Canyon and Mesa Verde settlements. At the height of its development, Aztec probably had 220 ground-floor rooms, 119 second-story rooms, and twelve or more third-story rooms, enough space to house 500 to 700 people. In total area, however, the pueblo covered less than two football fields.

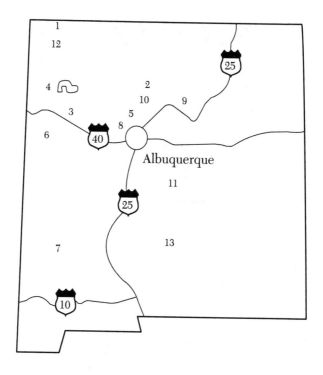

New Mexico
1. Aztec Ruins National Monument
2. Bandelier National Monument
3. Casamero Ruins
4. Chaco Culture National Historic Park
5. Coronado State Monument
6. El Morro National Monument
7. Gila Cliff Dwellings National Monument
8. Indian Petroglyphs National Monument
9. Pecos National Historic Park
10. Puyé Cliff Dwellings and Communal House Ruins
11. Salinas Pueblo Missions National Monument
12. Salmon Ruin
13. Three Rivers Petroglyph Site

Aztec Ruins National Monument

Earl H. Morris of the American Museum of Natural History, who began work here in the early twentieth century, excavated the ruin's Great Kiva in 1921. (He supervised its reconstruction thirteen years later.) The structure, 48 feet in diameter, might have been used for administrative purposes as well as a community and religious center. Its roof, which was supported by beams and four substantial pillars, may have weighed ninety-five tons. The kiva in the center is surrounded by fifteen roofed surface rooms with an exterior door to the courtyard.

Unlike other Anasazi kivas, most of the ceremonial structures at Aztec do not have the small hole in the floor called the sipapu, which, experts believe, symbolized the entrance to the spiritual world from which all life on earth once emerged. It is not certain whether the absence represents a cultural variation or whether the sipapu simply disappeared over the years.

A room within the pueblo that Morris excavated earlier, in 1918, revealed an interesting succession of uses. Originally it was a residential or storage room, then a trash repository (as evidenced by several feet of refuse), then a turkey pen, and finally a grave-yard. Morris excavated ten burials here. The heavy pine ceiling beams in this room, which support the upper story, were probably carried from mountains 20 miles away.

Most of the daily activities in the pueblo took place in the central plaza. The boundaries of the plaza can be seen in the excavation of the west wing of the settlement. An unusual tri-walled structure, 64 feet in diameter, which was probably used for religious ceremonies, can be seen at the Hubbard Site in the northeast corner. (The site was named for an early owner of the property.) Site markers indicate the location of small rooms wedged in between the outer walls and the ceremonial chamber in the center.

Aztec Ruins was made a 27-acre National Monument in 1923; it is one of the best-preserved Anasazi sites in the Southwest.

How to get there: In Aztec, a spur off Highway 550 leads to the monument.

Bandelier National Monument

Attraction: Large park with hiking trails to prehistoric sites; visitor center/museum
Hours: Memorial Day through Labor Day, 8:00 A.M. to 6:00 P.M.; rest of year, 8:00 A.M. to 4:30 P.M.
Admission fee: $5.00 per car
For more information: Bandelier National Monument, Los Alamos, NM 87544; (505) 672–3861

After descending into Frijoles Canyon for the first time on October 23, 1889, the Swiss-born anthropologist Adolph F. Bandelier wrote with typical enthusiasm that the caves and cliff dwellings were "the grandest thing I ever saw. . . . It is of the highest interest."

Bandelier, who grew up in Illinois, gave up a career in international banking at age forty to pursue his intense, lifelong interest in natural history and prehistoric societies. The Pajarito Plateau, on which the monument is located, was one of the first areas he visited (guided by Cochiti Indians) when he arrived in New Mexico in

1880. In 1890, Bandelier used this region for the setting of a novel, *The Delight Makers*, which is about prehistoric pueblo life. The 32,727-acre area of scenic wilderness, volcanic rock formations, and prehistoric dwellings is named for Bandelier, even though one of his successors, the well-known archaeologist Edgar Lee Hewett, the first director of the School of American Research and the Museum of New Mexico, did extensive work in the area and lobbied hard to have the entire Pajarito Plateau made a "National Park of the Cliff Cities"; instead, in 1916, a 42-square-mile area was designated the Bandelier National Monument. The monument includes over 23,000 acres of designated wilderness.

As far as archaeologists have determined, there was little permanent settlement on the Pajaritan Plateau until Anasazi people from the Four Corners region began migrating there about A.D. 1200. At first they lived in small, family-sized pueblos, which they often carved out of the soft volcanic tuff and which were spread out over a large area. As the population grew, these pueblos were enlarged or consolidated into larger villages. Because the soft volcanic rock made poor building blocks, the Anasazi made good use of the region's many cliffs by building their pueblos against them and carving additional rooms into their base. These settlements are sometimes called talus communities because they were built at the point where the talus slope, formed by falling rocks and other debris, and the cliff wall meet. A few larger communities, such as Tyuonyi (chew-OHN-yee), were built around a central plaza away from the cliffs in the bottom of canyons or, as with the pueblo called Tsankawi, on top of a mesa.

The Anasazi lived here for 300 years, growing corn, beans, and squash on the bottomlands, often with the aid of check dams and simple irrigation techniques. In the early sixteenth century, however, the Anasazi were forced to move to a lower elevation closer to the Rio Grande.

An easy, 1-mile trail makes a loop from the visitor center past the principal ruins, cliff dwellings, and kivas, coming first to Tyuonyi. This large, oval-shaped pueblo, which was excavated by Hewett between 1909 and 1912, had more than 300 small rooms and might have stood three stories high in places. There was a single entrance into a central plaza, where three kivas were located. From Tyuonyi, the trail continues up the north side of Frijoles Canyon to Long House, an 800-foot-long series of rooms that extends along the foot of the canyon. Starting again at the visitor center, a ½-mile trail leads along the banks of the Rio de los Frijoles to Ceremonial Cave, where Hewett discovered what appears to be large, well-preserved kiva sunk into the rock. (The Cave is located about 150 feet above the canyon floor and is entered by climbing a series of long ladders.) The semicircular kiva has been reconstructed and roofed over and is entered by a ladder through the roof. The cave's name might be misleading; instead of being used for ceremonial purposes, some scholars believe it housed turkeys.

The Bandelier National Monument also has some 70 miles of hiking trails. Some of these lead to the more distant sites. The intriguing Shrine of the Stone Lions, where two badly eroded cat-like stone animals are found surrounded by rocks, is a 10-mile round trip from Frijoles Creek. Present-day Pueblo Indians make pilgrimages to the shrine, which they consider sacred. Frijolito Ruin is a mere ½ mile off the main road, while the site known as Painted Cave is a 20-mile round trip.

A detached section of the monument, Tsankawi, is located about 11 miles north of Bandelier's main entrance. A self-guided trail leads to the mesa-top location of an unexcavated prehistoric village; the remains of pueblo dwellings can be seen at the base of the cliff. In places the ancient trail has been worn deep into the volcanic rock by centuries of passage. The top of the mesa, with its magnificent view of the Los Alamos area, is reached by a ladder. There are also petroglyphs—rock carvings of human figures, birds, four-pointed stars, and other images—on the cliffs.

The visitor center, which includes a small museum and an orientation program, is the starting point for a one-hour self-guided walking tour of the principal ruins. Free permits for overnight backpacking can also be obtained at the visitor center.

How to get there: The monument is located 46 miles west of Santa Fe. Take Highway 285 to Pojoacque, then turn west on Route 502 and south on Route 4.

Casamero Ruins

Attraction: Small Anasazi pueblo
Hours: Always open
Admission fee: None
For more information: Bureau of Land Management, Farmington Resource Area, 1235 La Plata Highway, Farmington, NM 87401; (505) 327-5344

This small pueblo, built about A.D. 1050, has only twenty-odd rooms, but it was probably the center for a number of small, one-family farms that were scattered through the broad valley in which it is located. As an outlying community of Chaco Canyon 50 miles to the north, Casamero had social, economic, and religious ties to that important center of the Anasazi civilization. One indication of Casamero's importance is the presence of a great kiva that, although unexcavated, is estimated to be slightly larger than the largest known great kiva at Chaco Canyon. The pueblo was excavated in 1966 and 1967.

How to get there: The pueblo can be reached from Route 40 (Prewitt exit). Contact the Bureau of Land Management (listed above) for more specific directions.

Chaco Culture National Historical Park

Attraction: Major archaeological site, visitor center/museum
Hours: Daily from Memorial Day through Labor Day, 8:00 A.M. to 6:00 P.M.; rest of year 8:00 A.M. to 5:00 P.M.
Admission fee: $4.00 per car
For more information: Chaco Culture National Historical Park, Star Route 4, Box 6500, Bloomfield, NM 87413; (505) 786-7014

The number of sites—more than 2,000 prehistoric ruins in a 32-square-mile area—the advanced state of the architecture, and the intricate irrigation system for diverting runoff water make this arid, 15-mile-long rift known as Chaco Canyon the most extensive group of Indian ruins north of Mexico and one of the most important archaeological sites in North America. Within the 34,000-acre monument, there are more than a dozen large buildings known as Great Houses and some 400 smaller pueblo sites. The larger, 60,000-square-mile San Juan Basin of northwestern New Mexico, in which Chaco Canyon is located, also has the remains of hundreds of segments of painstakingly built prehistoric roads. The purpose of these thoroughfares, which are wide, straight, and elaborately engineered, is a matter of continuing debate.

Although the canyon had been inhabited since 4000 B.C., construction of the pueblos did not start in earnest until about A.D 850 to 900. The population of the settlement eventually reached 5,000 people, according to some estimates. Why Chaco Canyon declined and eventually was abandoned is still a matter of speculation. A drought and the fact that the Chacoans caused environmental damage by cutting most of the timber in the region for construction and fuel undoubtedly hastened the decline.

Lieutenant James H. Simpson, a scientist accompanying the U.S. Army in actions against the Navajo, was the first, in 1849, to report on, measure, record, and name the sites at Chaco Canyon. In May 1877 the photographer William Henry Jackson spent five days mapping, sketching, and reconnoitering the canyon. Jackson also took 400 photographs with a massive view camera, but, unfortunately, none of them came out. In 1896 the pioneering guide and self-taught archaeologist Richard Wetherill began excavating at Chaco. Beginning in 1897 he led the Hyde Exploring Expedition to Chaco Canyon, where it spent four years excavating the canyon's principal ruin, Pueblo Bonito. (Wetherill stayed on at Chaco Canyon as a rancher and trader. He was shot to death by a Navajo man in 1910 in a dispute over a horse.)

In 1907 President Theodore Roosevelt proclaimed Chaco Canyon a national monument. In 1921 archaeologists began excavating Pueblo Bonito and uncovered about fifty rooms in Pueblo del Arroyo. A Smithsonian expedition of 1929 unearthed remnants of a late Basket Maker settlement called Shabik'eshchee, which predates the pueblos. Edgar L. Hewett of the University of New Mexico excavated Chetro Ketl, just east of Pueblo Bonito, in the 1930s. In the 1970s the National Park Service and the University of New Mexico established a modern research facility, Chaco Center, which uses remote sensing, an advanced form of aerial photography, and other up-to-date techniques to study the site. In December 1980 the monument was enlarged and its name changed to Chaco Culture National Historical Park. It became a World Heritage site in 1987.

Of the multistoried Chacoan Great Houses that were constructed in the period of great activity from A.D. 900 to 1115, Pueblo Bonito is the best known and most thoroughly studied; consequently scholars often refer to this period as the Bonito Phase. The meticulous construction of the Great Houses in grid-like patterns clearly indicates that they were the result of considerable architectural planning. The pueblo walls are built on solid foundations and taper as they rise, another indication that the additional floors were not simply an afterthought and that the Chacoans knew when construction started that the buildings would be multistoried. The structures were usually designed to descend in steps from a height of four or five stories to a central plaza enclosed by a wall of one-story rooms.

Although the same techniques were used elsewhere in the canyon and at other Anasazi settlements, the Great Houses represent the peak of Chacoan culture. "Not only are the buildings taller, the walls thicker and the stone patterns more intricate but also the individual rooms are larger than rooms constructed elsewhere during the same period," reported archaeologists Stephen Lekson, Thomas Windes, John Stein, and W. James Judge in 1988. Earlier archaeologists assumed that the Great Houses were simply large permanent dwellings. Further investigation indicates that they were used intermittently, probably by groups that came to Chaco on pilgrimages or for other spiritual reasons.

The network of roads that surrounds Chaco Canyon has been taken as an indication that the canyon was the center for large numbers of outlying communities, some of them quite distant, such as the outlier, now preserved as the Aztec National Monument, near the New Mexico–Colorado border.

Archaeologists have known about the roads for most of this century but most assumed that they were simply well-worn paths between settlements. Studies begun in 1981, however, showed that the roads had been meticulously engineered. Not only were they extremely straight over long distances, but many had roadbeds that had been dug beneath the surface. Also, long stretches were a consistent 29½ feet wide. The road network is one reason why modern archaeologists believe that Chaco Canyon was, as the archaeologists cited above wrote, "the heart of a vast regional system and a community of unprecedented complexity."

Chaco's two main roads—the Great North Road and the South Road—appear to have connected it with outlying settlements, but the reason for the construction of the other roads is uncertain. Archaeologists once thought the roads served the same function as any other thoroughfare: to move people and goods from one place to another. Now they are not so sure; the roads, they believe, are too grand for such utilitarian purposes. "These guys could get around just fine without 30-foot-wide roads cutting straight across the landscape," archaeologist John Stein was quoted as saying in a 1994 article in *Archaeology* magazine. Stein also described the roads as "overengineered and underused."

Current thinking portrays the roads as ceremonial in function, an interpretation that is bolstered by the presence of horseshoe-shaped shrines, called *herraduras,* along the routes. Archaeologists speculate that the roads could have been primarily used for religious processions or, as one team of archaeologists put it, "perhaps a power corridor to a sacred place."

There are self-guided trails through seven ruins: Pueblo Bonito, Chetro Ketl, Pueblo del Arroyo, and Casa Rinconada (all described in more detail) and three village sites. Some hiking is required to reach Penasco Blanco, Tsin Kletsin, Pueblo Alto, and Wijiji.

Pueblo Bonito

Pueblo Bonito, the canyon's most important community, is built in the shape of a giant D that conforms to the curve of the 100-foot-high mesa behind it (Chaco Canyon's north wall). The complex was mostly built between A.D. 850 and 1120. Much of the complex is surrounded by an 800-foot-long wall that is faced on both sides with small, intricately fitted stones and filled with rubble. Sections of the rear wall were five stories high. The pueblo might have contained as many as 800 rooms. Some of the older rooms were filled with trash to support newer rooms above.

Pueblo Bonito, Chaco Canyon

There are more than thirty-two small kivas and three great kivas, one 52 feet in diameter. The large number of kivas, as well as Pueblo Bonito's elegant and durable construction, is an indication that the complex had uses other than residential. One theory holds that Pueblo Bonito was built to temporarily house people from the outliers who came to the canyon for religious ceremonies.

The pueblo's large plaza is divided into two courts—one great kiva in the east court, and two in the west—by a single row of rooms. Some experts speculate that the division indicates the pueblo had two separate groups of inhabitants, each responsible for religious ceremonies at different times of the year. A similar division is found at certain present-day pueblos.

Casa Rinconada

This great kiva is one of the largest (62½ feet in diameter with a wall about 3 feet thick) ever discovered and the only one at Chaco Canyon that the public can enter. Although the kiva is now roofless, it was once at least partially covered by timbers connected to four massive posts of ponderosa pine. The interior is encircled by a masonry bench, logically a place for worshipers to sit, although in some present-day kivas they sit on the floor. The niches in the beautiful masonry walls, which were probably once covered with painted plaster, are evenly spaced around the interior; probably used for storing ceremonial objects, they were empty when the kiva was excavated in 1931. The square floor vaults might have been covered with planks and used as a floor drum, to amplify the beat of dancers' feet during ceremonies.

The ⁴/₁₀-mile-long trail leading to the kiva also passes three Anasazi house sites. These one- and two-story structures usually had little or no foundation and were not as massively constructed as the Great Houses. Archaeologists once believed that these simple dwellings were earlier than the Great Houses, but tree ring dating shows that the two styles are contemporaneous, although they served different functions.

Chetro Ketl

The name Chetro Ketl is probably derived from a Navajo word passed on to Lieutenant James Simpson by an Indian guide, but its original meaning has been lost. This extensive pueblo was five stories high in places and probably contained more than 500 rooms. Tree ring dating indicates that it was constructed between A.D. 1038 and 1054 and expanded and remodeled about A.D. 1100. The major part of the excavation was conducted in 1920–1921 and 1929–1934 by Edgar L. Hewett of the School of American Research and the Museum of New Mexico.

The pueblo is fronted by a large open plaza enclosed by a wall of one-story rooms. The long front wall facing the plaza was originally an open, cloisterlike porch or colonnade; at a later date, the space between the columns was filled in to create an enclosed passageway. Colonnades were common in prehistoric central Mexico but unknown in the Southwest before this time.

The great kiva at Chetro Ketl, just over 60 feet in diameter, is slightly smaller than the one at Casa Rinconada. It is built over a smaller kiva that had wall niches similar to those in the great kiva. When these earlier niches were discovered and opened in 1932, each one contained tourquoise pendants and strings of stone and

Chetro Ketl, Chaco Canyon

shell beads, one 17 feet long. Like the great kiva at Casa Rinconada, this one has four masonry-lined pits, which held the posts supporting the roof. When the kiva was excavated, the remains of a post 26½ inches thick were found. The four posts were connected with horizontal logs, which formed a square. Smaller roofing timbers connected the square with the perimeter of the kiva. Experts are not sure whether the center of the square was covered or left open.

The path through the ruin also passes the remains of a three-story tower formed by the rectangle of walls around it and filled with rubble. On the top was a room apparently used as a kiva.

Pueblo del Arroyo

This Great House takes its name from a now-eroded stream bed that was once the main channel of Chaco Wash before it shifted some 60 feet to the south. Like its eminent neighbors, Pueblo Bonito and Chetro Ketl, Pueblo del Arroyo is a multistoried structure, four stories high at the rear, that is stepped down to one-story rooms in the front. One-third of the pueblo was excavated by archaeologist Karl Ruppert in the summers of 1923 to 1926. The north wing of the pueblo is still unexcavated. Construction on Pueblo del Arroyo began about A.D. 1075, with the central section being built first. Although the architecture shows the same forethought and planning as in the other Great Houses, the pueblo is different in several aspects. For one, it faces east instead of south, and it is located out in the open instead of close to the canyon wall. In certain sections of the ruin, a softer-type sandstone is used in places, probably an indication that the denser, darker sandstone was becoming harder to find when the pueblo was built.

The circular walls of the largest kiva yet excavated at Pueblo del Arroyo were built so that they fitted within a rectangle of retaining walls; the empty spaces in the corners were then filled with rubble. The kiva has a typical subfloor ventilator. Although the kiva subsequently burned and was then filled with rubble, the offerings were undamaged when archaeologists recovered them—542 beads, pendants, and scraps of shell and turquoise.

The Chacoans probably obtained their turquoise from mines south of present-day Santa Fe and used it in trade as far away as central Mexico. Bones of the macaw, a bird native to southern Mexico, were found in one long room of the central section. Macaw feathers were used for ceremonial trappings. It is assumed that the birds were obtained by trading and not raised at Chaco since only bones of mature birds have been found.

Pueblo Alto

Between 1976 and 1979 a team led by W. J. Judge and T. C. Windes excavated about 10 percent of the previously unexcavated pueblo that is situated on top of the north rim of Chaco Canyon, commanding a 360-degree view. Pueblo Alto is unique among the Great Houses of Chaco Canyon because of its exposed location and its single-level construction. The archaeologists reported that Pueblo Alto was constructed between A.D. 1020 and 1060, with some remodeling done in the early 1100s. It was abandoned about A.D. 1132.

The team was surprised to discover that only five of the eighty-five rooms excavated were living quarters, as indicated by the remains of hearths, storage pits, and other evidence that food had been stored, prepared, and eaten there. A second type of room arrangement, which they called "big-room suites" (a storage room connected to a second room that may have been inhabited on a limited basis), was also found. The big-room suites had little evidence of habitation and no indication that cooking took place there. A third type of room, "road-related suites," consisted of interconnected storage rooms built along the outside of the building, each with a door opening on the road. The fact that these rooms were inaccessible from the inside was taken as evidence that whatever was stored inside was not for the use of the permanent inhabitants.

A small trench that archaeologists dug through a huge nearby trash mound produced more than 70,000 artifacts, among them potsherds, flaked stones, and food remains, far more than could have been produced by what the scientists believe was a small permanent population. Also the mound was layered as if large amounts of trash were deposited intermittently, a sign, perhaps, that large number of Indians gathered here periodically for ceremonies and other events.

How to get there: Chaco Culture National Historical Park is about 60 miles north of Thoreau via Route 57 and 29 miles south of Nageezl Trading Post via Route 44. The roads leading to the park are mostly unpaved and can be impassable in wet weather. The park visitor center and museum is located ½ mile from the south entrance.

Coronado State Monument

Attraction: Pueblo excavation and ruin, visitor center
Hours: Daily from May 1 through September 15, 9:00 A.M. to 6:00 P.M.; rest of year, 8:00 A.M. to 5:00 P.M.
Admission fee: $2.00
For more information: Coronado State Monument, Bernalillo, NM 87004; (505) 867–5351

The highlight of the 1930s excavation of this 1,200-room pueblo on the Rio Grande was the discovery of the square kiva with seventeen layers of polychrome ceremonial frescoes depicting hunting scenes on the walls, a rare example of prehistoric mural art. The multistoried pueblo, called Kuaua, consists of structures surrounding three plazas. For protection and defense, its high exterior walls were without ground-level entrances. The Tiwa-speaking Indians who began constructing the pueblo about 1300 farmed the rich earth of the Rio Grande valley and hunted in the Sandia Mountains across the river to the east.

Although the monument bears the name of the famous conquistador Francisco Vasquez de Coronado, his stopover at the pueblo during the winter of 1540–1541 was marked by conflict and discord. According to chronicler Pedro de Casteñada, the natives rebelled when a soldier ordered an Indian to hold his horse and then "ravished or had attempted to ravish his wife."

Kuaua was one of twelve pueblos grouped along the west bank of the middle Rio Grande. It was inhabited until about 1700, when the Spanish consolidated many pueblos by force.

The pueblo has been partially reconstructed and reproductions of the original murals can be seen in the kiva. There is a self-guided trail through the monument and a small museum at the visitor center.

How to get there: The monument is located 2 miles northwest of Bernalillo on Route 44.

El Morro National Monument

Attraction: Pueblo ruin, Inscription Rock, visitor center, trails
Hours: Visitor center/museum hours are 8:00 A.M. to 7:00 P.M. Memorial Day through Labor Day, 8:00 A.M. to 5:00 P.M. rest of year
Admission fee: $3.00 per car
For more information: El Morro National Monument, Route 2, Box 43, Ramah, NM 87321; (505) 783–4226

The first Indians from the Zuni area probably moved up to the top of El Morro Mesa about A.D. 1250 to take advantage of more rainfall at the higher elevation. At first they lived in scattered settlements, but soon gathered for defense into two nearly identical pueblos, Atsinna and Pueblo de los Muertos. (The latter is outside the monument and not open to the public.) Like other pueblos built for defense, Atsinna has two-story walls but no exterior, ground-level doors; the inhabitants apparently entered by ladders that could be pulled up in the event of an attack. The walls also offered an unobstructed view of the Zuni River valley. The pueblos were apparently abandoned when the drought ended at the end of the thirteenth century and the inhabitants returned to the valley.

Archaeologist Richard B. Woodbury excavated one wing of Atsinna in 1954–1955. The pueblo measured 200 by 300 feet and contained more than 500 rooms. Also visible are the remains of both a round and a square kiva. The short but steep trail from the visitor center continues past Atsinna to an undisturbed pueblo site.

El Morro, which means the headland or bluff in Spanish, was made a National Monument in 1906. The monument's main attraction is 200-foot high Inscription Rock, where, from prehistoric times on, passersby have left drawings, comments, and signatures, thereby creating a unique register of historical time. The petroglyphs and other rock art on the base of the rock probably date from the time of the occupation of Atsinna. The 500 readable names include Don Juan de Onate, the first governor of New Mexico, who passed by here in 1605 on his return from the Gulf of California; Diego de Vargas (1692), the Spanish general who reconquered New Mexico after the Pueblo Revolt of 1680; Lieutenant James Simpson (1849), the military observer who made some of the first scientific reports on many prehistoric sites in the Southwest; and, in 1857, Edward F. Beale, commander of the famed U.S. Army Camel Corps. Also here is the large pool of runoff water that attracted travelers to the site. There is a visitor center and small museum at the head of the trails and a small campground and picnic area.

How to get there: The monument is located off Route 53 just east of Ramah, 56 miles southeast of Gallup.

Gila Cliff Dwellings National Monument

Attraction: Cliff dwellings, trails, visitor center
Hours: Open daily Memorial Day through Labor Day, 8:00 A.M. to 6:00 P.M.; rest of year, 9:00 A.M. to 5:00 P.M.
Admission fee: None
For more information: Gila Cliff Dwellings National Monument, Route 11, Box 100, Silver City, NM 88061; (505) 536–9461

The location of these habitations in deep caves 150 feet or more above the canyon floor led the early anthropologist Adolph Bandelier, who visited the ruins in 1883, to observe that "while it would be difficult for an Indian to take the place by storm, its inhabitants could easily be cut off from water or starved." It took Bandelier, who was nursing a sore foot, twelve days to make the round trip—by horseback, wagon, and foot—from Mimbres in southern New Mexico to the site at the headwaters of the Gila (pronounced HEE-la) River.

Bandelier, who was the first scientist to visit and report on the cliff dwellings, also saw sandals made from strips of yucca, baskets, corn cobs, prayer sticks, and other evidence of the Mogollon occupation. His observations led him to conclude that the Mogollon Indians who lived here "were in no manner different from the Pueblo Indians in general culture." Indeed, the building techniques evident here also indicate that the Mogollons who built the cliff dwellings were influenced by Pueblo Anasazi to the north.

The Gila Cliff Dwellings represent 1,000 years of Mogollon occupation. They are also the only Mogollon habitations open to the public in the National Park system. The earliest Mogollons, who arrived at the site about A.D. 1,000, lived in pit houses; one pithouse village dating from this time was excavated to make way for a proposed road into the area. Research indicates that they began building surface dwellings about A.D. 100. Radiocarbon dating of the roof timbers revealed that the cliff dwellings preserved at the monument were built about A.D. 1280. (The dwellings were protected by projecting roofs as well as by overhanging cliffs.) The Indians lived here until 1300, when the site was abandoned. Gila is a corruption of an Apache word meaning mountain.

(Courtesy National Park Service)

Gila Cliff Dwellings

The Mogollon built their cliff houses in seven caves, five of which—a total of forty-two rooms—are open to the public via a self-guided trail. The 533-acre monument is located within the 3.3-million-acre Gila National Forest, a pristine wilderness area, where the Apache leader Geronimo and his warriors would take refuge after their raids.

How to get there: The monument is located 45 miles north of Silver City via Route 45. The visitor center is located 2 miles from the entrance.

Indian Petroglyphs National Monument

Attraction: Extensive grouping of petroglyphs, visitor center
Hours: Park open daily in winter 8:00 A.M. to 5:00 P.M., in summer 9:00 A.M. to 6:00 P.M.; visitor center open daily 8:00 A.M. to 5:00 P.M.
Admission fee: None

For more information: Indian Petroglyphs National Monument, 4735 Atrisco Drive NW, Albuquerque, NM 87120; (505) 839–4429

Recently upgraded from a state to a federal preserve, this is the first national monument devoted to prehistoric art. West Mesa, a 17-mile, serpentine stretch of volcanic rock west of Albuquerque, contains some 15,000 petroglyphs or prehistoric pictures—white or gray lines chipped into the desert varnish covering the rock. The Anasazi petroglyphs date from A.D. 700 to 1300. Between the fourteenth and seventeenth centuries, Tiwa Pueblo Indians carved animals, birds, people, flute players, and kachina figures. These petroglyphs are not as clear or as complex as those found farther north on the Colorado Plateau. Why prehistoric peoples chose this location for such a large concentration of rock art is unknown; perhaps it had spiritual meaning for them, or it could have been a hunting ground. Trails through the rock lead from turnoffs on the monument road.

How to get there: Take Coors Road exit from I–40, go north on Coors Road, turn left (west) on Sequoia, and go 1 block to Atrisco. Turn right (north) on Atrisco and go 1½ miles to visitor center. The monument is 1¾ miles beyond the visitor center.

Pecos National Historical Park

Attraction: Pueblo ruins, visitor center, self-guided trails
Hours: Open daily Memorial Day through Labor Day, 8:00 A.M. to 6:00 P.M.; rest of year, 8:00 A.M. to 5:00 P.M.
Admission fee: $3.00 per car
For more information: Pecos National Historical Park, P.O. Box 418, Pecos, NM 87552; (505) 757–6414 or 757–6032

In the history of American archaeology, Pecos National Monument is important because of the length of its documented history—more than 500 years spanning prehistoric and historic times—and the work of two pioneering and distinguished investigators, Adolph F. Bandelier and Alfred V. Kidder. In 1880 Bandelier spent a week photographing and documenting the ruined pueblo and Spanish mission church at Pecos and produced the first report ever published by the Archaeological Institute of America.

Kidder, who was sponsored by Phillips Academy of Andover, Massachusetts, excavated the extensive Anasazi pueblo at Pecos over the course of ten summers, beginning in 1915 and ending in 1929. When he started all that remained of the pueblo was two large mounds. In 1927 he invited colleagues in the field to Pecos to observe the results of his work, which changed the traditional emphasis in American archaeology from collecting artifacts to understanding and interpretating sites. The scientists also agreed at this time to adopt eight prehistoric cultural periods for this region: Basket Maker I through III and Pueblo I through V.

Kidder, who has been credited with "putting the Southwest on the archaeological map," was an innovative figure in American archaeology. He was one of the first archaeologists to use specialists outside his field to examine artifacts and human remains. He was also a pioneer in the use of aerial reconnaissance and made a number of flights with aviator Charles Lindbergh over Arizona and New Mexico searching for prehistoric sites. Kidder's *An Introduction to the Study of Southwestern Archaeology,* published in 1924, includes descriptions of his work at Pecos and remains a classic in the field.

Pecos Pueblo is located in a valley of the Pecos River, an area that provided the Pecos people with good farmland and hunting grounds. Indians began moving into this area about A.D. 800, but the pueblo itself was not founded until 1300, probably as protection against raids from Plains Indians from the north. Pecos became a buffer and a trading center between agricultural pueblos to the south and nomadic hunters from the Great Plains, particularly the Apache.

After A.D. 1500 the pueblo, which was built like a quadrangular fortress around an interior plaza, had some 700 rooms. Kidder estimated that the complex probably had more than 1,000 rooms, although not all of them were used at the same time. As at other pueblos, unused rooms often were filled with trash and became the foundation of additions to the structure. Coronado, the first Spanish explorer in the Southwest, stopped at Pecos in 1524, but the Indians lured him away with false stories of fabulous riches to be found in a city called Quivira to the northeast. In 1591 another Spanish explorer, Castaño de Sosa, attacked and overwhelmed the pueblo. In his account of his expedition, Sosa described the pueblo as being built "in the manner of houseblocks. . . . The houses are four and five stories. In the galleries there are no doors to the streets. [The inhabitants] go up little ladders that can be pulled up by hand through the hatchways."

In 1620 the Franciscans established a mission at Pecos. The impressive mission church, completed in 1625 with walls 8 to 10 feet thick and a nave measuring 40 by 133 feet, was burned during the Pueblo Revolt of 1680. The church was temporarily rebuilt after the Spanish reconquest in 1692. A smaller permanent structure was built on the debris of the 1625 church; its ruins are visible today. Despite a devastating Comanche massacre in 1750 and a smallpox epidemic in 1788, the pueblo remained inhabitated until 1838, when its eighteen remaining residents joined the Jemez Pueblo.

There is a visitor center with a film on the history of the pueblo and displays of artifacts from both prehistoric and historic times. A 1¼-mile self-guided trail through the park leads to the ruins of the churches and an adjoining convent, past the excavations of the South Pueblo, and onto the mounds marking the location of the North Pueblo. There is also a reconstructed kiva. Tours conducted by Park Service rangers are also available.

How to get there: The park is located 2 miles south of Pecos on Route 63.

Puyé Cliff Dwellings and Communal House Ruins

Attraction: Pueblo and cliff dwelling ruins
Hours: Daily 9:00 A.M. to 6:00 P.M.; guided tours on the hour 9:00 A.M. to 4:00 P.M., call to confirm
Admission fee: $4.00
For more information: Santa Clara Pueblo, Espanola, NM 87532; (505) 753–7326

Edgar Lee Hewett excavated this extensive mesa-top pueblo and cliff dwellings from 1907 to 1909. Anasazi Indians began construction on these dwellings in the late A.D. 1100s and abandoned the complex about 1580. The Puyé (poo-YAY) Mesa is part of the

Pajarito Plateau located between the Rio Grande to the east and the Jemez Mountains to the west. The ruins and the mesa on which they stand are owned by the nearby Santa Clara Pueblo (located 2 miles south of Espanola on Route 30). Present-day Santa Clarans consider the ruins their ancestral home and hold ceremonies here each summer.

The building material for the Communal House, or pueblo, was of lightweight but durable volcanic rock. The pueblo itself was one of the largest in the region, with more than 1,000 rooms stepped back in a multistoried arrangement and built in a quadrangle around an inner courtyard. Two levels of cliff dwellings extend for more than a mile along the bluffs below the Communal House. Some of the masonry rooms in the caves were three stories high and extended out beyond the face of the cliff.

How to get there: The site is located 11 miles west of Espanola via Routes 30 and 5.

Salinas Pueblo Missions National Monument

Attraction: Three separate mission ruins and prehistoric sites; visitor center
Hours: Visitor center open daily 8:00 A.M. to 5:00 P.M.; sites open daily in summer 9:00 A.M. to 6:00 P.M., rest of year 9:00 A.M. to 5:00 P.M.
Admission fee: None
For more information: Salinas Pueblo Missions National Monument, P.O. Box 496, Mountainair, NM 87036; (505) 847–2585

The center of interest at each of the three separate sites comprising this remarkable complex is the stately ruin of a Spanish mission church. But before the arrival of the Spaniards, there was a large Indian pueblo at each location, and evidence of Indian life before contact with Europeans has survived.

In 1980 the Gran Quivira National Monument and two nearby state monuments, Abó and Quarai, were combined under the present name. The stately remains of the mission churches rising from the desert floor have intrigued visitors for generations. In the late

(Courtesy National Park Service)

Salinas Pueblo Missions

1800s the writer Charles Lummis wrote of Quarai: "An edifice in ruins, it is true, but so tall, so solemn, so dominant in that strange, lonely landscape, so out of place in that land of adobe box huts, as to be simply overpowering. On the Rhine it would be a superlative, in the wilderness of the Manzano it is a miracle."

Quarai, eight miles north of Mountainair off Route 55, has ten large, unexcavated house mounds, the site of an Indian pueblo, and the ruin of Mission of Las Purísima Concepción de Cuarac, a church 100 feet long and 50 feet wide at the transept.

Abó is located off Route 60, 9 miles west of Mountainair. The impressive Mission of San Gregorio de Abó was built in 1620, but despite its massive size, it remained in use for barely half a century.

At Gran Quivira visitors can see the remains of one of the largest pueblos in the region, dating from about 1300, as well as the ruin of the Chapel of San Isidro, built between 1630 and 1636, and the 138-foot-long Mission of San Buenaventura, which was begun in 1659 and probably not completed when the pueblo was abandoned in 1672. Gran Quivira, a name somehow related to the fabled city that Coronado sought in vain, is located on Route 55, 26 miles south of Mountainair. There are self-guided trails at the three sites. The visitor center has a short slide presentation and a display of artifacts.

How to get there: The monument's visitor center is located in Mountainair, 1 block south of the junction of Routes 60 and 55.

Salmon Ruin

Attraction: Pueblo ruin and museum
Hours: Daily 9:00 A.M. to 5:00 P.M.
Admission fee: $1.00
For more information: San Juan County Archaeological Research Center and Library at Salmon Ruin, 975 Highway 64, Farmington, NM 87401; (505) 632–2013

Like Aztec Ruins National Monument just to the north, Salmon Ruin is the remains of two separate periods of occupation by Anasazi Indians. The settlement, on the San Juan River, was originally built by Anasazi from Chaco Canyon as a satellite community, or outlier, toward the end of the eleventh century. Several hundred emigrants from Chaco Canyon arrived in the year A.D. 1088 and spent the next decade building a pueblo that became, when they were finished, a sprawling, C-shaped, two-story building with some 250 rooms. The walls of the huge two-story-high Tower Kiva, which was built on a 20-foot-high platform, were shored up with buttresses similar to those used in the same period on fortresses and cathedrals in Europe. Like Chaco and Aztec, this pueblo was planned, not built at random as other prehistoric settlements often were.

For reasons we can only guess, the Chacoans abandoned Salmon after forty or fifty years. In the early thirteenth century, after being deserted for almost a century, the structure was again occupied by Anasazi, mostly nearby farmers of the Mesa Verdean culture, who lived here between A.D. 1225 and 1240. The Mesa Verdeans subdivided the spacious quarters of the Chacoans with walls built in a cruder style.

Salmon Ruin was fortunate to be on the property of the family of Peter Milton Salmon, who began homesteading there in 1877 and was vigilant in his efforts to protect the ruin from vandals and pothunters. San Juan County purchased the property in the early 1970s. Between 1972 and 1978, the remarkably untouched ruin was the site of the second-largest archaeological excavation in the country, directed by the late Cynthia Irwin-Williams and involving hundreds of scholars and students from around the world. An archaeological museum and research center opened at Salmon Ruin in 1973. Today the San Juan County Archaeological Research Center administers the site and a small museum.

How to get there: Salmon Ruin is located 2½ miles west of Bloomfield on Highway 64.

Three Rivers Petroglyph Site

Attraction: Large petroglyph collection, pueblo and pit house reconstruction
Hours: Always open
Admission fee: None
For more information: State Park and Recreation Division, 141 E. DeVargas, Santa Fe, NM 87503; (505) 827-7465

This fifty-acre preserve containing more than 5,000 petroglyphs carved into the volcanic rock is one of the largest collections of prehistoric rock art in the country. The petroglyphs are located on a ridge that rises from the desert floor near the base of the Sacramento Mountains. The pictures, which stand out as grayish lines against a dark background, depict humans, animals, fish, and reptiles but also include a variety of abstract designs, the meaning of which is not known.

Petroglyphs were pecked, scratched, or chiseled into the rock by people of the Jornada branch of the Mogollon people between A.D. 900 and 1400. Why the Mogollon chose this spot is unknown; perhaps it had religious significance, or maybe the artists were simply attracted by its tranquil beauty, which fortunately can still be appreciated today.

A mile-long trail leads through the rocks and passes many of the best petroglyphs, but many others can be seen by simply climbing across the rocks. The artists probably lived in a nearby settlement, part of which has been excavated and can be visited via a short trail from the parking lot. There is a replica of an early Mogollon pit house and two partially reconstructed pueblo dwellings. There is a picnic ground and camping facilities but no visitor center or ranger on duty.

How to get there: The site is located near Three Rivers, New Mexico, off Highway 64. Follow signs to parking area.

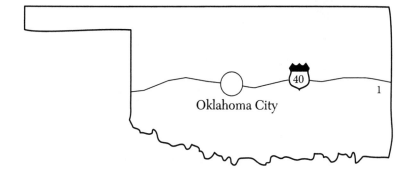

Oklahoma
1. Spiro Mounds Archaeological Park

OKLAHOMA

Spiro Mounds Archaeological Park

Attraction: Major Mississippian period mound site, interpretive center, trails
Hours: Wednesday through Saturday 9:00 A.M. to 5:00 P.M.; Sunday noon to 5:00 P.M.
Admission fee: None
For more information: Spiro Mounds Archaeological Park, Route 2, Box 339AA, Spiro, OK 74959; (918) 962–2062

This important center of Mississippian culture, religion, and trade was first occupied permanently about A.D. 800 but reached its height of development and influence in the years A.D. 1200 to 1350. The most elaborate burials also took place in this 150-year period, although most of the mound building was completed by 1250. Today the 140-acre site includes twelve mounds. Of these the largest is Craig Mound—300 feet long, 115 feet wide, and 32 feet tall—on the eastern side of the site.

More than 700 burials have been discovered in Ward Mound, which also had a clay crematory base and an earthen ramp extending northeast. Other mounds to the west were apparently used for "ongoing religious and political ceremonies for the living."

In 1933 Craig Mound was the victim of frenzied looting at Spiro. A group of commercial miners, calling themselves the Pocola Mining Company, leased the land and proceeded to dig into the mounds, unearthing an incredible number of ceremonial artifacts—stone effigy pipes in human and animal form, pottery, copper plaques, axes, shell carvings, and the like. Many valuable artifacts were destroyed in the excavation; the rest were sold right on the spot without any record being kept of their location or context.

This legal looting of the mound, which went on for two years, raised enough opposition to cause the Oklahoma legislature to pass its first antiquities preservation law in 1935. The next year the Works Progress Administration, in cooperation with the University of Oklahoma, the University of Tulsa, and the Oklahoma Historical Society, began a systematic excavation of Spiro Mounds, the first of several such investigations that have contributed vast amounts of information about the site.

These findings have shown that Spiro was an important trading and religious center. Its location in a narrow valley by the Arkansas River gave it access by waterway to settlements in both the Ozark Mountains to the north and the Ouachita Mountains to the south. Through trade, the inhabitants obtained conch shells from the west coast of Florida, flint from southern Illinois, quartz from central Arkansas, and copper from the Great Lakes and elsewhere. Situated between the eastern woodlands and the western plains, Spiro played a role in controlling trade between the Indians of the two regions. It was apparently so secure in its position of leadership that it had no need to defend itself; no evidence of a barricade, stockade fence, or moat has ever been found.

Archaeologists believe that the people of Spiro shared a common set of beliefs and practices, which included mound building and elaborate burial ceremonies, with other Indians at other mound centers throughout the Southeast. They call this belief system, which varied from place to place, the Southern Ceremonial Complex or Southern Cult. Spiro was on the western edge of the cults, the influence of which has also been detected at such important prehistoric settlements as Marco Key in Florida, Cahokia in Illinois, Moundville in Alabama, and Etowah in Georgia.

The similarity of decorative motifs and symbols found at Spiro and elsewhere is further evidence of the existence of the Southern Cult. These included the "weeping" eye, the cross, the sun circle, the hand and eye, and the bi-lobed arrow. At Spiro interesting finds include a mask made of a large seashell, which is etched with lines that could represent lightning, a symbol of power. Another find, a ceramic pipe, depicts a warrior clubbing an enemy. Ceremonial stone axes more than a foot long and carved from a single piece of stone were also excavated at Spiro.

After A.D. 1250 Spiro apparently ceased to be a thriving settlement, although burials of high-status leaders were frequent for the next 200 years. In fact, most of the burials found at Craig Mound were during this period. By A.D. 1450, however, the site was abandoned. The seeds of Spiro's decline were apparently planted when the climate began to become drier about A.D. 1200, causing, a booklet accompanying an exhibit on Spiro Mounds speculates, "ecological and social stresses that Spiro leaders could not resolve."

How to get there: Take Route 9 east of Spiro for 3 miles to the Spiro Mounds Road, then go 4 miles north.

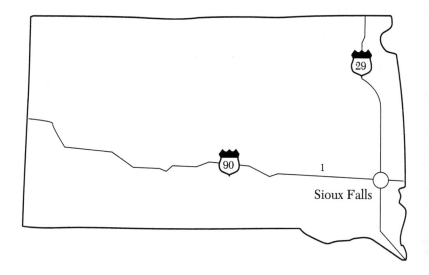

South Dakota
1. Mitchell Prehistoric Indian Village

SOUTH DAKOTA

Mitchell Prehistoric Indian Village

Attraction: Fortified, earthen lodge village, museum, visitor center
Hours: Open daily Memorial Day through Labor Day, 8:30 A.M. to
6:00 P.M.; May 1 through May 22, Monday through Friday, 9:00 A.M.
to 4:00 P.M.; September 8 through November 21, Monday through
Friday, 9:00 A.M. to 4:00 P.M.; winter open by appointment only
Admission fee: $3.00
For more information: Prehistoric Indian Village, Indian Village
Road, P.O. Box 621, Mitchell, SD 57301; (605) 996–5473

The only one of South Dakota's many archaeological land-
marks open to the public, the Prehistoric Indian Village is on the
site of a 700- to 1,000-year-old Plains Woodland habitation. The
settlement was located on Firesteel Creek, a tributary of the James
River, which has since been dammed up to form Lake Mitchell.
Today the central feature of the village includes a reconstruction of
a 20-by-40-foot, dirt-floor lodge that visitors may walk through.

The village once had a population of about 1,000 people who
lived in about seventy such lodges. The site also has a museum and
visitor center. In the museum's Patton Gallery, there are displays of
stone, bone, shell, and fired clay implements excavated at the site.

There is also a garden based on the plant remains found at the
site. Archaeologists speculate that the inhabitants had a five- to
ten-acre garden near the creek where they raised corn, beans,
squash, sunflowers, and tobacco. They also gathered wild prairie
turnips, known as Indian potatoes, and wild fruits such as choke
cherries, buffalo berries, wild plums, and wild grapes. The abundance of bison bone found there is an indication that animals came
to the creek to drink and feed, where they could be easily killed.
Elsewhere on the plains, the Indians cut the meat off the bones at
the kill spot for easier transportation home.

The remains of two parallel fortification ditches, about 95 feet apart, can be seen around part of the site. The conjecture is that the outermost ditch was built when the village expanded beyond its original borders. Evidence of wooden palisades between the settlement and the ditches have also been uncovered.

How to get there: Take Route 37 north out of Mitchell; turn west at the edge of town on Cemetery Road. Proceed ¼ mile and turn north on Indian Village Road.

TEXAS

Alibates Flint Quarries National Monument

Attraction: Prehistoric-historic flint quarries
Hours: Guided tours at 10:00 A.M. and 2:00 P.M., Labor Day through Memorial Day at the Bates Canyon Information Station; off-season tours by appointment
Admission fee: None
For more information: Alibates Flint Quarries National Monument, P.O. Box 1460, Fritch, TX 79036; (806) 857–3151

For some 12,000 years—from 10,000 B.C. to the 1870s—this extensive deposit of high-quality and brightly colored flint was used by Indians for making tools and weapons. Starting with people of the Ice Age Clovis culture, toolmakers chipped and flaked the flint to make knives, hammers, drills, axes, awls, scrapers, dart points, and arrowheads.

For most of this time, the peoples using Alibates were nomadic. From 10,000 B.C. to 6,000 B.C. groups of Paleo-Indians roamed the Plains hunting bison, mammoth, and other large game. Spear points and tools of Alibates flint have been found with the skeletal remains of these animals. During the Woodland period (A.D. 1 to A.D. 1000), farming was gradually introduced to the area and the Indians settled into villages built of adobe and stone and traded tools made of Alibates flint for Pacific seashells, catlinite from Minnesota, and painted pottery from the Southwest.

About A.D. 1450 the Apache Indians began to displace the agricultural peoples of the area; the Apache and several other tribes continued to control the region into the Historic period, which began in 1541 with Coronado's passing through the region. After the U.S. Army subdued the Indians, settlers of European descent began arriving. The quarries are named for Allie Bates, an early cowboy in this region.

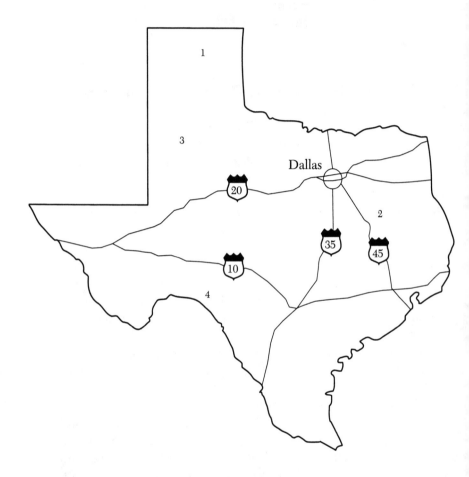

Texas
1. Alibates Flint Quarries National Monument
2. Caddoan Mounds State Historical Park
3. Lubbock Lake Landmark State Historical
   Park
4. Seminole Canyon State Historical Park

The quarries are located in a high, dry region of the Texas Panhandle known as the Llano Estacado, or Staked Plains, on bluffs that once overlooked the Canadian River. The construction of the Sanford Dam in the 1960s turned the river into a massive lake, Lake Meredith, with 100 miles of shoreline. The quarries, which consist of shallow pits from 5 to 25 feet across, can only be visited with a park ranger.

How to get there: Take Route 136 north of Amarillo for 30 miles.

Caddoan Mounds State Historical Park

Attraction: One burial mound and two temple mounds of the early Caddo culture; interpretive center, self-guided trail

Hours: Wednesday through Sunday 8:00 A.M. to 5:00 P.M.

Admission fee: None

For more information: Caddoan Mounds State Historical Park, Route 2, Box 85C, Alto, TX 79525; (409) 858–3218

The corn-growing people known as the early Caddos began work on the Caddoan Mounds about A.D. 800. The site today consists of two temple mounds, a burial mound, and part of the surrounding village. Archaeologists believe that Caddoan society was stratified by class, with the elite living near or on the temple mounds—the so-called inner village—and the common classes living in the outer village, in scattered dwellings amid work areas and farming plots. A small class of craftmen might also have lived there.

The site is located on a small alluvial prairie of a valley of the Neches River. The early Caddos introduced agriculture into the region and managed to subsist rather well. By controlling food surpluses and trade, they were able to dominate the peoples already living in this part of present-day East Texas. Since there is no evidence of defensive fortification or other signs of warfare at Caddoan Mounds, it can be assumed that the early Caddos enjoyed five centuries of relative peace.

A Frenchman working for Spain was the first known European to record, in 1779, a visit to the mounds, which are located near the famous colonial thoroughfare, the Camino Real. Another traveler, Amos Andrew Parker, visited there in 1834 and concluded: "I have seen no satisfactory explanation given of the origin and use of these mounds . . . and, at this late stage of the world, their origin and use may never be fully and satisfactorily explained."

The mounds were examined in 1919 by the Smithsonian's Bureau of American Ethnology and in 1933 by E. B. Sayles, an Arizona archaeologist, but they were not systematically excavated until 1939–1941, when H. Perry Newhall, with a grant from the Works Progress Administration, excavated half the large temple mound. From 1968 to 1970, Dee Ann Story of the University of Texas used modern methods, including radiocarbon dating, to establish that the early Caddos occupied the site from A.D. 800 to A.D. 1300.

Excavations have determined that the burial mound was built in six stages over a period of 400 to 500 years. The graves of the first five individuals to be buried here were found beneath the surface at ground level. Each successive stage above this also contained a number of individuals, probably a high-ranking chieftain plus members of his family and/or servants, who might have been sacrificed after he died. Over time, earth was added over the graves to make room for more burials. In all, the mound, which has not been completely excavated, appears to hold some ninety people buried in about thirty burial pits. The graves also held elaborate offerings, such as an effigy pipe, ax heads, ear spools, and arrow points that may have been imported in finished form from as far away as Florida and Illinois. The quality of these artifacts is another indication that the elite were buried here.

The temple mounds were also built in stages. Once a ceremonial temple was built, it was intentionally destroyed, often by fire, and covered with earth, whereupon a new temple would be built. This process was apparently repeated at regular intervals, and it is believed that the cycle is somehow linked to the burial-mound building increments. The largest building found at the site was almost sixty feet in diameter and was located at ground level beneath the three-stage Low Temple Mound. The remains of eleven structures were found within the High Temple Mound, which was also built in three stages.

The Caddoan Mounds Historical Park also contains the reproduction of an early Caddo house that was built by a team of experimental archaeologists using only materials and tools they believed were available to the early Caddos. The dwelling, which is about 25 feet tall and 25 feet in diameter, is somewhat smaller than most Caddo living structures, which averaged 35 feet in diameter. The thatch building is based on archaeological information plus accounts by early European travelers, who encountered descendants of the early Caddos in the seventeenth and eighteenth centuries. The modern-day builders of the reproduction dwelling used replicas of stone tools found at the site and wooden tools improvised based on educated guesses of what the early Caddos might have used. Their wooden tools naturally have not survived.

A model of the high temple mound and the village area is on view at the interpretive center. In addition to exhibits on the site, there is an audiovisual program and a self-guided trail through the mounds and village.

How to get there: Take Route 21 southwest of Alto 6 miles.

Lubbock Lake Landmark State Historical Park

Attraction: Excavation area, interpretive trails
Hours: Park open 9:00 A.M. to 5:00 P.M. Tuesday through Saturday, 1:00 to 5:00 P.M. Sunday; for tours of the main excavation area, inquire about current schedule
Admission fee: None
For more information: Lubbock Lake Landmark State Historical Park, P.O. Box 2212, Lubbock, TX 79408–2212; (806) 741–0306

Located in an area known as Yellowhouse Draw, this 300-acre park has been studied by archaeologists since 1939. The Lubbock Lake site is believed to be the only site in the Southern Plains to have been inhabited by all the prehistoric cultures known to have existed in the region.

There are three interpretive trails in the park. The trail into the main excavation area is by guided tour only. A ¾-mile, self-guided trail leading around the twenty-acre excavation area has many interpretive exhibits along the way. A 3-mile trail meanders through Yellowhouse Draw, with interpretive wayside exhibits and shade shelters.

How to get there: The park is located on the northwest edge of Lubbock, near the intersection of Loop 289 and Clovis Road (Highway 84).

Seminole Canyon State Historical Park

Attraction: Shelters containing prehistoric rock paintings
Hours: Park open daily year-round; tours of Fate Bell Shelter given Wednesday through Sunday at 10:00 A.M. and 3:00 P.M.
Admission fee: None
For more information: Seminole Canyon State Historical Park, Box 820, Comstock, TX 78837; (915) 292–4464

This area, just a short distance downstream from the confluence of the Rio Grande and the Pecos River, was visited some 12,000 years ago by Ice Age people hunting now-extinct species of elephant, camel, bison, and horse. The vegetation was lusher and the climate more temperate until about 7,000 years ago, when the climate changed, producing the arid and desertlike conditions of today. About that time a new people settled in the region. The newcomers, who settled in small groups, were hunter-gatherers and subsisted by harvesting plants like sotol and yucca, hunting small animals, and fishing.

These people produced the pictographs that are found today in caves and shelters throughout the Lower Pecos River country, which includes a portion of the Rio Grande and Devils River as well. More than 200 pictograph sites have been located, including the Fate Bell Shelter located within the park.

These pictographs, perhaps 4,000 years old, are thought to be among the oldest examples of rock painting in the country. The Indians of this period and region painted in a distinctive style— clearly recognizable hunting scenes and elongated, nearly life-size human figures.

Seminole Canyon is believed to have been named for a group of black U.S. Army scouts who escaped slavery by fleeing to live with the Seminole Indians in Florida. They were stationed at Fort Clark, near present-day Brackettville, in the 1870s.

The visitor center at park headquarters has exhibits on the prehistoric inhabitants of the region and a life-size cave diorama based on artifacts and rock art found nearby. Visitors can only visit Fate Bell Shelter with a guide from the park headquarters.

How to get there: Go 9 miles west of Comstock on Highway 90 to park entrance, which is located just east of the Pecos River High Bridge.

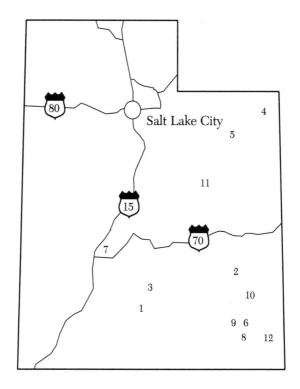

Utah
1. Anasazi State Park
2. Canyonlands National Park
3. Capitol Reef National Park
4. Dinosaur National Monument
5. Dry Fork Canyon/McConkie Ranch
6. Edge of the Cedars State Park
7. Fremont Indian State Park
8. Grand Gulch Primitive Area
9. Mile Canyon Ruin
10. Newspaper Rock State Historical Monument
11. Nine Mile Canyon
12. Three Kiva Pueblo

UTAH

Anasazi State Park

Attraction: Excavation site and replica
Hours: Open daily May 16 through September 15, 8:00 A.M. to
6:00 P.M.; rest of year, 9:00 A.M. to 5:00 P.M.
Admission fee: $1.00
For more information: Anasazi State Park, P.O. Box 1329, Boulder, UT 84716; (801) 335–7308

Eighty-three rooms were uncovered when the University of Utah excavated this large Anasazi village in 1958–1959. The site was then re-covered with plastic and dirt until it was re-excavated beginning in 1978. A number of excavated rooms are now on view for the public. There is also a replica, built in 1978, of a room block

Habitation room at Anasazi State Park

233

consisting of three habitation rooms and three food storage rooms. A small museum displays artifacts found here.

The Anasazi who settled at this mountainous site probably came from the Kayenta Anasazi region of northeastern Arizona about A.D. 1050 and stayed for 150 years. Tree ring dating of wooden beams used in the construction proves that the trees were cut between A.D. 1129 and 1169. There is also evidence showing that sixty-seven of the structures burned when the building was abandoned. Although the fire could have been accidental or set by enemies, some believe the inhabitants burned the village themselves when they left.

The self-guided tour includes the grave site of a young adult female who was buried with thirteen whole pots, 143 pieces of pottery, sixteen arrowheads, a bone awl, seventy-four turquoise beads, more than 1,000 stone and shell beads from a bracelet, and many squash seeds. The structures on view include habitation rooms with fire pits in the center and nine rooms used for storage—or so it is assumed, since the rooms are smaller than the habitations rooms and have no fire pits. Two types of construction are evident in the ruins: Kayenta masonry, in which walls are made of sandstone blocks and mud mortar, with smaller stones sometimes used as chinking; and Jacal masonry, in which poles are placed upright around the floor of the room and the spaces between them are filled with sticks, small stones, or both. There are also three mealing bins on the site, where the Anasazi ground their corn into a fine meal.

A short trail leads through the park, which is in Boulder, a small ranching town once considered the most remote town in the country.

How to get there: The park is located on Route 12 in Boulder.

Canyonlands National Park

Attraction: Rock art in national park
Hours: Visitor center (in Moab) open daily 8:00 A.M. to 4:30 P.M., with extended hours in summer
Admission fee: $3.00 per vehicle

For more information: Canyonlands National Park, 125 West 200 South, Moab, UT 84532; (801) 259–7164

Scenic beauty is the main attraction of this 337,570-acre park. After exploring the Green and Colorado rivers in 1869 and 1871, John Wesley Powell described "a wilderness of rocks; deep gorges where the rivers are lost below cliffs and towers and pinnacles; and ten thousand strangely carved forms in every direction; and beyond them, mountains blending with the clouds." The Green and Colorado rivers divide the park into three districts: Island in the Sky, the Needles, and the Maze. Each section has its own entrance.

The Fremont and Anasazi peoples hunted and farmed along the rivers from about A.D. 1000 to A.D. 1250. The walls of the park's Horseshoe Canyon contain superb examples of rock art, probably painted and carved by the Fremont. These images include huge anthropomorphs, hand prints, animal tracks, bows and arrows, and unusual shield figures with circular bodies. One rock painting, called The All-American Man, is particularly well known; it is a red, white, and blue representation of a shield figure. There are ruins of Anasazi pueblos and granaries at the area known as Salt Creek.

How to get there: Take Route 313 or 211 from Highway 191. The park's visitor center is located in Moab, at 125 West 200 South.

Capitol Reef National Park

Attraction: Rock art sites in national park
Hours: Visitor center open daily Memorial Day through Labor Day, 8:00 A.M. to 7:00 P.M.; rest of year, 8:00 A.M. to 4:30 P.M.
Admission fee: $3.00 per vehicle
For more information: Capitol Reef National Park, Torrey, UT 84775; (801) 425–3791

Fremont Indians lived along the Fremont River for about 400 years and their petroglyphs depicting bighorn sheep and human forms can be seen carved in the rocks along the river. Some of the human figures are wearing distinctive fringed headdresses that are similar to those found in rock art in western Colorado and northeastern Utah. The Fremonts stored corn and beans in bins made from wood and rock, called moki huts, and these structures, preserved by their protected locations, are visible along some trails. The Fremont River is named for John Charles Fremont, who crossed its headwaters in the 1850s. Mormons arrived in the area during the late 1800s and founded the town of Fruita, which is now within the park. There is a nature trail, scenic drive, and many hiking trails. Information on prehistoric sites and rock art as well as the park's well-known scenic wonders is available at the visitor center, which is open daily except holidays.

How to get there: The entrance to the park is located 5 miles east of Torrey on Route 24.

Dinosaur National Monument

Attraction: Rock art sites
Hours: Visitor center open daily in summer 8:00 A.M. to 7:00 P.M.; winter 8:00 A.M. to 4:30 P.M.
Admission fee: $5.00 per vehicle
For more information: Dinosaur National Monument, P.O. Box 210, Dinosaur, CO 81610; (801) 789–2115

As the monument's name implies, this area has been known for dinosaurs ever since 1909, when Earl Douglass found a nearly complete skeleton of a brontosaurus in a ledge near the Green River. Douglass was on assignment for Andrew Carnegie, who wanted "something big" to put in his museum in Pittsburgh. The national monument, which was established in 1915 and later enlarged to the present 325 square miles, is also rich in Fremont Indian rock art, produced by carving or chipping through the magnesium oxide, known as desert varnish, covering the rock face. The park's Cub Creek Archaeological Area is particularly rich in the large, easily identified trapezoidal figures of the Classic Vernal style, named for the town of Vernal in northeastern Utah.

Radiocarbon and tree ring dating of archaeological sites in the monument indicate that the rock art was produced between A.D. 600 and 1000, when the Fremont left this area. Often Fremont rock figures are heroic, nearly life-size figures, trapezoidal in body shape with broad shoulders, body decorations, and headdresses. What appear to be phallic images might identify males, and what has been interpreted as a couple holding hands is located near the top of a cliff in the park.

Fremont rock art sometimes combines petroglyphs and paintings. It has been observed that some petroglyphs at Dinosaur are more abstract than others. Some experts believe this is indicative of evolving styles, but another theory holds that erosion and other wear and tear over the centuries have eliminated certain details, leaving what appears to be an abstract representation.

How to get there: Dinosaur National Monument is located in both Utah and Colorado. The park's headquarters are in Dinosaur, Colorado, but the visitor center and the archaeological areas are in Utah. To reach the visitor center, take Route 149 off Highway 40 at Jensen. The monument's Dinosaur Quarry Visitor Center is located 7 miles north of Jensen.

Dry Fork Canyon/McConkie Ranch

Attraction: Rock art
Hours: Daily
Admission fee: Nominal fee
For more information: Dinosaurland Travel Board, 235 East Main, Vernal, UT 84078

Starting about 8 miles northwest of Vernal, Utah, the sandstone cliffs on the north side of Dry Fork Valley contain a wealth of petroglyphs in the Classic Vernal style. The most accessible and greatest concentration of rock art in the valley is located on the privately owned cliffs behind the McConkie Ranch, about 10 miles from Vernal. For a nominal fee (pay at a hut by the parking area), visitors can scramble up well-marked paths to the rock art panels. Here they will find an abundance of human figures with the distinctive trapezoidal bodies, headdresses, and necklaces of the Classic Vernal style of Fremont rock art. Many of the figures hold shields and other objects that appear to be masks to some viewers and scalps or severed heads to others. The dates of the rock art are

Fremont rock art at McConkie Ranch

uncertain. One habitation site on the ranch has been radiocarbon dated to A.D. 1350, but the possibility exists that the rock art is much earlier. The McConkie Ranch affords an excellent opportunity to see well-preserved rock art at close hand.

How to get there: In Vernal at the intersection of Fifth Street West and Main Street, turn north onto Route 121. After 3½ miles turn right onto Dry Fork Canyon and proceed to site.

Edge of the Cedars State Park

Attraction: Anasazi village, museum
Hours: Daily 9:00 A.M. to 5:00 P.M.
Admission fee: $1.00
For more information: Edge of the Cedars State Park, 660 West 400 North, Blanding, UT; (801) 678–2238

Mormon settlers of this remote section of southeastern Utah came across the remains of this Anasazi village in 1905. Portions of the settlement were finally excavated and stabilized from 1969 to

1972. Anasazi Indians lived here from A.D. 750 to about A.D. 1200 in a series of six village clusters. The pueblo is located on a ridge overlooking Westwater Canyon, where the Anasazi went for water. To the north are the Abajo Mountains, where they hunted and gathered wild plants and berries.

A trail behind the state museum leads to the sites; only Complex Four has been excavated and partly restored. The others are visible only as depressions in the earth.

Visitors may enter a pit house by a ladder through the entrance in the rebuilt roof. The interior walls are original. The complex includes the remains of a Great Kiva, which was used as a community center and for ceremonies. Its large size indicates that prehistoric Indians from the region might have traveled to Edge of the Cedars for ceremonies. Archaeologists from Weber State College in Ogden, Utah, are continuing with the excavation and stabilization of the site.

There is a view of the ruins and the surrounding mountains from an observation tower in the museum. Made of native stone, the museum opened in 1978. Among the well-displayed exhibits is a fine collection of Anasazi pottery. On view are storage and ceremonial objects, kitchen vessels (including ollas, or water jars, with concave bottoms that women carried on their heads), duck pots and bird effigies probably used for ceremonies, and an interesting assortment of corrugated pottery for cooking. The distinctive markings on the pots were produced by pinching the clay coils as the pieces were being made. There is a shop featuring American Indian arts and crafts in the museum and a picnic area on the museum grounds.

How to get there: Take Center Street west from Highway 191 and follow signs for about 1 mile.

Fremont Indian State Park

Attraction: Numerous rock art sites, visitor center/museum
Hours: Open daily mid-May to mid-September, 9:00 A.M. to 6:00 P.M.; rest of year, 9:00 A.M. to 5:00 P.M.
Admission fee: $1.00

For more information: Fremont Indian State Park, 11550 West Clear Creek Canyon Road, Sevier, UT 84766; (801) 527–4631

The decision to run a highway through central Utah's Clear Creek Canyon resulted in the 1983 discovery of the remnants of the largest Fremont Indian village ever uncovered. The Fremont, with distinctive unfired pottery and petroglyphs with trapezoidal bodies, were a separate culture from the Anasazi, their neighbors to the south.

The fourteen-month-long excavation of the Fremont village was conducted by Brigham Young University beginning in 1984. The 103 excavated structures included eighty residences, pit houses, and storage granaries. Several tons of pottery, arrowheads, and grinding stones were also uncovered. Although the site subsequently was destroyed by highway construction, the Utah Legislature established the Fremont Indian State Park in 1985 to house the excavated artifacts and to preserve the rock art in Clear Creek Canyon.

The 900-acre park contains more than 12,000 examples of rock art on more than 500 rock panels. There are both pictographs and petroglyphs, which the Fremont created by chipping or chiseling through the dark rock surface (magnesium oxide, called desert varnish) to reveal a lighter layer of rock below. As with all prehistoric rock art, the meaning of the panels in Clear Creek Canyon is largely indecipherable. The park has adopted as its symbol a commonly found, humanlike figure with arms, legs, five fingers on each hand, and what appear to be two horns growing out of its head.

The museum displays include a large pot (14½ inches tall) that was unearthed during the excavation in 1983 and the peculiar unfired clay figurines that were found in the pueblo. There is also a replica of a Fremont pit house and granary outside the museum. A short, paved interpretive trail starts at the museum/visitor center and leads into Joe Lott Canyon, where there are panels of petroglyphs engraved with forms that appear to be deer, sheep, and people.

Information about hiking trails (including Rim Rock Trail, which requires a guide) and other examples of rock art is also available. Indian Blanket, the largest pictograph in the park, is among the rock art that can be seen from the frontage road that parallels I–70. Its design resembles the pattern on a modern Navajo blanket.

How to get there: Located on I–70, the park can be reached from either Highway 89 to the east or I–15 to the west. If coming from I–15, take exit 17 at Cove Fort.

Grand Gulch Primitive Area

Attraction: Rock art and ruins in wilderness area
Hours: Always open
Admission fee: None
For more information: Bureau of Land Management, San Juan Resource Area, 435 North Main Street, Monticello, UT 84535; (801) 587-2141

According to the Bureau of Land Management, which administers and patrols the area, Grand Gulch is a 50-mile-long "outdoor museum" for backpackers. The rancher Richard Wetherill, who turned up so many important archaeological sites in the Southwest, explored the gulch in 1893–1894 and 1896–1897. There is plentiful evidence of Basket Maker people in the region, although their subterranean pit houses did not survive as well as the habitations of the later Pueblo Anasazi, who lived there until the late 1200s. There is also a great deal of rock art from both the Basket Maker and Pueblo periods.

Grand Gulch is not for the casual tourist. The actual sites are not marked on any map, and visitors must carry their own food and water.

How to get there: The primitive area extends in a northeasterly zigzag direction from the San Juan River on the south almost to the junction of Routes 95 and 261. For specific directions contact the Bureau of Land Management in Monticello (address above).

Mule Canyon Ruin

Attraction: Anasazi ruin
Hours: Always open
Admission fee: None

For more information: Bureau of Land Management, San Juan Resource Area, 435 North Main Street, Monticello, UT 84535; (801) 587-2141

This accessible site has a room block that probably housed two Anasazi familes as well as a kiva and tower with connecting tunnels. The kiva is well preserved and has features typical of such ceremonial structures as a fire pit, wall niches, and a ventilator shaft. The small pueblo was probably inhabited in the eleventh and twelfth centuries.

How to get there: The site is located on a turnout loop along Route 95, 26 miles west of Blanding.

Newspaper Rock State Historical Monument

Attraction: Grouping of petroglyphs on rock face
Hours: Always open
Admission fee: None
For more information: Canyonlands Travel Region, 117 South Main Street, Monticello, UT 84535; (801) 587-2231

Newspaper Rock—called Tsé Hané, or Rock that Tells a Story, by the Navajo—consists of a crowded group of more than 350 petroglyphs carved into the desert varnish on a smooth rock face under a protective overhang. Scholars believe that the images were produced over a period of 3,000 years by the prehistoric Archaic, Basket Maker, Anasazi, and Fremont peoples; in historic times images were added by the Ute and Navajo Indians and even by white settlers.

The panel includes Ute petroglyphs from historic times superimposed over some earlier rock art and shows human figures with headdresses, equestrians (including one rider shooting an arrow at an elk or deer), and many human footprints and bear paw prints. In her book *Legacy on Stone, Rock Art of the Colorado Plateau and Four Corners Region,* Sally J. Cole makes the point that Ute art remained traditional in style even after they came into contact with Europeans. She singles out one bowlegged figure wearing both a traditional headdress and American-style chaps (and holding what may be a quirt in its left hand) as a "rare example of art combining aboriginal subjects and themes with Euro-American subject matter." There is a short nature trail and picnic area by the site.

How to get there: Go 14 miles north of Monticello on Highway 191, then follow Route 211 west for 14 miles to the site.

Nine Mile Canyon

Attraction: Rock art sites along scenic unpaved road
Hours: Always open
Admission fee: None
For more information: Bureau of Land Management, Diamond Mountain Resource Area, 170 South 500 East, Vernal, UT 84078; (801) 789–1362

This canyon, which is closer to 40 miles long, takes its name from Nine Mile Creek, which was named by a topographer with John Wesley Powell's 1869 expedition. The canyon is a rich repository of pictographs and petroglyphs carved and painted by the Fremont Indians, who inhabited the canyon between A.D. 300 and 1200. The Fremont rock art is characterized by horned, trapezoidal, humanlike figures and stylized animals. Figures holding bows and arrows are assumed to be part of hunting scenes. Among the many different depictions are small walking figures, known popularly as "backpackers"; the humps on their backs could represent a burden or load.

After the Civil War the U.S. Army built a road through the canyon linking Fort Duchesne with the railroad at Price. Remains of iron telegraph poles and settlers' cabins can still be seen along the route.

The canyon road is two lanes with a graded gravel-and-dirt surface and is easily navigated by passenger vehicles during good weather. There are no services available along the route, although camping is allowed on Bureau of Land Management lands.

How to get there: The 78-mile-long road through Nine Mile Canyon runs roughly northeast from a turnoff on Highway 191 approximately 2 miles east of Wellington to a point on Highway 40 about 1 mile west of Myton.

Three Kiva Pueblo

Attraction: Anasazi pueblo ruin
Hours: Always open
Admission fee: None
For more information: Bureau of Land Management, San Juan Resource Area, 435 North Main Street, Monticello, UT 84535; (801) 587-2141

The photographer William Henry Jackson explored this fourteen-room Anasazi ruin in 1886, but the pueblo itself was not excavated until the Brigham Young University Field School of Archaeology undertook the task between 1969 and 1972. At that time one of the three kivas for which the site is named was reroofed and the outside masonry repaired. Starting about A.D. 900, the site was occupied over three periods; the last period of occupation was by Anasazi farmers and lasted from A.D. 1000 to 1300. There is also a masonry room used for a turkey run and three milling bins for grinding corn.

How to get there: The site, located in the middle of the wide Montezuma Canyon bottom, is reached by an unimproved road leading east out of Blanding. For specific directions contact the Bureau of Land Management (address and phone above).

WYOMING

Big Horn Medicine Wheel National Historic Landmark

Attraction: Unusual arrangement of rocks in a large, imperfectly shaped circle
Hours: Always open
Admission fee: None
For more information: Big Horn National Forest, District Ranger's Office, 1969 South Sheridan Avenue, Sheridan, WY 82801; (307) 672–0751

Medicine Wheel, Big Horn Range

(Courtesy U.S. Forest Service)

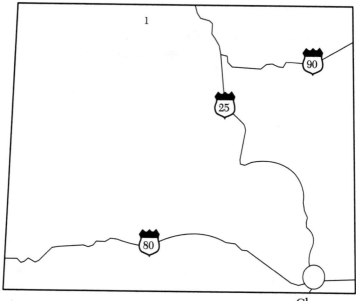

1

90

25

80

Cheyenne

Wyoming
1. Big Horn Medicine Wheel National
   Historic Landmark

Located just above the timberline on a shoulder of Medicine Mountain in northern Wyoming's Big Horn Range, the stone Medicine Wheel has inspired many legends but its true age and purpose are still a matter of speculation. The "wheel," although far from a perfect circle, being blunt on one end, is 80 feet across, with twenty-eight unevenly spaced spokes radiating out from a central rock pile or cairn. There are also five open rock circles irregularly spaced around the wheel's perimeter.

The wheel was built by indigenous inhabitants of the region about 200 years ago. (Tree ring analysis of a piece of wood found in one of the cairns produced a date of 1760, although the wheel could be older.) Nomadic tribes in the area at the time included the Crow, Sioux, Arapahoe, Shoshone, and Cheyenne. These early Plains Indians were not builders; tepee rings, circles of rocks used to hold down the flaps of their shelters, are the most common evidence of their existence. Archaeologists know of a few other medicine wheels throughout the Rocky Mountains from northern Alberta to southern Wyoming, but the Big Horn Wheel is the largest and the only one in the United States open to the public. In Indian dialects, incidentally, medicine and magic are the same words.

Theories about the purpose of the wheel abound, although it is generally conceded that there is a definite astronomical aspect to it, with the twenty-eight spokes somehow relating to the length in days of the lunar month, which the Indians used to mark the passage of time. In an article on the site, astronomer John A. Eddy observed in 1977: "And two of the cairns are placed symmetrically on either side of a north-south line, making it possible that they served as horizon markers for sunset and sunrise. Could it be that they were placed to mark distinctive directions where the sun rises and sets, just as parts of Stonehenge are thought to have been used on another continent and in another age?" Eddy also pointed out similarities in the designs of the wheel and the Plains Indian sun-dance lodge.

How to get there: The site is off Highway 14A about 27 miles east of Lovell.

GLOSSARY OF TERMS

alluvial: Relating to sediment deposited by rivers, as in *alluvial plain.*

anthropomorphs: Representations of humans, as in the rock art known as petroglyphs and pictographs, defined below.

atlatl: A spear-throwing stick designed to increase accuracy and distance.

bastion: Projecting part of a fortification, probably used as a lookout post.

blank: A roughly shaped but unfinished artifact, such as an arrow point.

bola: A hunting tool consisting of weights attached to ropes.

borrow pits: Pits dug by prehistoric peoples to obtain soil for earthworks, such as mounds and fortifications.

cache: From the French *cacher,* meaning "to hide." Archaeologists use the term to indicate a grouping of identical objects.

caliche: A reddish clay found in the desert.

charnel house: A structure containing the remains of the dead; sometimes, when full, a charnel house would be covered with earth to form a burial mound.

chert: a flintlike stone used for making prehistoric tools.

coprolite: Fossilized feces, often a valuable indicator of diet.

dart: The projectlike launched by an atlatl.

daub: A covering of clay or mud spread on a foundation of wattle (see below) used in the construction of primitive buildings.

dendrochronology: The science of tree ring dating.

desert varnish: Patina caused by chemical change on rock surface in the Southwest, sometimes analysed in an attempt to date rock art.

diffusion: The theory that culture, ideas, and technology are advanced by the contact of different peoples either through trade or migration.

dig: Popular term for an archaeological excavation.

effigy: Likeness or image of a person or animal, as in an *effigy mound.*

flake: A piece chipped off a stone in the process of shaping a projectile point.

fluting: Depression that runs lengthwise on certain projectile points; its purpose may have been decorative.

gorget: Neck ornament carved from shell or stone.

grid system: Method used by archaeologists to block out a site to be excavated so that they can record the precise location of every item found.

intrusive burial: Usually a burial near the surface of a burial mound, which was placed there by a later, non–mound building culture.

kiva: A word meaning "room" in the Hopi language, it refers to the subterranean structures believed to have been used for spiritual and religious purposes by prehistoric peoples in the American Southwest.

lithic: Pertaining to stone, as in *lithic material.*

metate: Grinding stone.

midden: Deposit of prehistoric trash or debris.

obsidian: Sharp-edged volcanic glass used for tool making.

palisade: A stockade fence made of pointed sticks or posts.

petroglyph: Rock carving.

pictograph: Rock painting.

pishkun: An Indian word for buffalo kill site, it refers to a cliff or precipice over which Plains Indians drove buffalo to their death.

point: The killing tip of a projectile, be it a spear or arrow, made of stone, bone, or metal. Also called spearheads and arrowheads.

potsherds, potshards: Pieces of broken pottery.

prehistory: Human history before the advent of writing.

radiocarbon dating: Method of determining the age of a prehistoric object by measuring the amount of the radioactive isotope, carbon 14, it contains.

remote sensing: Various techniques used to acquire archaeological information without disturbing the earth; for example, aerial or satellite photography, radar, or measurement of variations in the magnetic field of the area being studied.

sipapu: Spirit hole, found in Anasazi kivas in the Southwest, believed to be symbolic openings to the spirit world.

talus: A slope of rock debris at the base of a cliff. Often a rich source of archaeological finds.

wattle: Construction of posts interweaved with splints, twigs, reeds, or similar material. Often used as the foundation for a coating of daub (see above).

GLOSSARY OF CULTURES

Adena: A mound-building culture of the Ohio Valley that first appeared around 1000 B.C. and lasted until about A.D. 200. The name comes from the Chillicothe, Ohio, estate of a prominent white settler, on whose property a large mound was located.

Anasazi: An indigenous people who lived in the Four Corners region starting about A.D. 100. The Anasazi lived in pit houses during the early Basketmaker phase and in cliff dwellings during the later Pueblo period. Anasazi cliff dwellings were largely abandoned by the early fourteenth century. Present-day Pueblo people in the American Southwest are believed to be descended from the Anasazi.

Archaic Indians: The people that lived in North America after the Paleo-Indians, from roughly 5000 to 1000 B.C. The Archaic people had a more varied diet and developed a wider variety of tools than their predecessors.

Caddos: A people named for the Caddodacho Confederacy, a group of tribes that ocupied parts of Texas, Louisiana, and Arkansas when European settlers arrived. As the westernmost part of the Mississippian tradition, the Caddoans were mound builders and fine potters.

Clovis: The first defined Paleo-Indian culture, dating to the first human occupation of this continent, by some estimates as early as 10,000 B.C.

Copena: An offshoot of the Adena culture that migrated from Ohio south along the Tennessee River. The Copena built mounds and worked with copper and the lead ore known as galena.

Fremont: A culture that developed in Utah perhaps as early as A.D. 400 and had mostly disappeared by 1300. The Fremont left a rich legacy of rock art and were influenced by the Anasazi.

Hohokam: An agricultural people that developed elaborate settlements, including networks of canals, along the Salt and Gila Rivers in Arizona about 300 B.C. The Hohokam began to abandon their settlements about A.D. 1350.

Hopewell: A mound-building culture that was centered in the Ohio Valley and extended much farther along the Mississippi Valley than the earlier Adena culture. According to some estimates, the period of Hopewell activity lasted from 300 B.C. to A.D. 700.

Mimbres: This subgroup of the Mogollon culture settled along the Mimbres River in New Mexico and is distinguished by its black and white pottery.

Mississippian: This culture first appeared in the lower Mississippi Valley about A.D. 700 and spread across much of the eastern half of North America. Intensely agricultural, the culture began to decline during the thirteenth century, although some phases survived until the arrival of European settlers.

Mogollon: An Indian culture that flourished in the Southwest from about 300 B.C. to A.D. 1300. The name, pronounced mo-goi-YONE, is that of a mountain range in southwestern New Mexico.

Paleo-Indian: In North America, the period from the earliest human habitation to roughly 5000 B.C.

Salado: A people of northeastern Arizona that settled near the Hohokam in the vicinity of the headwaters of the Salt and Gila rivers. In the early 1300s they moved from the valley to massive dwellings such as the ones at Tonto National Monument in Arizona.

Sinagua: A hybrid culture that drew on the Hohokam, Mogollon, and Anasazi traditions. They thrived between A.D. 1100 and 1300 in the Verde Valley of central Arizona. The Sinagua, from the Spanish for "without water," were first recognized as a separate culture early in the twentieth century.

Southern Cult: A set of burial practices that possibly originated at Spiro Mounds about A.D. 800 and spread to other important Mississippian sites, such as Etowah ad Moundville. Also known as the Southern Death Cult and the Southeastern Ceremonial Complex.

Woodland: A number of related cultures that developed in the forests and along waterways of the eastern part of North America from about 1000 B.C. to the time of European settlement. The term includes such principal cultures as the Adena, Hopewell, and Mississippian.

INDEX

A

Abó, 213
Adair, James, 64
Adena, people and culture, 31, 90–91, 96, 97, 98, 111–13
Adena Mound, 97–98
Alabama Museum of Natural History, 5, 7
Alibates Flint Quarries National Monument, 225–27
American Antiquarian Society, 92, 117
American Bottom, 33, 37
American Museum of Natural History, 187, 193
Anasazi, xiii, 93, 127–31, 138, 140, 144–46, 163–65, 168, 170, 173–75, 178, 189–90, 191–94, 195, 197, 199, 202, 211, 212, 215, 233–34, 235, 238–39, 241–42, 244
Anasazi Heritage Center, 163–65
Anasazi State Park, 233–34
Ancient Ones. *See* Anasazi
Ancient Monuments of the Mississippi Valley, 88, 96
Angel Mounds State Historic Site, 41–42
Antiquities of the Southern Indians, 26
Anza, Juan Bautista de, 155
Anza-Borrego State Park, 155
Apache, 144, 146, 208, 209, 211, 225
Arapahoe Indians, 247
Archaeological Institute of America, 210
Archaeology magazine, 200
Archaic
    people 28, 59, 73, 242
    period 60
Arkansas Archeological Survey, 13, 15
Assiniboine Indians, 185

atlatl, 9, 56, 59, 60, 102, 171, 249
Atsinna, 207
Aztalan State Park, 117
Aztec, 117, 136, 152, 191
Aztec Ruins National Monument, 191–94, 199, 215

B

Bandelier, Adolph F., 132, 144, 194–95, 208, 210
Bandelier National Monument, 194–96
Bartram, William, 27, 29
Basket Maker, 127, 130, 144, 174, 189–90, 198, 211, 241, 242
Bates, Allie, 225
Beale, Lt. Edward F. "Ned," 148, 207
Bear Creek Mound (Natchez Trace), 65, 67–68
Benthall, Joseph, 3
Betatakin, 138–39
Bickell Ceremonial Mound, 21
Big Horn Medicine Wheel National Historic Landmark, 245–47
Bird Mound (Poverty Point), 55
Black, Glenn A., 41
Blackduck culture, 59
Blackfeet Indians, 179, 183, 185
Boone, Daniel, 73
borrow pit, 36, 55, 249
Boyd Mounds, 66
Brackenridge, Henry, 35
Brain, Jeffrey, 70
Brigham Young University, 244
British Museum of Natural History, 73
Bullen, Ripley, 22
Bureau of Land Management, 156, 163, 168, 169, 182, 183, 187, 197, 241, 243, 244

busk ceremony, 79
Bynum Mounds, 66

C
cache, 37, 88, 249
Caddo people, 227–29
Caddoan Mounds State Historical
Park, 227–29
Cahokia, 33–38, 75, 117, 220
Cahokia Mounds State Historic Site,
33–38, 69
Calico Early Man Site, 155–57
Camel Corps, U.S. Army, 148, 207
Camp Tupper Earthworks, 90
Canaveral National Seashore, 17
Canyon de Chelly
National Monument, 127–31
Casa Blanca (White House Ruins),
129
Canyon del Muerto, 128, 130
Canyonlands National Park, 234–35
Capitol Reef National Park, 235–36
Capitolium Mound, 89–90
Cardenas, Garcia Lopez de, 145
Carnegie, Andrew, 236
Carson, Christopher "Kit," 129
Carver, Jonathan, 45
Casa Grande National Monument,
131–33
Casa Malpais site and museum,
133–35
Casa Riconada (Chaco Canyon),
201–2, 203
Casamero Ruins, 197
Casqui, 12
Casteñada, Pedro de, 206
Castle Windy Midden, 17–18
Caywood, Louis, 146, 147
Chaco Canyon, 93, 129, 131, 138, 165,
169, 191, 197–205, 215
Chaco Culture National
Historic Park, 197–205
Chapin Mesa (Mesa Verde), 172, 178
Charboneau, Baptiste, 183

charnel house, 87, 249
Chata and Chickasaw, 63
Chattahoochee National Forest, 31
Chaw'se Regional Indian Museum,
160
Cherokee Indians, 63
chert, 36, 38, 249
Chetro Ketl (Chaco Canyon), 198,
202–3
Cheyenne Indians, 247
Chickasaw Indians, 63, 64, 66
China Lake Naval Air
Weapons Station, 161
C. H. Nash Museum—Chucalissa,
103–5
Choctaw Indians, 63–64, 103
Choctaw Mother Mound, 63–64
Chucalissa, 103–5
chunkey, 50
Churchill County Museum,
Fallon, Nevada, 187–88
Citadel Ruin, 152–53
City of the Dead, 86
Civilian Conservation Corps (CCC),
6, 7, 103, 145, 171, 189
Civil Works Administration, 28, 137,
142, 146
Clark, William, 182–83
Cliff Dwellers of Mesa Verde, 170
Cliff Palace (Mesa Verde), 170, 175–77
Clovis, New Mexico, xi
Clovis culture, 74, 225
Coe, Dr. Joffre, 79
Cole, Sally J., 242
Coles Creek culture, 69–70
Colton, Harold Seller, 135, 149
Comanche, 212
Conus Mound, 89–90
Coolidge, Calvin, 151
Copena culture, 3
coprolite, 188, 249
Cornelius, Rev. Elias, 25
Coronado, Francisco Vasquez de, 206,
211, 215, 225

Coronado expedition, 145, 225
Coronado State Monument,
    205–6
Costanoans, 158
Coyote Hills Regional Park, 157–58
Cree Indians, 185
Creek Indians, 63, 79
Criel Mound, 111–12
Crow Indians, 247
Crystal River State
    Archaeological Site, 18–19
Cummings, Dr. Byron, 138, 146
Cushing, Frank H., 132, 143

D
daub. *See also* wattle and daub, 249
Davenport Academy of
    Natural Sciences, 45
Davis, E. H., 87, 88, 92, 96, 106
Dayton Society of Natural History,
    100
Death Mask Mound, 88
Death Valley National Monument, xii,
    158–59
Delight Makers, The, 195
dendrochronology, 250
Deptford culture, 18
desert varnish, 236, 240, 250
de Soto, Hernando, 3, 12, 25, 66, 68,
    103
De Soto Caverns, 3–4
d'Iberville, Sieur, 63
Dickson, Dr. Don F., 38–39
Dickson Mounds, 38–39
Dinosaur National Monument,
    236–37
Dirst, Victoria, 120
Dominguez ruin, 165
Doney, Ben, 151
Doran, Edwin B., 53
Douglass, Dr. Earl, 236
Drumond, D. E., 124
Dry Fork Canyon, 237–38
du Tisne, Charles Claude, 74

E
Edge of the Cedars State Park, 238–39
Eddy, John A., 247
effigy, 46, 56, 103, 118, 145, 228, 250
Effigy Mounds National Monument,
    43–45
Emerald Mound (Natchez Trace), 65
El Morro National Monument,
    206–7
Escalante ruin, 165
Etowah, Georgia, 220
Etowah Indian Mounds State
    Historic Site, 24–25

F
Fagan, Brian, 156
Fairbanks, Charles H., 26, 31
*Fantastic Archaeology, The Wild
    Side of North American Prehistory,*
    114
Far View Visitor Center
    (Mesa Verde), 172
Fewkes, Jesse Walter, 132, 142, 151,
    166, 171
Flint Ridge State Memorial, 83–84
Florence Indian Mound
    and Museum, 4
Ford, James A., 29, 51, 54, 55
Fort Ancient
    site, 84–85
    people and culture, 84–85, 96,
        99–102
Fort Carondolet, 75
Fort Hill State Memorial, 85–86
Fort Rosalie, 63
Fort Walton
    culture, 19–21
    period, 19–21
    pottery, 20
Four Corners region, 163, 172, 195
Fowke, Gerard, 51
Fowler, Melvin L., 37
Fremont, John Charles, 236
Fremont Indian State Park, 239–41

Fremont people, 235, 236, 239–41, 242, 243
Futhark, xi

G
Gallatin, Albert, 35
geofacts, 156
Geronimo, 209
Gibson, Jon L., 54, 56
Gila Cliff Dwellings National Monument, 208–9
Gila Polychrome, 143
Gopher, The, 7
Graham Cave State Park, 71–73
Grand Canyon National Park, 144–46
Grand Gulch Primitive Area, 241
Grand Mound Center, 57–59
Grand Village of the Natchez, 61–63
Gran Quivira National Monument, 213–14
Grave Creek
  mound, 91, 112–15
  tablet, x, 114–15
Great Bear Mound, 43
Great Circle Earthworks, 94
Great Journey: The Peopling of Ancient America, 156
Great Kiva, 168–69, 193
Greber, N'omi, 90
Gros Ventre Indians, 185

H
H. Earl Clack Memorial Museum, 184–85
Hampson, James Kelly, 11
Hampson Museum State Park, 11–12
Harris, Thaddeus Mason, 114
Harvard University, 114
Harvard's Peabody Museum, 96
Haury, Emil, 146
Hemenway Southwestern Archaeological Expedition, 132
Hewett, Edgar Lee, 195, 198, 202, 212
Hidden Cave, 187–88

Hill, Alfred J., 45
Hodge, Frederick Webb, 132
Hohokam, 131–33, 137, 142–43
Holmes, William H., 166
Hoover Dam, 189
Hopewell, people and culture, ix, xii, 31, 43, 45, 46, 51, 53, 59, 85, 86, 87, 90, 91–96, 98
Hopewell Culture National Historical Park, 86–88
Hopi, 127, 134, 142, 148, 149, 150, 151, 152
Hovenweep National Monument, 165–68
Huntington, W. D., 165
Hyde Exploring Expedition, 198

I
Illinois State Museum, 74
Incinerator Site, 100
Indian Grinding Rock State Historic Park, 159–61
Indian Petroglyphs National Monument, 209–10
Indiana Historical Society, 41
Indian Temple Mound and Museum, 19–21
Inscription House, 140
Introduction to the Study of Southwestern Archaeology, 211
Irwin-Williams, Cynthia, 216

J
Jackson, Earl, 137
Jackson, William Henry, 166, 170, 198, 244
Jefferson, Thomas, 35
Jeffers Petroglyphs, 59–60
Jennings, Jesse D., 156
Joliet, Louis, 77
Jones, Charles C., Jr., 26, 30
Jones, Doug, 8
Jones, Walter B., 7
Judd, Neil M., 139, 145

K

Katmai National Park and Preserve, 123–25
Kayenta Anasazi, 138, 150, 234
Keet Seel, 140
Kettering, Charles F, 91
Kidder, Alfred V., 210–11
Kimmswick Bone Bed, 73–74
King, Colonel Fain White, 50
Kino, Father Eusebio Francisco, 131
kiva, 127, 129, 131, 133–35, 145, 152, 167, 168–69, 172, 173, 174, 175, 177, 178, 193, 196, 197, 201, 202–3, 205–6, 207, 212, 215, 239, 242, 244, 250
Knapp, Gilbert, 13
Kolomoki Mounds Historic Park, 25–27
Kymulga Cave, 3

L

LaBatt, Dennis, vii
Lapham, Increase A., 117
Laurel culture, 59
Leakey, Louis S. B., 156
Legacy on Stone, 242
Lepper, Bradley T., 92, 93
Lewis, Captain Meriwether, 113
Lewis, Theodore H., 45
Lewis and Clark, 182
Lilly Endowment, 41
Lincecum, Dr. Gideon, 64
Lindbergh, Charles, 211
Little Miami River, 84
Little Petroglyph Canyon, 161–62
Lizard Mound County Park, 118–19
Lockett, Samuel, 54
Lomaki Ruin, 151, 153
Long House (Mesa Verde), 178
Long Walk, 129
Lost City Museum, 188–89
Lost Tribes of Israel, 92
"Lost John," 47–49
Loughridge, Robert, 49

Louisiana State University, 53
Loveberry, Clarence, 97
Lowry Pueblo Ruins, 168–69
Lubbock Lake Landmark State Historican Park, 229–30
Lummis, Charles, 214
Lupton, Nathaniel T., 7

M

McClenahan, Patricia, 125–25
McConkie Ranch, 237–38
McKinley, William, 26
Madira Bickel Mound State Archeological Site, 21–22
Madison Buffalo Jump State Monument, 179–81
Madoc, Prince, 106
Mammoth Cave National Park, 47–49
Mangum Mound, 66
Marching Bear Group, 43, 45
Marco Key, 220
Marietta Earthworks, 88–90
Marksville culture, 51–53
Marksville State Commemorative Area, 51–53
Martin, Paul S., 169
Marquette, Jacques, 77
Mastodon State Park, xi, 73–74
Maturango Museum of Indian Wells Valley, 161
Maxwell, Thomas, 7
Meadowcroft Rock Shelter, xi
Mearns, Edgar Alexander, 137
Memphis State University, 103–5
Mera, Henry P., 142
Mesa Verde, CO, 131, 138, 191
National Park, xiii, 165, 168, 170–78
Museum, 174–75
Miami River Valley, 100
Miamisburg Mound State Memorial, 90–91
Mica Grave Mound, 87–88
Mindeleff, Cosmos, 130
Minnesota Historical Society, 59

Mississippi River, 43, 45, 49
Mississippian
culture, 24, 39
people, 28, 38, 42, 49, 65, 66, 69, 70, 75, 84, 103, 105, 108, 117, 219
period, 41, 66, 68
Missouri Indians, 76–77
Mitchell Prehistoric Indian Village, 223–24
Mitchem, Jeffrey, 13
Miwok people, 159–60
Modified Basekt Maker period, 171, 174, 175, 178
Mogollon, 133–35, 208, 216–17
Monks Mound (Cahokia), 35
Montana School of Mines, 182
Montezuma, 136
Montezuma Castle National Monument, 135–37
Montezuma Well, 136–37
Mooney, James, 31
Moore, Clarence B., xi, 6, 18, 20, 54, 70
Morris, Earl H., 193
mortar cups, 159
Mound B, 55–56
Mound Builders, x, 227–29
Mound Builders State Memorial, 91, 94
Mound Cemetery, 89–90, 98
Mound City, 86–88
Mound of the Fossils, 88
Mound of the Pipes, 88
Moundville, Alabama, 108, 220
Moundville Archaeological Park, xiii, 4–8
Moundville Historical Society, 7
Mound State Monument, 7
Mule Canyon Ruin, 241–42
Mulloy, William, 182
Murray State University, 50
Museum of New Mexico, 195, 202
Museum of Northern Arizona, 149
Myer, William, 107, 108, 109
Myths of the Cherokees, 31

N
Nanih Waiya, 63–64
Nash, Charles H., 103
Narbona, Antonio., 128
Natchez Indians, 61–63, 64, 65
Natchez Trace Parkway, 64–68;
visitor center, 67
National Geographic Society, 9
National Park Service, 9, 64–65, 88, 159, 198
National Register of Historic Places, 123
National Road, 84
Navajo Indians, 127–31, 198, 202, 240, 242
Navajo National Monument, 138–40
Neitzel, Robert S., 53
Newark Earthworks, x, 91–95
Newark Holy Stones, 92
Newhall, H. Perry, 228
Newspaper Rock State Historical Monument, 242–43
Nine Mile Canyon, 243
Nodena culture, 11
Nodena point, 11
Nodena red and white pottery, 11
Nordenskiold, Gustaf, 170, 177
Norona, Delf, 115
North Rim Drive, 130
Nutt, Rush, 68

O
Oakley, Carey, 5
Ocmulgee National Monument, 27–29
Octagon State Memorial (Newark, Ohio), 91, 94
Oglethorpe, James, 27
Ohio Company, 89
Ohio Historical Society, 83, 84, 85, 90, 91, 94, 95, 97
Ohio Museum of Indian Art, 94
Ohio River, 42
Ohio State Archaeological and Historical Society, 87

Oklahoma Historical Society, 220
Old Stone Fort State
    Archaeological Area, 105–7
Onate, Juan de, 207
Oneota Indians, 43
Osage Indians, 74–75
Osage River, 74
Osage Village State Historic Site,
    74–75
Owen Mound, 94
Owl Creek Mounds, 68–69
Ozier Mound, 108

P

Paiutes, 189
Paleo-Indians, 83, 225
Palmer, Edward, 14
Parker, Amos Andrew, 228
Parkin Archeological State Park,
    12–13
Pecos National Historical Park,
    210–12
Pee Dees, 79
Penicaut, Jean, 61
Penutian language, 158
Petersen, Robert, 87
Petrified Forest National Park,
    140–42
petroglyphs, 31, 59–60, 120, 135, 141,
    159, 161–62, 167, 172, 182–83,
    189–90, 196, 209–10, 216–17,
    234–35, 236, 237–38, 240, 241,
    242–43, 250
Pharr Mounds, 67
Philadelphia Academy of Sciences, 70
Phillips Academy, Andover, MA, 25,
    211
Pictograph Caves State Park, 181–82
pictographs, 120, 155, 181–82, 230,
    234–35, 240, 251
Pinson Mounds State
    Archaeological Area, 107–9
pishkun, 179–81, 183–85, 251
Plains Indians, 211, 247

Pleasant Point, Colorado, xiii
Pleistocene era, 73
Pocola Mining Company, 219
Pompey's Pillar National Historic
    Landmark, 182–83
Poverty Point
    State Commemorative Area, vii,
        53–56
    culture, 51, 53–56
    objects, 56
Powell, John Wesley, 145, 235, 243
Pueblo Alto (Chaco Canyon), 204–5
Pueblo Anasazi, 189, 208, 241
Pueblo Bonito (Chaco Canyon), 198,
    199, 200–201, 203
Pueblo del Arroyo (Chaco Canyon),
    198, 203–4
Pueblo de los Muertos, 207
Pueblo Grande Museum and Ruins,
    142–43
Pueblo people, 129, 196
Pueblo period, 127
Pueblo Revolt of 1680, 207, 212
Putnam, Frederick Ward, xi, 96
Putnam, Gen. Rufus, 89
Puyé Cliff Dwellings and Communal
    House Ruins, 212–13

Q

Quadranaou, 89–90
Quarai, 213–14
Quivira, 211

R

radiocarbon dating, 251
Red Ochre culture, 43
Ritzenthaler, Robert, 118
Roche-a-Cri State Park, 119–20
rock art, 234–38. *See also* petroglyphs
    and pictographs
Rock Eagle Effigy, 30–31
Rockefeller, John D. Jr., 171
Rogan, John, 25
Roosevelt, Franklin D., 29, 189

Roosevelt, Theodore, 142, 198
Roosevelt Dam, 144
Ruppert, Karl, 204
Russell Cave National Monument,
    xi, 8–9

S

Sacajawea, 183
Sacra Via, 89–90
Safety Harbor
    culture, 18
    period, 22
St. Francis River, 11, 12
Salado people, 143–44
Salinas Pueblo Missions National
    Monument, 213–15
Salisbury, James and Charles, 92
Salmon, Peter Milton, 216
Salmon Ruin, 215–16
San Juan County Archaeological
    Research Center, 215–16
Santa Clara Pueblo, 212
Sayles, E. B., 228
Sayre, Melville H., 182
Saul's Mound, 108
School of American Research, 195,
    202
Schoolcraft, Henry Rowe, 114
Sears, William, 25, 26
Seip Mound, 95–96
Seminole Canyon State
    Historical Park, 230–31
Serpent Mound State Memorial, xi,
    96–97
Setzler, F. M., 51
Shetrone, Henry Clyde, 95
Shiloh Church Mounds, 69
Shoshone Indians, 159, 161, 247
Simpson, Lt. James H. 129, 198, 202,
    207
Sinagua, people and culture, vii, 135,
    146, 147–53
Sioux Indians, 247
Siouan Indians, 60, 79

sipapu, 175, 251
Smithsonian Bureau of
    American Ethnology, 14, 25, 31,
    112, 145, 171, 228
Smithsonian Institution, 7, 26, 28, 31,
    51, 75, 107, 112, 149, 166, 198
Sosa, Castano de, 211
Southern Cult, 220
Spicer, Edward, 146, 147
Spiro Mounds Archaeological Park,
    219–21
Springerville, Arizona, 133–35
Spruce Tree House (Mesa Verde),
    173–74
Squier, Ephraim, 35, 87, 88, 92, 96, 106
Stein, John, 199, 200
stelae, 18
Step House Cave (Mesa Verde),
    177–78
Stevenson, James, 149
Story, Dee Ann, 228
Story Mound, 97–98
Sunwatch, 99–102

T

Talwa, 80
tepee rings, 181, 247
Thomas, Cyrus, x, xi, 14, 37, 75, 112
Thomas, David Hurst, 187
Three Kiva Pueblo, 244
Three Rivers Petroglyph Site,
    216–17
Tiltonsville (Ohio) Cemetery Mound,
    xiii, 98–99
Tiwa Pueblo Indians, 206
Toltec Mounds Archaeological
    State Park, 13–15
Toltec Research Station, 15
Toole, William L., 46
Toolesboro National Historic
    Landmark, 45–46
Tonto National Monument, 143–44
Town Creek Indian Mound, 79–81
Towosahgy State Historic Site, 75–76

Track Rock Archaeological Area, 31–32

Travels Through the Interior Parts of North America in the Years 1766, 1767, 1768, 45

Turner, Ted, 184

Turtle Mound, 17–18

Tusayan Ruin and Museum, 144–46

Tuzigoot National Monument, 146–48

U

Ulm Pishkun State Monument, 183–84

U.S. Forest Service, 31, 69

University of Arizona, 146

University of Arkansas, 15

University of Chicago, 39, 182

University of Missouri, 76

University of New Mexico, 198

University of North Carolina, 79

University of Oklahoma, 220

University of Oregon, 124

University of Tennessee, 106–7

University of Texas, 228

University of Tulsa, 220

University of Utah, 233

uranium-thorium dating, 156

Ute Indians, 166, 242

V

Valley of Fire State Park, 189–90

Van Meter State Park, 76–77

Vargas, Diego de, 207

Vikings, xi

W

Wahkpa Chu'gn Buffalo Jump and Archaeological Site, 184–85

Walnut Canyon, 136, 148

Walnut Canyon National Monument wattle and daub, 50, 100, 148–50, 189, 251

Weber State College, 239

Weedon Island
culture, 18, 20, 26
period, 22

Wendorf, Fred, 142

Wetherill, Al, 138

Wetherill, John, 138

Wetherill, Richard, xi, 138, 166, 170, 198, 241

Wetherill Mesa (Mesa Verde), 171, 177

Wickliffe Mounds, 49–50

Williams, Stephen, 114

Winterville Mounds State Park and Museum, 69–70

Wisconsin Archaeologist, 119, 120

Woodbury, Richard B., 207

Woodhenges, 36

Woodland, period and people, 35, 38, 49, 60, 66, 73, 105–7, 119, 223, 225

Works Progress Administration, 41, 53, 220, 228

World's Columbian Exposition (1893), 96

Worthington, Thomas, 97

Wright Earthworks, 94

Wupatki, 136

Wupatki National Monument, 150–53

Wukoki, 152

Wyrick, David, 92

Y

Yale University, 70

Z

Zuni Indians, 134, 206–7